THE ELECTRIC CITY

The Stehelins of New France

THE ELECTRIC CITY

The Stehelins of New France

The fabulous true story of a legendary family
who carved out of the forest wilderness
a beautiful life
and a prosperous business —
the saga of their
struggles, loves, war and dispersal.

by
Paul H. Stehelin

The Electric City
Copyright © Paul H. Stehelin, 1983

All rights reserved. No part of this book may be reproduced, stored in a retrieval system or transmitted in any form or by any means without the prior written permission from the publisher, or, in the case of photocopying or other reprographic copying, permission from CANCOPY (Canadian Copyright Licensing Agency), 1 Yonge Street, Suite 1900, Toronto, Ontario M5E 1E5.

ISBN 978-1-55109-307-9

(Previously published by Lancelot Press: ISBN 0-88999-186-3)

Nimbus Publishing Limited
PO Box 9166,
Halifax, NS   B3K 5M8
(902) 455-4286

Cover photos courtesy of Public Archives of Nova Scotia

Printed and bound in Canada

CONTENTS

Preface 7
Acknowledgments 11
Jean Jacques Sets Foot in Acadie 12
A Family at the Crossroads 26
Three More Sons to Canada 38
The First Winter 60
A Beautiful Spring 84
The Summer of Decision 91
The Family Settles in the Wild 121
New Home, Old Ways 136
The Weymouth and New France Railway 154
Social and Business Weymouth 173
The Call of Adventure 193
A Grandson is Born 211
Death Comes to New France 222
Another War, Another Blow 235
Soldiers Reunion 251
New France Fades into Legend 260
Epilogue 270

PREFACE

This is the story of New France, a family settlement and lumber enterprise, conceived and built in Digby County, Nova Scotia, by my Alsatian grandfather, Emile Charles Adolphe Stehelin, from Normandy, France, his wife, eight sons and three daughters. The colony was situated on the banks of the Silver River, hard by Langford Lake, seven miles through the dense forest from Southville, the nearest habitation, and seventeen miles from Weymouth.

I began work on its story about thirty years ago, at the urgings of the family, especially my cousins, grandchildren of the founder, most of whom never saw New France, nor indeed Canada. Time marches on and now only one grandchild born at New France remains, Sister Jacqueline, who lived her very happy early days there.

There are many living descendants of people who worked at New France or were guests at the Big House, who would also like to know more about this now legendary village, lost in the woods which the Acadians and The Blacks sometimes called "The Electric City". Finally, I was greatly encouraged by the interest young people displayed in this small segment of local history. So often it is thought that history, to be interesting and useful, must recall events and ways of life of the far distant past. I believe, however, that because changes in ways of life have been so swift and far reaching in the last near one hundred years since our story took place, the reader will be provided a link to a vastly different past era.

As I began my search, I was surprised to find so much information in family records, letters and pictures. Besides, most uncles and aunts were still living then, and they wrote or recounted to me many stories and gave me valuable explanations of certain vital decisions and events. It was their adventure and they never ceased living it.

I found much useful information in *L'Evangeline* and *The Weymouth Times*, newspapers published in Weymouth at the time, and the *Digby Courier*. From old homes around Weymouth and along the French Shore, I received old surveyor's maps, postcards, pictures and valuable oral tradition, some too fantastic to be true. I was also able to talk with some picturesque old timers who had worked at New France, especially Zozime (pronounced Zozeem), all fine raconteurs.

My father, Emile Jean, left considerable written material which provided detailed background information about family history, life at St. Charles, the early beginnings of New France and Life there until he left in 1909. I have drawn heavily on his material.

My Uncle Paul had a fine sense of history and to him conceiving, building and living New France was romance and a near heroic deed. It remained his lifelong Odyssey. He encouraged me to write its story and until his death at St. Charles in 1962, he was my most reliable source of information. We exchanged a coutinuing correspondence over the years through which he gave me detailed accounts of events, documents, pictures and what was most valuable to me, objective critiques of my early efforts. As he often said, he was the best informed of all because he had lived the adventure from its inception to its demise and "I knew New France like the insides of my pockets". No one loved New France more than he did and no one worked as hard to keep it in the family and alive.

Unfortunately, but then perhaps fortunately too, my grandfather's detailed diary covering those exciting years was lost. Undoubtedly, it would have unlocked many secrets and answered many questions. Fortunately, we have a few letters written by him to his sister Mathilde, which came to me from family sources in Switzerland. I must mention that their translation purposely retains a French flavour. Purists may feel they could be rendered in better english, but then that would detract from their french form.

I drew heavily from my own recollection of life in the family, which goes back to just before the first world war, when I was nearly five years old. When several Stehelins got together, the discussion was always about the family, its history, of which everyone is very proud, its characters, their grand deeds and not so grand escapades and, of course, New France. The conversation at my grandfather's table, to me at that tender age, seemed interminable and boring. But we grandchildren were expected to sit quietly, and be seen and not heard. After the passing of my grandfather, the tenor of these family discussions changed and there seemed unbridled disagreement about the affairs and fortunes of the family. All this talk must have slumbered in my subconscious for many years, only to surface and tumble with great force before my mind when I set to work on this book.

I well remember the last family dinner I attended at St. Charles in 1949, with twelve members, of varying ages, present, including three uncles and two aunts. While much old wine, some buried through two great wars, much Champagne and Calvados were drunk until two o'clock in the morning, the conversation was almost exclusively about New France. There was even a heated argument about the correct location in the garden of the horseradish patch, which was not settled. Upon rising from the table, however, they all agreed, with great nostalgia, that their years at New France had been the best ones of their long lives.

Upon reaching the end of our story, we are left with the same thoughts that have occupied the minds of many before us. We see the price a man of courage and faith in himself was willing to pay for a simple life of peace and tranquility for himself and his wife and for a better future for his many children. In this new land of Canada, his eight sons especially would find opportunities that did not exist in France, for a useful and satisfying life, spared from the sufferings and ravages of ever recurring wars in Europe.

For himself, he found the life he sought and restored his health. However, his grand design for his family, in part, miscarried when the war he had foreseen engulfed even Canada, an outcome he had not foreseen. When the call to arms came to Weymouth, he rose to accept the sacrifice that was now demanded of the family. We can share his sad moments however, when in the solitude of his declining years, he asked himself why man should plan and labour so when destiny, it seemed, brought the same end to all.

His descendants alive today are not very numerous and are widely dispersed. Four grandchildren are in Nova Scotia, one in the United States and five in France. Great grandchildren are more numerous, but also widely dispersed. Four live in California, four in Alberta, one in England, one in Ottawa and five in France.

More distant relations, bearing the name, live in Switzerland, mostly in Bâle, where the family began around the year 1519. There the family history and genealogy is carefully kept up to date. Cousin Fritz has devoted much of his time over many years to this work. Other family members administer the Stehelin Family Assistance Fund, which was set up and augmented by many ancestors to provide financial assistance to members in need.

The family home, Saint Charles, near Gisors in Normandy, built by my grandfather when he had to leave Alsace, is still in the family. It passed to Uncle Paul and the present owner is his son also named Paul.

ACKNOWLEDGMENTS

I would like to acknowledge, with very sincere thanks, the valued assistance of many friends: Mr. Russell Lenz, for the detailed maps and the drawing of the village plan; Mr. Norman Creighton, for his inspiring advice and assistance; Mr. and Mrs. Ralph Morton, for their assistance in the preparation of the manuscript; Father Leger Comeau and other Eudist Fathers, for the valued information about Father Blanche and for the kind permission to use his photograph; Robb Engineering of Amherst, for the photograph of the locomotive Maria Theresa and copies of correspondence between Mr. Robb and my grandfather; Mrs. Barbara Hanson, who laboured long and patiently over my handwriting and typing to produce the final manuscript; Mr. Sandford Archibald, for his assistance in technical matters of production.

I am also indebted to members of the family for their continued interest, support and contributions of materials; more especially, Sister Jacqueline Stehelin, who has been my reliable source of information over many years; my cousin, Paul, who gave me access to very old family documents and pictures kept in the home of Saint Charles.

I wish to thank also the many people, too numerous to name individually, around Weymouth, Southville and the Acadian villages, French, Blacks, English and Indians for the materials and oral tradition they gave me.

Last, but certainly not least, I am gratefully indebted to my wife, Jean, for her unfailing support and encouragement through many years of work on the Story of the Stehelins of New France.

JEAN JACQUES SETS FOOT IN ACADIE

On a beautiful, sunny, warm July midmorning in 1892, a well dressed young man stepped down from the mail horse drawn carriage in front of a little store, which also housed the Post Office at Church Point, in Nova Scotia. Jean Jacques had stepped off the Yarmouth morning train just an hour before, at the little Dominion Atlantic Railway station, three miles back from the village, sitting practically in the woods. He had crossed the night before on the Boston boat and about ten days before that he had left his father's home in Normandy to sail for New York and the New World.

Standing there in his stylish Parisian cut grey checked suit, his shining black dress ankle boots buttoned down the sides, his melon shaped Edwardian dark grey hat, his high collared pinkish coloured shirt with wide necktie neatly held in place by a gold stickpin, he looked out of place alongside the few unshaven Acadian men standing there in overalls and dirty work boots. For a few minutes, they just starred at him without uttering a word, then slowly they tipped their worn caps and smiling slightly greeted him in words he hardly understood. Soon the store owner and Postmaster, Louis A. Melanson, dressed in a dark brown suit, came out of the store, introduced himself, extended his hand and with a smile, very simply said, "Bienvenue Icite". Welcome here, indeed, Jean began to feel, as the men, over their initial surprise, also shook his hand.

Jean Jacques Stehelin had just passed his twenty-first birthday, as he stood there in a very strange country, among people so different from his own countrymen, a difference more pronounced because they were supposed to be french-speaking and he hardly understood what they said. This was a new world indeed and perhaps he had not prepared himself for something so different.

This dusty, rutted and crooked path was quite unlike the cobbled roads of France. The houses he could see were made of wood, drab and unpainted and around them not a flower or a tree. And this little horse in front of him, unkempt, thin and dejected looking, hitched to a frail looking wagon, dirty, its paint long ago worn off, with a harness that was also dirty and patched here and there with pieces of rope.

For a moment, his mind flew back home, his father's large house with its manicured lawns, the multi-coloured flower beds and the family "atelage," waiting at the carriage entrance. The coat of that chestnut gelding was always shining clean, the harness polished every day and the graceful and sturdy looking landeau, black and green, always clean. Glancing at the little old maildriver standing by, untidy and unkempt like his horse, Jean saw in his mind's eye, Leon, the liveried coachman at home, sitting erect on his little high seat, working the reins expertly and with style in gloved hands. He remembered his own Arabian thoroughbred saddle horse, Bombe, bobtailed as was the style then, immaculately turned out every morning, ready for perhaps a day's hunting party, the exhilerating chase of the fox, to the voices of the hounds and the calls of the horn or perhaps just a canter to visit friends.

But he had tired of all that, as later on he had also tired of the gay and debonair life of the Paris salons, the music halls and the grand balls. His merry companions and the beautiful women of his set he could perhaps not afford any longer. Anyway, it was time he found a niche in the world for himself. Unfortunately too, the call up for his year's military service was approaching and he did not relish the prospect of life as a recruit at the lowly rank of "simple soldat". And so, after long soul searching sessions with his father, it had been decided that he would tempt his luck in America, more specifically in Nova Scotia, by all accounts a fabulous country.

Needless to think of the past now, here he was in Canada and he had better think about the future. Looking around, he noticed that these peasants, as he already thought of them, were smoking short stemmed, blackened clay pipes, which prompted him to pull out his fine gold ringed briar and nonchalantly fill it from his pigskin pouch, lighting it with a match he pulled out of a little silver box. Jean very much enjoyed this first smoke. It seemed to settle his nerves somewhat and put him in a better frame of mind to digest his present situation and ponder over his future.

Jean was soon awakened from his reverie by Vitale the mail driver, who asked him to step back into the wagon. He would drive him to the college, his final destination. There he sat on the not too clean seat, with his violin on his knees as the little horse, willing but tired, was goaded into starting off once more.

On the way down the hill, looking around, the only pleasing sight Jean saw, was the blue shining waters of Saint Mary's Bay in the distance, over the green trees of a little woods. As the wagon turned the bend at the foot of the hill, College Sainte Anne and the big white church of Sainte Marie came into view. It was not long before the wagon pulled up in front of the college door. The building, of wood, was nearly square, much in the style and architecture of colleges in France, with the all important bell in a belfry sitting on the centre of the roof. It was painted brown, probably to look more like stone Jean thought. Upon entering the long wide hall, he saw carpenters busily at work finishing the walls and hanging doors. Once again, Jean felt that he was being critically inspected. The men did not stop working but they "took in" this strange young man in fine clothes and flowing black moustache.

Standing there, Jean soon saw the figure of a priest coming towards him from the other end of the hall. There was no mistaking that he was a Eudist. Jean knew the dress very well from his college days. The flowing black soutane with little black buttons all the way down the front, the elbow length little cape, also with black buttons all the way down the front, the flowing wide black linen sash and, of course, the very fashionable clerical headdress at that time, the biretta. As the priest came closer, Jean recognized him, yes, it was Father

Morin, his old latin professor at St. Jean. Vitale was impressed by the warm welcome extended to Jean. His passenger, this young man, must be very important to be addressed in such high fashion. Nobody was a "monsieur" around here.

Father Superior had his room cum office, in the parish glebe house a few minutes walk towards the church. He lived there rather than at the college, because as well as being Superior, he was also Parish Priest. Walking along, Father Morin and Jean exchanged the type of small talk usual in circumstances such as these, very casual and very proper. But then Jean had not been Father Morin's model student. In the language of the day; his studiousness and piety had "left something to be desired".

The glebe house was old and much in the style of all the other buildings around the village, except that it was much larger and at one time had had a coat of white paint, now somewhat faded. The church, alongside the cemetery on the other side of the road, was obviously not of French architectural inspiration but it was simple and neat in appearance. Father Morin knocked on the first door on the left as the two men entered the center hall. A sonorous and warm voice inside responded instantly, "Entrez, Entrez". Hearing this familiar voice, Jean Jacques felt joy and comfort even before the door opened, and then there in front of him, standing tall and erect, smiling at him, was his old prefect of discipline of Ecole Saint Jean, Father Blanche. Even before a word was uttered, the good man was already clasping the young man's hands in his.

The welcome Father Blanche extended his former pupil, the son of his comrade in arms, was warm and genuine and Jean fell under that old spell of admiration and instinctive willingness to follow the leadership of this big man, with shaggy white hair, pinch nose glasses and the friendly piercing eyes. The atmosphere was very relaxed and friendly as the two men sat down and lit their pipes. For an instant, both must have visualized themselves back at St. Jean, to those days they had spent in the relationship of Master and Student. Sure, Jean had been an impetuous young man who needed to be held in check, but he had also been full of wholesome energy, intelligent, spirited in sports, even if he had the dash of modern youth. It was the soldier's background that made Father Blanche discover and admire such qualities. This was the human clay that challenged and fascinated him. His tools to mould it into men of worth were only his leadership qualities, his self-discipline and his love of his fellow human being. Indeed the bravery and sacrifices of young men like this one now before him, had been the only source of pride for France in the disastrous war of 1870. He had led in battle those young men and he remembered. Jean only needed to find himself and he would succeed.

The opening talk was mostly about the family. It had been distressing to learn that the health of Jean's father had given cause for concern, but happily remedial action had been taken and serious consequences avoided. Father Blanche then launched into an explanation of his own presence in Canada. The task he and Father Morin had undertaken in November of 1890 had seemed well nigh impossible. To lay the foundation of a college and operate it with very meagre resources, was a challenge that tested his self-confidence to the limit. Somehow, with the help of the devoted Acadians and many friends in France, Ste. Anne was built and the first year of instruction had begun in September of 1891. He hoped that the worst was now behind, as he looked forward to the second year starting next September.

Father Blanche then touched upon the country and the people, especially the Acadians. As he had done in his letters to his friend, Jean's father, he eulogized the country, its effective government, its climate and above all the opportunities it presented for newcomers as well as for the natives. There was therefore no reason to doubt that Jean would find a suitable and profitable opening for himself. He had education, training and some means to get started. While orientating himself, Jean would live at the college as agreed and could find many ways to be helpful.

Jean had always felt free to open his most inner thoughts to Father Blanche. Very frankly, he told him he had realized the problems of his contemporaries and he had wondered what future might lay ahead for himself. He was confused. His father told him France was adrift in a chaotic economic and political morass created by the Godless government. But life had been very pleasant and at times he had resented restraints suggested by his father and the sermons of his mother. Like many of his worldly friends, he was now tiring of that life of pleasure and he was grateful for this opportunity to come to Canada.

Father Blanche would always be there to help and advise and Jean was confident and happy now, anxious to start his apprenticeship and investigation. Father Blanche seemed pleased also as he was reminding Jean that he must learn English, right away. He himself was working at it now. The college bell rang for "déjeuner" (lunch).

The refectory was very simply furnished and the meal was frugal, very monastic and without wine. The conversation over the next half hour was naturally about France, then mainly for Jean's benefit, it turned to Canada, with which all four priests were enthused. The Acadians were discussed with great feeling and hope for their advancement. This contact encouraged Jean further.

That first night, Jean, lying on his small unpainted wooden bed in a sparcely furnished little room on the top floor of the college, surveyed his experience so far. He felt somewhat dazed and certainly confused and uncertain, the change of environment was so drastic. He had no financial worries. Besides sending him an allowance, his father had arranged to pay the college, generously no doubt, for his board. He would heed Father Blanche's advice and follow his guidance. He was enthused about what he had heard and was curious to start his looking around. Tomorrow would bring his second day of discovery of Canada.

During the next month, Jean Jacques listened, looked around and asked questions. Nearly every day he had at least a brief chat with Father Blanche and very often he walked up to the Post Office to listen to Louis Melanson tell about the past of the Acadians, the present day politics of the country, its economy and its way of life. Jean quickly came to like the Acadians. They were a happy people in spite of their hard life. The entire family worked on the land, in the fishing boat and in the forest. Very little money circulated in trade but the bartering of goods and services flourished. During this same time, Jean started learning English, a task he found interesting and not too difficult.

By the end of the first month, Jean felt ready to explore further afield. He would go to Weymouth, the nearest town, which he was told was quite large and very prosperous. The train journey was interesting and his first view of the town was surprisingly impressive, although he quickly gathered it was not really large. On both sides of the Sissiboo River, he saw the activity of what appeared to be a thriving commerce. Stores, great piles of lumber, tall ships and teams of oxen and horses on the road. On the high ground, he saw nice houses and churches. Making his way across the bridge to the office of the *L'Evangeline* newspaper, he formed the impression that this was a prosperous and flourishing area.

Jean Jacques had, by this time, discarded, at least for every day wear, his fine clothing, but he still looked a stranger in these surroundings, clad in high leather boots, a longish jacket and a soft felt hat. The editor of the paper welcomed him warmly and introduced him to his staff. They had heard of this young man and now all eyes were on him. Jean was not slow in taking stock of the situation and resting an eye on the rather pretty girls, more stylishly dressed than the ones at Church Point, as they answered his low bow with what he mused the same coquetish smiles of young ladies everywhere. Decidedly, this might be a very good place in which to settle one's roots.

Being shown the town, Jean learned many useful things from the many people he was introduced to and he was pleasantly surprised that already he was able to converse in his new language, albeit with some difficulty. That afternoon, boarding the Halifax train for Church Point, he felt very satisfied with his day.

September and the opening of the fall term at the college arrived very quickly, at least it seemed to Jean, and he found himself helping wherever he could. He did some tutoring in French, undertook the supervision of study periods and helped in putting on concerts and performed as a violinist.

Through the fall, he continued his visits to Weymouth, looking around, visiting places of business, lumber operations and ships in harbour. He kept enlarging his circle of friends and business contacts. He talked with woodsmen, millmen and other tradesmen and relaxed and talked with Uncle John, sitting by the warming fireplace of the Goodwin Hotel.

Jean's letters home were always informative and interesting. He described the country, its people, Acadians, English, Blacks and even Indians. He kept his father informed as he learned, as he went along, travelling and mixing with all the people. He assured his mother that he was very happy, that he was attentive to the advice Father Blanche was good enough to give him. She would be pleased to learn that he followed the custom of the good people at Church Point and went to church every Sunday.

Jean had missed his horse very much and it was at this time that he bought one for forty dollars, a good price at the time, and a saddle at Campbell's in Weymouth for nine dollars. It was a novel sight for the people to see Jean, dressed in his riding habit he had brought from home, cantering along the road. He liked to ride in the woods, where the ever changing scenery of colour, lakes and paths was a new sight to him. A few miles in the woods at the back of Church Point, he found a small water powered sawmill. He visited it many times, intrigued by its mechanism and marvelling at its simplicity and perfect functioning. He loved the smell of fresh sawdust and newly sawn lumber drying in piles along the road. Some days he brought a lunch and at noontime sat with the men as they ate their lunch brought from their homes. They explained the workings of the mill and regaled him with tales of the woods.

During the winter, Jean had to curtail his wandering through the country somewhat, but he did find back of Grosses Cocques an interesting logging operation. He watched the men cut the trees, limb them and haul them with their ox teams to the mill pond of another water powered sawmill, ready for spring sawing. It was also during the winter of 1893 that he gave violin and equitation lessons, for which he received no pay. Pursuing the arts was not generally highly regarded by the population. Much better for a boy to learn to be a good carpenter, mason, blacksmith and how to fish, farm and cut trees. It was considered perhaps a good thing for one boy in a large family to have some higher education, but not all the children. In order to change this spirit of passive resistance to education, the college had started evening classes for adults. The people, thusly exposed, began to see the value to knowledge and acquired a taste for finer things. Midnight Mass that Christmas brought a sense of appreciation of colourful religious ceremonies with singing by a few trained voices and the sweet music from Jean's violin. The people were deeply moved and even the Indians squatting at the back of the church, sat immobile as if in a trance.

By springtime, Jean Jacques was able to manage quite well in English and was off to Halifax. The hours of the day-long train trip passed quickly as he was completely absorbed by the changing scenery, woods, lakes, towns, mountains and finally the city which looked quite big. In Halifax, he stopped at the Queen Hotel, which he found comfortable and with a good table.

The French Consul arranged several introductions for him, through which he visited a number of businesses, lumber dealers, merchants, shipping companies and even a fish processing plant. Jean was also introduced to the social life of the city and he was not one to miss opportunities in this very necessary side of one's life. He was introduced at the Yacht Club, the Gun Club and the Riding Club. Everywhere, he met very fine young people. He was surprised to see that young ladies were members of these clubs, a freedom which was unheard of in France. In his fine Parisian clothes and displaying his finest manner with the ladies, Jean could guess that he had been a grand success if not a devastating one. Friendships that he made on this visit remained close over the years ahead.

Back in his familiar surroundings, on a beautiful afternoon in May 1894, Jean was on his horse riding up river to visit the Sissiboo Pulp Mill. He had come up from Church Point that morning, had lunched at the Goodwin and planned to stay there the night.

Cantering along the tortuous road, he was soon

enthralled by the picturesque scenery, unfolding on every side. The forest of varying hues of green rose from the very shoreline of the Sissiboo to the top of the steep hills on both sides. The banks of the river, studded at intervals with rocky cliffs, presented varied and well proportioned vistas, continually surprising and fascinating his esthetic sense. Further along, he was enchanted by the sight of a delightful little bay called Green Cove, surely the place to recline on the soft green grass along its edge, and dream in the tranquility of a freed soul, floating in perfect unison with the lively ripples moving along the mighty river.

Suddenly he came face to face with a wonder he had never seen before; the majestic falls. Over sixty feet of tumbling water, cast in whirling white foam, rolling along, eternally it seemed, to the rhythm of its frightening roar, in hundreds of changing patterns until it swirled in an eddy before returning to placid waters to continue in a quiet flow to the sea. While Jean stood there in awe, he realized the value of this unlimited energy, that could be harnessed to produce goods and wealth. Sissiboo The Sublime.

He visited the pulp mill, now being built, situated on one side at the top of the falls. Only a fraction of the energy was used to run the machinery. The peeled wood was crushed by huge rollers into a yellowish paste that was then compressed, dried and bundled into packages of slabs about three feet square. The finished product was taken to ships at Weymouth, destined for markets in the U.S.A.

Jean Jacques continued his exploration and by the time the college year ended in early June, he had pretty well decided he would try his luck in the lumber business. Father Blanche had given much of his valuable time to Jean, looking into possibilities and discussing projects with him. Jean's letters home were very enthusiastic about prospects and the beauty of the forest, much of it still in its virgin state. The climate was healthful and life was peaceful. It was therefore not a great surprise when Jean's father received a definite proposal to buy timber lands in Digby County. Father Blanche recommended the purchase. Beside providing a start for Jean, it would be a good investment. Without delay, Jean's father agreed to finance the venture and with this good news, Jean started his feverish search for land. Well wooded land near the shore was not available any more. What could be bought was badly deforested. Weymouth offered the best shipping facilities, therefore, it would be wise to search for land further inland at the back of the town.

The news quickly spread that the young Frenchman, with money, was looking for land to buy and offers began to come in, of course, at unreasonably high prices. Jean and Father Blanche realized at this point that expert advice was needed and they turned to two experienced and highly recommended woodsmen, Howard Steele and Ben White, both living at Southville and knowing the surrounding country well. The first lot they looked at consisted of about five hundred acres, situated between two lakes called Little Tusket and Langford. Jean went on the cruise with his two advisors and learned something about the art of estimating the stumpage content of a given piece of land. The final report was very encouraging. No timber had been cut there for many years and very little had been cut then. It was practically virgin forest, in a healthy state and it would produce very high quality spruce and pine lumber.

The experts then looked into the feasibility of exploiting that land. The two lakes were connected by less than a mile of river and at the Landford end, down stream, a water saw mill had operated long ago. No trace of its ruins were visible. There was no reason why another mill could not be installed on the same site. The six miles of road from Southville were bad, but then all roads were bad, and with a little work on it, ox teams could negotiate it easily. Ox teams were the accepted means of transporting lumber, or indeed any freight, at the time.

Negotiations for the purchase of the land began in earnest. The price was much too high but Jean knew the seller was anxious to sell. He bargained hard and long, at the same time, looking at other lands. Finally, a price was reached, a little above market price, but still below the land's value. Armed with a six month's option, Jean hired a millwright from Church Point by the name of Fric Thibodeau, to look into the feasibility of setting up a sawmill on the site of the previous one. Fric visited the area with Jean and after a few days' assessment, he assured him that a large capacity water powered sawmill could be built there. Two dams would be needed, one at the foot of Tusket Lake to build a large reservoir of water and the other at the mill.

By this time, Jean had gone over the old road on horseback many times. He had spent many nights alone on the banks of the Silver River at the old mill site, sitting by the fire and sleeping on the perfumed fir boughs. He was completely captivated by the beauty of this peaceful corner of the world. He must have it and he dreamed of the day when he would settle down there. Father Blanche was closely involved in the transaction up to its final closing, so much so in fact that he confreres felt they should report his involvement to the General of the Order in France. They reported that the people knew of Father Blanche's involvement in these negotiations and were beginning to think he himself was buying the land. They might think he was a rich man and it would be disastrous if the people, as a consequence, withheld their donations to the cause. It is unlikely Father Blanche ever knew of these reports. He probably had an idea that his associates, who, in theory, were his subordinates, felt that he concerned himself too deeply with the social and economic development problems of the community and that he was somewhat authoritarian. But he pushed ahead towards his goal. The passing of the years have heightened his stature in the eyes of the people, as they realize that without a man of his stamp, the difficult foundation of Ste. Anne might well have foundered. Over the many years and in this day, his memory is literally revered.

The land was bought and the plans for its development started to take shape at once. Before the autumn rains, 1894, the dams would be completed, as well as the under structure of the mill. The rains would fill Long Tusket and Little Tusket lakes, while some logs would be cut alongside the river and near the mill to begin the production of lumber. Before that, the timbers for the understructure had been squared by hand on site. In the early fall, a crew of men with a yoke of oxen went to work improving the old road by laying hardwood trees across it in the marshy spots and blasting a few boulders.

By November, a little cabin had been built by the mill site to house Jean and the carpenters who would finish the mill during the winter. As soon as snow came, a logging crew settled in very rough cabins along Tusket Lake and began cutting logs and hauling them onto the ice.

From the first moment Jean discovered the woods, he was captivated by its charm. His letters home displayed growing enthusiasm as time went on. He had a good imagination and he wrote in a vein that was sure to arouse the minds of his brothers, especially the younger ones. At that time, there was wild excitement all over Europe about America, generated by stories by Jules Verne and other writers, and by the sight of life and adventure depicted in Buffalo Bill's Wild Shows. It seems every young man wanted to go to this fabulous land. The Stehelin boys were even more excited about the mysterious forest, the wild animals, the freedom of life spent hunting, and fishing. Any young man would thirst for this sort of adventure. The parents were also greatly taken by these descriptions of the free life, but they were chiefly relieved and pleased to gather that their son Jean was making progress in settling down to a good life.

Jean's stay at the College had been most beneficial in many ways. Father Blanche could feel that he had done all he could to help him get started and had succeeded in his set task. Jean would find his way in the business world and he could still be his friend and advisor.

Jean Jacques was finally on his own and he was very happy and confident. It was not too soon for him to leave the monastic life of Sainte Anne. The yoke was beginning to chafe, as his father gathered from his letters of late, in which he complained that the good sisters in charge of the kitchen were lacing the food with salt-petre.

It was not long afterwords, that my grandfather received the shattering news from Jean, that he had decided to marry an Acadian girl. The whole family was shocked, all the more so because Jean did not ask permission of his father, as was the custom for young men to do in those days.

A letter from Father Blanche came not far behind. Obviously, he was very upset, stating very firmly that such a union was unthinkable and Jean must be dissuaded from it. There was such a gulf between Jean's and Katie Thiboudeau's backgrounds, that there could be no compatibility. Nothing derogatory could be said about Katie's character, but she was not in Jean's class. In fact, she could hardly read or write. He had tried to reason with Jean and as a last resort had told him he would refuse to perform the marriage ceremony.

In a desperate effort to stave off Jean's plans, his father sent him a cablegram, asking him to postpone his marriage until he recieved his letter which was on the way.

Jean persisted stubbornly in going ahead with his plans. He informed his family he would not come home as asked to do. In a last cablegram, the distressed father made his desperate move. He told Jean he refused his consent to the marriage. Jean brushed aside all objections, advice and entreaties and left Church Pointe with Katie to be married in a neighbouring parish. For a time, the newlyweds set up their home in Weymouth, but it was not long before they were back at Stuart's Hotel at Church Point. Katie, the country girl, had never been away from her village and her family and she was too lonesome to stay in Weymouth.

Although very upset and perhaps very discouraged, my grandfather did not disown Jean and cut off his income and the capital for the new venture, now well underway. The marriage was never mentioned again. It was accepted as an unalterable situation and it was the duty of the parents to try to make it work. They had nothing against Katie as a person and even from the great distance that separated them, they tried to be kind to her.

This turn of events, precipitated the next decision, which was in the background of my grandfather's thoughts for some time in the future. In the summer of 1894, he decided to send Emile Jean, his oldest son, to Canada to look over the situation. Perhaps in the deep recesses of his mind was geminating the idea that some day he would himself cross the Atlantic.

A FAMILY AT THE CROSSROADS

Approaching the closing decade of the last century, Emile Charles Adolphe Stehelin was living very comfortably in his spacious home, St. Charles, near Gisors, in Normandy, France. His successful felt factory stood adjacent to his home. In the setting, he worked and lived with his wife and eleven children, three daughters and eight sons, ranging in ages from twenty-four to four years.

Emile had not always lived in this part of France. He had been born in Alsace, a rich industrial province on the Upper Rhine River on July 28, 1837. His family from far back had been connected with the iron foundry and the machine tool business at Bitschwiller where he was born. His father, Charles, with a cousin, had run the business.

Under the management of Charles, the company had branched out into the construction of locomotives. They built the first Alsatian engines and on October 25, 1838, with Charles at the throttle, the line Paris-St. Cloud, was inaugurated. The Duc d'Orleans, eldest son of Louis Philippe was on board for this memorable occasion. The firm built twenty locomotives following this first one. In 1843, Charles and Edouard started a felt manufacturing business, having developed a new type of steam engine, ideally suited to the process involved.

Alas, for the family and the business, Charles died suddenly at the age of forty-four in 1848, at the height of his success, just recently decorated by a grateful government with the Legion of Honour. He left three daughters and two sons, the younger being my grandfather, Emile Charles Adolphe.

Emile was only eleven years old when his father died and the felt factory, which was his inheritance, had to be managed by trustees, his mother Amelie and his uncle Edouard, until he reached majority. When he did come of age, due to his trustees wise management, he took over a thriving business. His future was assured, prosperous and bright. In 1869, he married Marie Therese Buisson and the year following, the happy couple shared the joy of the birth of their first son, Emile Jean, my father.

The successful career, the happy family life, the dreams for the future, were brutally dashed with the outbreak of the Franco-Prussian war of 1870. Emile, like all young Frenchmen, was called to his regiment. It was an Infantry regiment and he held the rank of major in the Reserve. It was a disastrous war for France, humiliating in the extreme, more so because she had declared war and the Germans occupied Paris. It was a very short war and the treaty ending it imposed harsh terms on the vanquished, the most humiliating of which was the loss of the two northern provinces of Alsace and Lorriane. Neapoleon III was banished, ending his days in England, and the Third Republic was born.

Emile, demobilized, returned to his young family and his business, which seemed to give promise of continuing success. He soon realized, however, that he could not function and be happy under the heel of the Prussian boot. The citizens, the conquered, were to be made to feel their new masters. The land and its Frenchmen were to be totally germanized, the French language was to disappear, supplanted by German and the product of industry was to be oriented towards the needs of Germany, already building armaments for future aggression. In future, young men as they came of age would be drafted in the armies of the hated enemy for a period of compulsory service. For Emile, it was unbearable to have to contemplate the possibility of himself, his son and perhaps other sons born in the future finding themselves forced to face brother Frenchmen on the battlefield.

Like many Alsatians, Emile opted to remain a French citizen and leave the land of his ancestors, the province of Alsace, to settle in unoccupied France. Those like Emile who refused to swear allegiance to the conqueror were given a period of three years to wind up their affairs and leave the country.

Setting up a new felt factory in France presented many problems. Emile found that after two years of peace, the social and political conditions under the new Third Republic were still unsettled. To him, a business man from the calm and prosperous north, the situation seemed hopelessly chaotic. The government, new to power, was struggling to govern a divided people, mostly uneducated and in an underdeveloped industrial setting, if one compared it with that of America, England and Germany. Much of the instability was due to the ignorance of the masses, class warfare and the poverty of the peasantry. The monarchy and its privileged classes, although brought down by the revolution, were still powerful and bitter opponents of social change. Their forces united in a common effort to wreck democracy.

Among the businessmen and bankers of Paris, Emile had many friends. Business enterprises were owned by rich families and since time immemorial, the rich banking families, mostly immigrants, had controlled the fiscal and monetary business of government, of the kings, the Emperor and now the Republic. It was through these friends that he acquired his factory, from a rich banking family, who ran other factories at Gisors.

In 1873, the Stehelin family, now comprising four children, Emile Jean, born 1870, Jean, 1871, Charles, 1872 and Therese, 1873, moved to Gisors. As much of the machinery as could be dismantled, was moved from Alsace and reinstalled at Gisors. About thirty of his Alsatian workers and their families moved with their employer and within a very short time, the factory was operating and prosperous. Before leaving Bitschwiller, Emile tore down his house and sold the land, so bitter was his contempt for the Boche. Through respect for the memory of his mother, he did, however, retain a piece of the Forest of Remiremont in Lorraine, which she had given him.

Some day it would be part of France again and so would Alsace.

Gisors was fast becoming a highly developed industrial area. There were cotton, leather, linen and paper factories and now a felt factory. Gisors is only forty kilometers from Paris where Emile maintained an office. These factories were owned by rich and powerful families, some titled, whom the government feared, remembering that they had brought down two Republics and had prospered again during the Empire. To Emile, it looked much like the old order being revived with the old and the new nobility allied to the new rich and politically powerful families.

Being a democrat, in the circle in which Emile moved, was like being a socialist today. He approved steps taken by the government to raise the standard of life for the labouring class. He believed in compulsory education, which would bring equality of opportunity to all and with it, a stronger economic base and a rich intellectual development. Of course, he believed in free enterprise, providing it was free and competitive. Such an egalitarian philosophy was frowned upon in the chateaux of Gisors.

My grandfather decided to send his sons to the public school, run by the Christian Brothers. This caused raised eyebrows among his friends, because this new type of school was frowned upon, even by the ordained clergy who tended to snub the Brothers. After all, Emile was a successful businessman and he was expected to line up with the elitists and bring up his children above the masses, very necessary, of course, for labour and the army. This attitude naturally drifted down to the sons of the higher society which caused many fist fights between them and the Stehelin sons.

Having settled this problem, at least for the time being, Emile returned to his worrying thoughts about the state of the French nation. It was a continuing source of concern and doubt to see the government unable to govern effectively, impeded by the shortage of leadership resources and the continuing opposition from the remnant of the Old Order. Unfortunately the bitterness which this situation engendered, caused the adoption of anti-clerical legislation, which further split the nation and isolated France from important external contacts.

As time went on, however, younger men of worth seemed to appear on the political scene. One of these was Clemenceau, a young doctor turned politician. He was highly applauded when he spoke the mind of many Frenchmen declaring, "We must vote for the biggest idiot if we want to save France".

Comparing France with other nations, only heightened Emile's sense of frustration. As much as he hated the Boche, he had to watch Germany forging ahead towards its probable goal of world domination. The presence of the British Empire was perhaps the only stabilizing force in the world. The peace and progress of that vast empire worked mightily on the minds of Frenchmen. Its story was one of unbelievable success, apparent happiness and prosperity. At its head, a constitutional monarch, an orderly functioning Parliament, people at work developing a mighty industry. Queen Victoria was held in affection well beyond the confines of her Realm. She was affectionately called, The Grandmother of Europe.

From appearances, however, one would never have thought that Emile should have had too many causes to worry about his life and his family. His wife had given him more healthy children since the family had moved to Gisors. By the year 1880 had been born, Adeline Sophie in 1874, Louis in 1875, Roger in 1876, Paul in 1878 and Germaine in 1879. Yet, even in lighter moments, as he drove with his beautiful wife beside him in his shining bright landeau, with his Alsatian coachman, Leon, performing with style, to a dance or perhaps a garden party to one of his friends' chateau, his mind never strayed very far from his nagging concern about the future. Another war, bringing perhaps complete collapse. The Revanche was hoped for, but how could such a weak government bring it about. Now with six sons, and maybe more in the future, what chance would they have.

It was soon time to think of higher education for Emile Jean, Jean and Charles. Taking the advice of his friends, he sent Emile Jean and Jean to a college at Vaugirard, run by Jesuits disguised as laymen. One of the objectives of the school was undoubtedly to prepare the upper class youth for the destruction of the Republic. Physical fitness was given high priority and fencing was taught as an asset for acceptance into the army officer corps. The teaching inflamed the minds of the students with a sense of "Divine Mission". They would become the elite, that led by the masters, would restore France to her former greatness and bring glory upon themselves. They would form part of that illustrious company, Deus Machina (The Machine of God).

Young minds were easily inflamed, when subjected to this type of indoctrination and the Stehelin sons were proud to tell their father of their future glorious destiny. Their father, however, was not so taken with the type of training his sons were receiving. In fact, he would have nothing to do with Deus Machina and this plotting against the established government to destroy it.

After much searching, Emile decided to send his three sons to the Ecole St. Jean at Versailles. It was run by Eudist Fathers, who, although also Royalists at heart, were not plotting like the Jesuits. They held on to the old values, but more so because they felt they alone formed character and self-discipline. They could not keep out of their institution the new wave of modernism that was sweeping the country. Reluctantly, they had to allow a certain freedom of thought and independence in their students. But they did succeed in maintaining some vestiges of the old line discipline.

My grandfather was greatly relieved and encouraged when he found at St. Jean, as prefect of disciple, his old army comrade, Gustave Blanche. It was a joyous reunion, a recementing of a friendship born in the hardships of military service together during the disastrous war, still vivid in their minds. And now, they both agonized over the sorry fate of the homeland, adrift in a storm of politics and impotence and the wave of Moderism which was sweeping away solid old values, creating a vacuum which brought independence of thought and action and a breakdown of restraining moral values. Not only the youth were affected. The men who had recently risen to power and opulence were now able to adopt the loose morals, reserved in the past to the nobility. The cachet of a liberated successful man was keeping a mistress in luxury.

Paris was the free city of pleasure where a new romanticism inspired the writings of emancipated poets. A difficult environment in which to bring up sons.

Gustave Blanche was born in Brittany in 1848, in a comfortably well to do family. When the call to arms came in 1870, he was articled to a notary, studying law. He joined his Regiment as a private soldier, but his valour and leadership qualities were recognized and he was soon commissioned an officer on the battlefield. He went on to successfully command his platoon and finally his Company. He was then sent north, to a staff appointment. It was at the headquarters of General Martenot that Emile Stehelin met Captain Blanche. The two men cemented a friendship which lasted throughout their service. Like so many Frenchmen, they were humiliated by the treaty of Frankfort, which made their country feel the sting of defeat. They agonized over the loss of France's richest northern provinces. Demobilized, each went back to civilian life, not seeing each other during the intervening years.

Gustave Blanche did not go back to his law office. During the turmoil of the war, he had felt a great desire to serve his fellow man in his deepest need. Entering religious life, in due time, he received Holy Orders and became a member of the Eudist Congregation.

Three more children were added to the family; Maurice in 1882, Simone in 1885, and finally Bernard in 1886. Therese was already a young lady, attending the Convent of the Ladies of the Sacred Heart at Beauvais, a town near Gisors. Germaine was attending a day school run by sisters in Gisors, in preparation for continuing at the Sacred Heart.

As the last decade of the century approached, life seemed serene at St. Charles. The social circle, Paris-Gisors, lived a life all its own, for the young as well as for their parents. Rich families became more powerful, consolidating fortunes through the marriages of their children. The ladies vied with each other in their Haute Couture. Sunday Mass was a special occasion to parade themselves at their best. Young men seemed to do nothing but amuse themselves. They had their own saddle horses, attended afternoon parties, evening parties, the horse races, and took their places in the grander society of

Paris. They were learning to be gentlemen, which went with the yearning for the Revanche. If they could not all be admitted to St. Cyr, the top military school, they could be perfect horsemen for a cavalry regiment. The young ladies danced under the benign eye of their mothers, whose burning ambition was to make their daughters desired by young men, so that with a substantial dot (dowry), their fathers would arrange a "good marriage".

Emile Stehelin could not help wondering if the present state of affairs could really be real and could lead to a calmer future for France and especially for his sons. His concern became real as his sons, one by one finished at St. Jean. The eldest, Emile Jean, went to the army for his compulsory one year service. Jean, while awaiting his call up, became the dashing young man of his set, which through connections made at college, now extended to Paris. He was an accomplished horseman and a good violinist. He soon became popular and made his friends among the debonair and ultra modern young men and women of Paris.

The antipathy between the Government and the Clergy was getting progressively more bitter. The Clergy felt unable to transfer their loyalty and allegiance to the Republic, which was getting stronger and more determined to demand it. The Eudists, like many orders, started to look for a haven in another country. They made their choice for America, Canada if possible. They had some knowledge of Canada. Years before, one of their brother priests had been a friend of Bishop Laval of Quebec. Later a young Eudist had ministered to the people along the St. Lawrence. He had heard of the Acadian people and had come upon their story by Longfellow, and had translated Evangeline into French.

In Nova Scotia, about this time, among the Acadians, a movement for the building of a French college for boys was gathering momentum. The years following the exile had been unbelievably difficult, full of suffering and humiliation. Finding no home anywhere, the drift back to the province began quite early after the deportation of 1755. They found no welcome on the part of the government. They were refused grants of land but they were allowed to occupy desolate lands along Ste. Mary's Bay "temporarily". By 1871, the condition of this unfortunate people had improved considerably. There had been no serious opposition by the English colonists to their resettlement, perhaps because it was well known that the land they squatted on was arid and rocky, ill suited to rewarding cultivation. The government began to make generous concessions of land to the Acadians. As the need for more land grew with the rapidly increasing population, further grants were made.

Social and political progress had been very slow in developing, due to the lack of education and therefore leadership. The people, however, had maintained their language, culture and religion. They were a mission to the priests who visited them infrequently. The Irish priests were not particularly interested in helping them to remain Acadian, and it was not until the arrival of Abbé Signogne that they began to make progress. Abbé Signogne, born in France, had been banished from his country at the Revolution, because he would not swear allegiance to the new government. In England, he found refuge and was given a teaching job. The British government, through some chance of circumstance, sent him to the Acadians. Not only did this energetic man minister to the religious needs of his flock, but he also became their lawmaker, administrator and arbiter of their disputes. That he was a ruler with a firm hand there is no doubt, but he was able to negotiate successfully for the Acadians.

Between 1885 and 1889, the Acadians, having developed sufficient strength, put pressure on the Archbishop in Halifax, who controlled the education of his faithful, to allow them to operate a French College for boys. This concession was not won easily, because the Archbishop held the opinion that the best solution to the Acadian problem, from all standpoints, was to assimilate them into the English (Irish) culture and education system.

The Acadians were known to be hard headed and they persisted in their demand, until the Archbishop agreed to the foundation of an academy, not a college, at the expense of the Acadians themselves, reserving the right to select the religious order to build and operate it.

Negotiations were undertaken with several orders, but they all in turn refused the assignment. Finally, someone in Quebec recommended the Eudist Fathers, and a letter was sent to their General, Father Le Doré. The Eudists replied, accepting the charge, but somehow the letter was lost and negotiations with another order were undertaken. Not hearing back from Halifax, Father Le Doré decided to send two confreres to look over the situation. He selected Father Blanche and Father Morin for this assignment and they left in September 1890.

It was a surprised and embarrassed Archbishop in Halifax, who, one day late in September, 1890, opened his door to these two Frenchmen. He had practically promised the task to another order and he told them he needed a few days to decide what to do. Indeed after a few days, Father Blanche was called in to learn the final decision, which happily was in his favour. After final negotiations, the two Eudists were on their way to Church Point on Ste. Mary's Bay. To sustain them and their new work, they were given the cure of three parishes, with all benefits and revenues, but no money.

Father Blanche threw himself, energetically and confidently into his new task. He encountered a very hospitable but poor people. The building of Ste. Anne College began at once. The people gave of their labour and lumber, but money was not available in sufficient amounts to provide the materials that had to be bought. They asked for and received donations from France and from friends of their families. The Acadian clergy aided financially, to the limit of their resources, and the college was soon abuilding.

Father Blanche and his friend in Gisors kept up a correspondence, which from the outset revealed the enthusiasm of Father Blanche for the New World. The country was beautiful, peaceful and full of opportunities. Religion flourished like in the olden days in France and the morals of the people were wholesome. In spite of many hardships, letters from Canada reflected joy, love of the country and its people and great enthusiasm and hope for the future.

The following summer, Father Blanche returned to France, chiefly to get financial assistance from friends and associations. He visited many people and returned to St. Jean to see some of the young men he had started on their way to an education. He enthused all those he spoke with and his superiors were well pleased with his work.

Emile met Father Blanche on this visit and they talked about mutual problems and no doubt about the future. For good reasons, Emile was worried about the future of his sons. Jean was becoming a source of concern. He was caught up in the wave of modern ideas, rebellious to authority. He was burning away his energies on living the life of the youth of Paris. Perhaps Canada would provide him the incentive he needed to make something of his life, once removed from the life of youth in modern France. It was something to think about.

Father Blanche returned to Church Point and correspondence between the two men continued. Eventually Emile had to face the fact that there seemed no issue to Jean's problem. After much thought, it was decided that he would go to Canada. There, under the guidance of Father Blanche, he would try to make his way into some kind of occupation. Jean willingly accepted the prospect of leaving for new adventure.

Towards the end of 1891, the family had been shocked to learn, that their father's health was impaired to the point he would have to curtail his activities. Unfortunately, work at business and worries at home could not be put aside easily, and continued to mine his health. Early in 1892, Emile was confronted with the solemn edict of his doctor that he must stop work completely and take an enforced rest. He accepted the inevitable, although he nursed in his mind some misgivings about entrusting his affairs to his manager and his inexperienced son, Emile Jean. The only solution was for him to go away, removing himself from the causes of his worries. Accordingly, accompanied by his wife, he went to Divonne-les-Bains, a health spa on Lake Geneva.

Emile and his wife spent most of 1892 at Divonne-les-Bains. He returned home, much improved in health. His doctor was encouraging, but he cautioned against his patient getting once again fully involved in the business. Emile realized that part-time involvement would be impossible, and after mature thought, considering that he was fifty years of age, he took the momentous decision to retire and sell the factory.

Shortly after the death of his brother in 1893, Emile felt the urge to visit Alsace and Lorriane. He had never returned there since he had left in 1873. Firstly, he wanted to revisit the town of Remiremont, the home of his mother and the small piece of land he was still holding. He went on to visit his brother's widow and his nephews and nieces at Pont d'Aspach. It was a sad reunion, filled with apprehension lest another war break out too soon. These two families shared common anxieties over the future of their younger members, whether they lived in Alsace or in France.

Emile found the situation so depressing that he vowed never to return until the day Alsace would be French again. In a melancholy mood, he crossed into Switzerland to visit relations and family landmarks in Bâle. Being in this country of peace, prosperity and culture and mingling with his cousins and relations, who extended their warm hospitality, rekindled his spirits. Returning to St. Charles, to the turmoils of France and the worries of his family, he consoled himself somewhat in the thought that his life was not, after all, the most difficult in these trying times.

THREE MORE SONS TO CANADA

The decision to send Emile Jean to Canada to look over the situation was taken in the summer of 1894 and he started preparing to leave France in the autumn. He was then twenty-four years old, had finished university, his military service and had had some experience at the felt factory.

It always seemed that each decision taken by Emile brought on a new problem. At this point, Roger who was eighteen and Paul who was sixteen, declared that they too wanted to go to Canada with their older brother. After much thinking, soul searching and a lot of persistence on the part of the two boys, the father consented to let them go, but on the firm undertaking that they would enroll at Sainte Anne College on arrival and finish their education there. Father Blanche was consulted and he agreed to enroll them. Calm was restored but the father and mother could not help some feeling of concern and regret as they saw the beginning of the dispersal of their family. In those days, families clung together as long as possible.

One can easily imagine the upheaval in the minds of these young men and the general air of excitement in the home, as preparations went on. Going to Canada where one would live among the Indians and wild animals was a thought indeed unbelievably exciting and daring. Among the friends of the family, there was amazement and doubt at the wisdom of the whole project. Canada was so far away, almost unknown to people in Europe, engrossed in their own busy lives. The whole of America was still thought of as a land of snow and mystery.

Preparations were made as for a very dangerous expedition. Trunk upon trunk were filled with woolens, heavy clothing, rifles, shot guns, harness, and varied accoutrements, in fact with everything that ignorance of the country and inexperience in this sort of adventure could suggest. The pictures of the Canadian forest, in the novels of Jules Verne, glowed ever so brightly in the imagination of these young boys. Over and above this enchantment, in plain truth, the change promised them relief from the boredom of the idleness of their lives. The future looked exhilarating especially so because it seemed so far fetched and so daring to their friends.

Farewell parties were held in the chateaux around Gisors. They had many young friends in the fashionable large families of their community. It was for good reason that these spoilt young people were known as the "Jeunesse Dorée" (gilded youth).

One notable farewell event was a hunting party known as "La chase à courre", hunting the stag on horseback behind a pack of hounds, in proper dress and with all the niceties of the sport carefully organized. To the sound of the hunting horn, the chase went on all day, through hill and dale, over obstacles and through water. By dusk, the exhausted stag was standing in the river up to his knees, wet with sweat, perfectly still in the early moon light. The pack of dogs on the bank howled savagely but were not brave enough to attack him. There the noble animal stood, antlers high, looking with disdain at all these men who were going to make him die for their sport. The Picqueur (whip of the hunt), approaches and stabs the exhausted animal. "St. Hubert, patron of hunters, what crimes are committed in your name." Naturally, a big dinner followed and festivities carried on into the small hours of the morning.

On the 8th of December, 1894, at last the day of departure had arrived. The train from Dieppe picked up the three boys at Gisors for Paris, where they transferred to the boat train for Le Havre. The family and a large number of friends were at the station to wave a last farewell with wishes for a bon voyage, as the station master blew his trumpet and the train disappeared into the darkness. Among those left behind, young and old, many shook their heads in doubt. Perhaps the parents felt some apprehension and questioned in their inner thoughts, the wisdom of allowing this adventure to an uncivilized Mission Country. Perhaps they even wondered if they would ever see their sons again. But the excited and seemingly foolhardy trio felt like heroes and would not have traded their places for an empire.

On the train to the boat, left to themselves and their thoughts in the darkened compartment, the young men, for the first time were really alone, engaged in serious reflection on the portent of their adventure, now begun. They became a little apprehensive too, and it was even with some real feelings of misgivings that they embarked on the liner, *Normandie*, of the French Line, bound for New York. It suddenly occurred to them that they had never even seen the sea, let alone a huge steamer that sailed an ocean. Their brother Charles had gotten leave to come aboard ship to see them off and at the sight of him, their spirits bounced again. As they toasted in champagne, the New World and then the Old World, the thought of everything they were leaving behind, left a little lump in their throats.

The big ship's siren, sounding its mournful wail into the night, brought home the hard realization that the approaching departure was into the unknown. Leave taking, perhaps forever, of the shores of their homeland, brought, even though only momentarily, a deep feeling of immense sadness, almost regret as expressed in the old Alsatian refrain they recalled,

> "quand il faut quitter son patelin
> Sa ferme, ses cochons et sa Rose
> On a beau faire le malin
> Cela fait toujours quelquechose."

> "When one has to leave his village,
> his farm, his pigs and his Rose,
> one may put on a bold front
> but it does one something just the same."

The last glimpse of Home was their brother Charles in

his resplendent sergeant's uniform of the Cuirassiers, standing motionless on the mole, his arm raised in farewell. Thrown in relief by the enormous floodlights along the dock, they watched his image disappear gradually, finally swallowed up into the darkness.

Very comfortably settled in cabins of the luxurious Normandie, the young adventurers soon found their nerve again and immensely enjoyed their next ten days at sea. Everything was new, interesting and even seasickness was a new experience. They soon made friends and seemed to dance all night with nice American girls, the first they had ever met. They liked the easy going freedom of these young ladies which disconcerted them at first, as they compared the French way, where a girl was closely chaperoned and had very little freedom. They even began to learn some useful English words. The food was of course very good and they were having a very nice time.

New York came into view one early morning. Accustomed to Paris with its gardens and parks, this huge city viewed from the ship seemed like a monstrous apparition. Indeed it was grandiose but very ugly. They didn't see the nicer parts of New York, as they only passed through a small part of it, on their way to Fall River and another ship that was to take them to Boston. Their first encounter with the English language was not too difficult. They were helped by friends made on the Normandie and they found the Americans very helpful and patient.

The Fall River boat was, to Europeans, astonishing in the extreme. An excellent brass band on the upper deck played lively marches. The promenade decks were simply full of people but what was most astonishing, because they were completely new to them, were the black waiters, dressed in white, of solemn and obsequious mein, serving in the restaurant.

They saw quite a bit of Boston on their way to another ship that would take them to Yarmouth, Nova Scotia. They liked Boston because it reminded them of French cities, with twisting streets made of cobblestones. Not attractive, but more familiar. The elevated railway was indeed a revelation to them.

They had seen nothing like this before.

On the good ship *S.S. Yarmouth*, a far cry indeed from the *Normandie*, they made their first contact with some people who spoke French. They were Acadians, of whom they had only recently heard about, through letters from Father Blanche and their brother Jean. They were, therefore, very interested in meeting some of them. At first, they had difficulty understanding their French. The idioms were archaic, but the source of the greatest problem in understanding them, was their use of so many English words. Giving English words a French pronunciation did not help either.

The *Yarmouth* left Boston in the evening, and the trip was without incident except that the sea was very rough. After all, it was in December and the winter gales had arrived. The young men slept well in cabins which they found very small and poorly equipped. They had outside cabins and in the morning, they saw sea water sluicing about the floor. For supper, as the evening meal was introduced on the menu, they ate for the first time, corned beef hash and apple pie. For breakfast, they tried bacon and eggs, a dish not served in France.

They sighted Yarmouth at seven o'clock in the morning. Seen from a distance, this town looked like any other small seaport town; A cluster of houses and commercial buildings along the waterfront with the forest behind it. However, inspected closely as they came up the harbour and tied up at the wharf, this place was very different from anything they had ever seen before. For one thing, the streets were unpaved and very muddy. This mud made everything look dirty, especially the horses, wagons and carts moving about. The buildings, houses, stores, and warehouses were all made of wood. This was a strange sight indeed, giving them the impression that the whole town was nothing but a temporary flimsy theatre backdrop. These buildings were painted different colours, clashing all over this strange panorama. Here a blood red clashing with a bright yellow, on to a vivid green and other tints. A real orgy of colour. In the old world, one saw only the natural subdued colours of brick and stone blending together to give a pleasing effect to the eye.

Upon disembarking at Yarmouth, the trio entered the

nearest building they saw, which was a very small restaurant on the wharf. Happily, here they met a French speaking Acadian waitress who coaxed them to try moose meat. She explained that the moose was an animal of the forest, abundant, and that its meat was succulent and greatly appreciated. The meat was hard fried and they found its aroma very pungent. When they tried to eat it, they found it very tough and flat tasting, a far cry from the tender, rare red "bifteck" of their home province of Normandy. However, it was accepted as another new experience.

In a little while, a train backed up alongside the boat, on a track built on the wooden wharf, which, to their amazement, was held up simply by pilons of wood, driven into the muddy bottom. The bell of the train was ringing constantly, warning people and horses to get off the track. Looking at a scene of hurried activity, the newcomers' attention was attracted to the low hung platform carts, busily engaged hauling freight to and from the pier. The horses seemed small in comparison to the Percherons of Normandy. The make up of the harness was puzzling, a conglomeration of leather straps and pieces of rope. But the team seemed very practical.

Finding one's self in a strange country, one automatically begins by comparing with things left behind. In this frame of thought, they examined the train, which proved to be another discovery. Here, there were no First, Second, and Third class compartments. Indeed there were no compartments at all, just long coaches with a central passageway with seats on both sides. The seats were padded, and covered in velour, some red, others green. There was a small room at the end of each coach where men could go if they wished to smoke. Naturally, the women did not smoke. The lighting was by gas and the heating was by steam piped from the locomotive. In Europe at that time, the trains had three classes. The First Class was very luxurious; the Second Class was comfortable and way ahead of the Third Class which was uncomfortable with wooden seats, strictly for the peasants.

In Canada, apparently one just got onto the train and took a seat anywhere. There was no official on hand to collect one's fare before embarking. In fact, unlike in France, there were no officials at every turn, fatuous in their gold braided uniforms, pushing people about. There was no station master visible anywhere like in France, dressed in a fancy gold braided uniform, gold stripes and a fine cap, strolling about looking very important with a sheaf of papers under his arm, a long polished brass trumpet in one hand and a bright red flag in the other. He was very important and no train could move without the "agent de Gare" blowing his trumpet three blasts and waving his little red flag. Here things were different and simple. The train just started off after the conductor who seemed to appear from nowhere, growled something unintelligible to them, and waved his arm as he stepped into the last coach. After skirting the harbour for a little distance, they were amazed to see the train going over the road right through the town. There were no crossing barriers with a little man waving a flag as in France. Apparently here the train had equal right of way with the carts and the carriages. Nobody seemed concerned.

No one had told them before leaving Yarmouth that they had to obtain "billets" (tickets) for the train and so they were very amused to think that travellers didn't have to pay any fare. Very soon they discovered that they were very wrong on this point, as a commotion seemed to be arising over their heads when a little bearded old man in a very plain uniform and a funny little flap cap with a little gold braid here and there, stood in front of them saying something which they did not understand. They smiled at him politely but fixing his little beady eyes behind steel framed glasses on them, he continued to say something which was all gibberish to them. They thought he was very funny and they burst out laughing. Obviously, the wrong thing to do. The old man's face turned scarlet as he waved his arms in all directions, talking very fast and thrusting his hand in front of the boys hollering "ticket, ticket". He really thought these boys were putting him on, trying to travel free. The situation was saved and calm returned to the coach when a Religious Sister, who was an Acadian, explained to the Frenchmen that this man was the conductor, an important man, and that he wanted their fares. At the same time, she explained to the conductor that these young men spoke no English and had just landed from France. The incident was amicably closed when the fares were paid and everybody smiled again.

It was a cold December day and they enjoyed the warmth of the train. In Europe, trains were not heated. It was not deemed necessary as travel was not supposed to be comfortable and train journeys were not long anyway. The countryside along the route presented nothing attractive, to say the least. The land one could see appeared very wild and very poor. Here and there an opened field with little vegetation, usually strewn with big rocks. The appearance of the forest disappointed them. They had expected huge trees and soft clearings underneath them, just like the drawings in Jules Verne's books. Instead they looked at small stunted trees, all in a jungle. Here and there along the way appeared small villages, no more than a few drab unpainted houses and small barns which quickly disappeared again into the woods as the train sped by. The names on the signs were novel also; Ohio, Brazil, Hectanooga and others. Near old barns, they saw small and scrawny animals looking half frozen as they sought shelter from the bitter cold wind. It seemed so cold out there that no human being ventured out. One redeeming feature of this whole panorama of apparent desolation was the beauty of the frozen lakes, nestled in the trees and sparkling white in the bright sunshine.

It was at Meteghan Station that they saw the first sign of life. Some men were standing in front of the railway station, a little wooden building on stilts, painted green with maroon trim in front of which the train stopped for the first time since leaving Yarmouth. On a frozen road nearby, covered with a thin layer of snow, they saw big red wheeled carts drawn by bullocks, which they learned were called oxen, somehow yoked together and somehow harnessed to the cart. The houses looked better here, although very few were painted. Still, to the boys, this whole world was frozen and the wind so bitter. Would Siberia be like this?

Coming to a place called Saulnierville, the first French place name they encountered, they saw, way in the distance, the blue waters of Saint Mary's Bay and on the other side, the shoreline of the cold looking, blue hills of Digby Neck. The sun seemed to be warming up the countryside now, enlivening the whole scenery, even the people standing around at the station. As the train went along, they could see grey little houses in the distance, lining the bay for mile upon mile. Sister Bernard, who since the ticket episode, had taken these young men under her wing, explained that the whole length of this shore was like one long street in France. More like one great big village which was called La Ville Française. When the train passed, without stopping, at a place called Little Brook, Sister told them to get ready to get off soon at the next station which would be Church Point. In no time, the train stopped in front of another little station with a wooden platform along a short piece of track. The train blew and was off again, and there they stood on the ground, in the middle of nowhere.

They went inside the station, where they saw their first pot bellied coal stove standing in the middle of the room, giving off comfortable warmth. There were benches nailed to the walls on all four sides of the room. Looking out the window, the countryside looked cold and desolate.

Eventually a little man arrived, poorly dressed and rather unkempt. He was Vitale Thibodeau, the mail driver. He guessed who these young men were. They were Jean Stehelin's brothers and he had been expecting them any day now for the last week. He directed them outside and without more ado, invited them to climb aboard his conveyance which was to take them three miles to Church Point village.

This horse drawn contraption was called a wagine (corruption or francization of the english word wagon). It was an atrocious looking affair, which it seemed, passed for a carriage in this part of the world. It consisted of four large wheels between which somehow two seats had been mounted. Obviously, it was a rough home made affair, a far cry from the *landeau* and brake of St. Charles. Some suitcases were loaded in a box at the back and here and there whereever some spare space could be found. The trunks were left behind in the stations, to be brought out, a few at a time later on.

There was no room for Vitale in the wagine, so he walked alongside driving the scrawny little horse. They soon realized that Vitale had chosen the better part. Walking was much more comfortable than riding over this so called road, which was nothing but a myriad of frozen ruts, hard as rock. They wondered how this poor lean little old horse was going to haul this load. The boys got out of the carriage and started walking but they soon realized that they could not walk in their fancy shoes and they had to get back into the wagine.

The trip took more than one hour and it seemed long in the cold wind, to which they were not accustomed. There was nothing interesting to see along the road; more trees and a house here and there, no people to be seen anywhere. About one mile from Church Point, from open high ground, the sight they beheld took their whole attention. Against the beautiful blue backdrop of the bay, they saw the houses in the distance as if perched on a cliff.

The first men they saw out of doors wore woolen trousers coming just below the knees, heavy home made grey long stockings and heavy short coats. They wore grey mittens and big caps which covered their ears. They wore strange looking boots, which were called mocassins. Some were ankle length and some were knee high length, but all were home made. In fact, most clothing for men and women was home made, from the weaving of the cloth to the sewing and finsihing.

Looking beyond the houses, they saw the wooden white church and looming high, College Sainte Anne. They recognized the new rectory built very recently. It looked like St. Charles, only larger. Standing there in the midst of all the little houses, it gave these newcomers some nostalgic feeling of home. There were no trees anywhere and this, with the constant wind, gave the whole place an air or mournful sadness.

The first stop was at the Post Office and Louis Melanson, the postmaster, was the first man they shook hands with in Canada. He welcomed them warmly and invited them to warm themselves by the big stove in the middle of the floor. He introduced them to some men standing around or sitting on the counter, not seeming to be doing business, just passing away the time of day. Louis Melanson was a distinguished looking gentleman, refined and very kind, and they were friends from the first meeting.

They were introduced to another man, who also impressed them very much. His name was William à Johnie. His real name was William LeBlanc, but as they soon learned, surnames were seldom used here. Rather, people were described by tacking onto their christian names, the christian name or names of their fathers, and sometimes their grandfathers also, if considered necessary to identify an individual correctly. William was, therefore, the son of Johnie. His son might be called Emile à William à Johnie. William, they thought, had a distinguished look about him. He was big and fat with a highly coloured face which seemed to smile pleasantly all the time. They put him down as a shrewd Norman horse trader which, in fact, he was. Thus began another friendship which was to last well over many years ahead.

The first house they entered was the village hotel, where they were to stay until they went to the woods, where Jean was carrying on operations. Stuart's Hotel was half way between the Post Office and College Sainte Anne. It was run by Captain Johnie Stuart and his wife and although they bore a Scottish name, they were completely Acadian. The family consisted, at the time, of one son and a number of daughters.

When the young men from France arrived, Captain Stuart was away on his packet, a two masted pink, which he sailed between the Bay, Boston, the West Indies and St. Pierre Miquelon freighting lumber and fish and bringing home molasses, salt and some liquor, mostly rum. Mrs. Stuart received them very cordially, making them feel at home, telling them she had been anxiously awaiting their arrival. She seemed about forty-five years of age, with dark hair, dark complexion and somewhat fat. With her slightly hooked nose and black eyes, dressed in black, she reminded them of the Basque red blooded people in the south of France and the Pyrenees.

The hotel was larger than other houses in the village but really not very large. It had a centre entrance into a hall with stairs on one side. The living room on the left was heated by a base burner. This was a popular hard coal burning stove, quite tall with two tiers of mica paned doors all around. It was filled from the top, morning and evening. It was a beautiful stove, gave a good heat and was decorated with lots of nickel. It was named Half Moon and was made at the Burril Foundries in Yarmouth. The dining room with one large table was on the right, and the kitchen was at the back.

It was here that they met Katie, Jean's wife, their new Canadian sister-in-law. As Jean had married her over the objections of their father and the advice of Father Blanche, they were anxious to know her. Reports that had reached France made no adverse comments about her except that she was not a suitable wife for Jean. Difference in background and almost complete lack of education could hardly make for a compatible marriage. They found her pretty, but not a raving beauty. She was tall with brown hair and hazel eyes and she seemed to have an instinctive grace and a pleasing manner. Katie's background was interesting and her charm may have come from her supposed ancestor, The Baron de St. Castin. He was a French nobleman from the Basque country who had come to Quebec as a young enseign with the famous regiment, de Salieres et Carignan. The regiment was eventually disbanded, the officers being given seigneuries and the men farm lands around Quebec. The Baron chose to move to the area at the mouth of the Penobscot River which was the boundary between French Canada and the New England states. Many stories are told about the Baron who married a squaw, became the chief of her nation and had many children. He was such a gentleman with the ladies that when he came to Port Royal, the governor had him put in jail in order to preserve the peace and decorum of the settlement. In spite of these precautions, the Baron left a numerous progeny around Port Royal. Katie showed no sign of Indian blood and she had the swagger of nobility, but her sister could easily have passed for a full blooded Indian squaw.

Katie and Jean lived at Stuart's hotel and receiving her new brothers-in-law in what was her only home, should have been easy, but the first contact was a bit awkward. It was a meeting between people of different worlds. They seemed to have nothing in common and hardly understood one another, in their effort to make conversation. It must have been awesome for her, meeting three brothers-in-law at one time, coming from so far away, from a country of which she knew so very little. However, the blood of the old Baron must have come through, because the young men felt she received them with a certain grace, friendliness and good manners. Katie explained that Jean was in the woods for the week but would be back that night.

So much had happened since they landed at Yarmouth on the very morning and it was yet only eleven o'clock. They decided to walk to the college and pay their respects to Father Blanche. They were somewhat downhearted as they stumbled over the frozen, rough road to Sainte Anne. It was only a few moments ago that they had been introduced to their cold, drably furnished little rooms at Stuart's Hotel. After a morning full of surprises, it was really only then, in these little rooms, that the full impact of their presence in this strange new country made itself felt. The vision of the life they had left behind hit them with full force. Saint Charles, Paris, horses, very comfortable living, even luxurious, sports, parties, and so many other niceties of life. Here, nothing but a frozen barren countryside, an uncomfortable hotel and the wind, always the wind, cold, penetrating and mournful. Everything seemed leagued to discourage them and raise doubts in their minds, perhaps feelings of deep regret.

When they met again the beloved prefect of Versailles, their friend, so warm, so gracious and so sincere, they quickly regained their laughter and their courage. As Father Blanche talked, he appeared solid as a rock. Having sensed their not too well hidden fears and regrets, in an atmosphere of friendliness and cheerfulness, his warmth banished from their minds the anxieties and the disillusionment of the first contact with their new environment.

They stayed for lunch and at the table, they met Fathers Louis leDoré and Morin whom Emile had known at Versailles. It was a happy hour for all, Frenchmen from France, talking about the homeland, the days at Ecole St. Jean, old friends and comrades. These priests loved their fatherland, even if they were being expelled from it. They were happy here and showed no regrets at having left everything, especially their families, to come and work among these Acadians who so needed help and who were so grateful to these men, their Frères de France (brothers from France) as they called them.

Later that afternoon, the young men returned to Stuart's Hotel, much happier, encouraged and secure in the feeling that with Father Blanche so near, they would never feel alone and could go to him for any needed paternal counselling. That evening, they tasted Acadian cuisine for the first time. In their first letter home, they termed this encounter, with what was called "souper", a very disagreeable experience. It consisted of dried fish, hard and somewhat smelly, with potatoes served in their jackets and for desert, again something new; molasses with bread. The boiled tea was too much. Indeed, the morale sank again as they dreamed of dinners at St. Charles and only three days ago of dining on the *Normandie*. Bifteck, gigot à l'ail, poularde à la Toulouse, etc. and for desert, Baba au rhum, Nougat, cheeses, with wine and coffee. After such a dinner, they spent the evening in a beautiful ship's lounge sipping liqueurs and dancing with nice American girls. Here not even a comfortable chair, not even a very ordinary wine. They were told that rum was a favored drink here. Unfortunately, there was none in the house at the moment, but Captain Stuart would surely be home before Christmas, only a few days away, his pink loaded with the "stuff". Another new word, it was contraband because apparently in this country it was forbidden by law to drink wine and spirits, but no one paid attention to this law and ordinarily there was lots of rum for everyone.

Towards the end of this strange meal, eaten in silence, as they were very dejectingly ruminating over the low state of their fortunes, they heard the sould of a wagine driving up on the driveway alongside the house and on towards a big barn at the back. "That is Jean returning from the woods", said Katie, and everyone rushed out of the house and ran towards the barn. The four brothers embraced and wept with joy. Jean Jacques had left France three years ago. Just seeing him inspired confidence. After all, he knew the country and being with him would help adjust and learn the ways of things. Jean was setting up the mill on the Stehelin property and that winter was also cutting the first logs to feed the mill in the spring. The site was about twenty miles from Church Point and Jean and his crew went into the woods on Sundays and came home on Saturdays.

There has always been a sense of the fantastic and with it a matching tendency to role playing in the Stehelin character. Well knowing that he might meet his brothers that night, Jean had prepared himself to play the role that would dazzle them and enflame their imaginations. Throwing the rich looking buffalo robe off his lap, he jumped to the ground, the true picture of the hunter, woodsman, they had expected to see. On his head he wore a large fur cap and on his feet knee high moccasins. At the waist of his checkered mackinaw coat down to his knees, he wore a wide leather belt from which hung a long and dangerous looking hunting knife. In his hand, he carried his carbine at the ready. To his three brothers, this was a sight to their taste and very much in line with the kind of adventure in the forest they had been dreaming of, the mirage they had travelled so far to overtake.

Jean had a big black dog at his heels, a mongrel, no doubt of collie and labrador background. His horse General Nox was the object of great interest and careful inspection. He was black, as his name suggests, standing quite high with a narrow head, lean legs, and lean pasterns and a short back. He had a magnificent neck and chest surmounted by a long flowing mane. General was then five years old and at the height of his good looks and full strength, Jean said he could trot two minutes and thirty seconds to the mile, which was very good, and which, according to Jean, made him unbeatable. It may seem strange that these men showed so much interest in a horse, but in those days, it was the great interest of everybody, just like cars are the thing today. There was a number of good horses in the area. Horse racing on the main highway, such as it was, for years, had been the great sport of Acadian men.

Sitting in uncomfortable chairs in the parlour, Jean regaled his brothers, very green and avid novices, in the ways of the woods, with stories about life in the forest. Firstly, the road was very bad. In the winter, the snow made the going by sleigh much easier and very pleasant. Jean found a bottle of rum somewhere and as the night wore on, the stories got bigger and better. He told his brothers of almost daily encounters with bears and wild cats, the latter resembling small tigers. There were also lots of moose, birds, small game and abundant trout in the many streams and rivers. One can readily imagine the excitement of these wide-eyed boys as they listened to such wild tales.

When three o'clock came, they went to bed, overexcited and so anxious to get into those woods. Adieu the glamourous civilization of the old world. The devil with all the glitter and pomp of society and goodbye to all its restraints. Give us the forest, give us the bears and the wildcats, the fishing, hunting and the freedom. But, worse luck, they would have to wait until after the Christmas and New Year festivities before they could get on their way to the Silver River, to the mill that Jean was building, to the wild woods.

The first night at Stuart's Hotel was another miserable experience. To them, the room was as cold as they imagined the North Pole must be. They went to bed fully dressed, with their long coats on top of the homemade quilts, poor substitutes for woolen blankets. By morning, they felt lucky they had survived.

They did not relish the idea of having to spend another week or ten days here, but there was nothing they could do about it, so they might as well control their impatience and use this time to further orient themselves in the ways of this country. Their first breakfast, called "Déhouner," was as much of a surprise as the souper had been the night before. They had never eaten fried salt pork, cut in strips, served with fried eggs, bread and the already ubiquitous molasses and boiled tea. In France, breakfast, "petit déjeuner", consisted of café noir (black coffee), croissants, with preserves, cheese or some creamy custard.

Madame Stuart did her best to help orient these young men by instructing them in the ways of life in this country. To cheer them up on that second day, she told them the secrets of the contraband rum trade and that her husband Captain

Johnie would soon be home with a load. They would all have a very fine Christmas. She told them about the ways of the people and assured them all would be well for them in the end.

That second day, Sunday, they went to church like everybody else did. The old church was a very simple wooden structure, very small by European standard but quite large for this country. There were no detailed architectural effects such as one sees on the stone churches of France. This was the parish of Ste. Marie and so the one statue in the whole church, that of the Virgin, adorned the main altar. On three sides overlooking the nave were galleries, supported by pillars. The church was full. People were cramped in the wooden pews both upstairs and downstairs. Parishioners came long distances, even some on foot to attend Sunday mass. There were many horse carriages, which belonged to the more well to do. At the back of the church, Indian families were squatting on the floor. Our young men sat upstairs where they could see the entire congregation. The Indians interested them and they noticed how happy they looked, smiling and talking among themselves.

The men sat on one side of the nave and the women on the other. Even husbands and wives did not sit together. The dress of the people was also different. Most men wore caps, but the more affluent wore wide brimmed black felt hats, of the type and style in vogue at the time in Brittany. Very few men wore collars and ties and very few seemed to have shaved that morning. The women wore mostly black cotton dresses with woolen black shawls, and black kerchiefs over their heads, tied under their chins. With their dresses to the ground, they certainly looked mournful and without sex appeal, which was probably the purpose of such dress. Husbands and wives seldom walked side by side. Going to church, the women formed groups and walked ahead of their husbands, who also formed groups. Looking at these couples, seemingly so detached one from another, one could wonder how they managed to produce the large families they all had!

When Father Blanche entered this packed congregation in colourful vestments and with an energetic stride, the whole scene seemed to acquire life and an air of some pomp and ceremony. His voice filled the church and the people listened to his words with obvious respect.

After mass, the men gathered outside. Here the "brothers from France" were introduced and welcomed. They did not meet any women, because it was their role to quietly leave for home without delay. This was the time and place for the men to exchange news and do some bargaining. In french villages, the markets were nearly always located near the churches and they were always in business on Sunday.

The different types the newcomers met interested them immensely. Here a big handsome man of swarthy complexion, reminded them of a Basque, even to the same big moustache. A smaller man with a white beard looked like a Norman for sure. All these men showed signs of hard work and rugged living. Hands knarled like the roots of old oak trees, stooped shoulders, serious, stern countenances, even if ready to crack a smile at a good salty joke.

That Sunday afternoon, there was a horse race on the road. The event had to be finished by two thirty in time for everybody to go back to church for vespers. The contenders that day were General, Dan, a reddish Bay belonging to Louis Melanson and Dab, a Chestnut belonging to William-à-Johnie. They raced with very light two wheeled affairs called gigs. The correct name of this type of racing vehicle was the American Spider. They looked very light and frail but they gave the horses nearly complete freedom to run his best. That day, Dan won.

On the Monday following, Mrs. Stuart came in all excited and told the boys that Captain Johnie had been sighted coming up the bay, tacking his ship against a stiff northerly breeze. Within a few hours, the little old pink was tying up at the wharf, where many men had gathered to welcome the Captain home. He was busy at the helm but soon had everything ship shape and was onto the wharf. He was a big dark complexioned man with a limp. He was chewing tobacco, when the men from France were introduced to him. To them, all this activity was very exciting because the rum traffic was illegal, but they soon discovered there was nothing exciting about it. Unloading the rum became a community chore. The ox carts were there to carry the kegs away somewhere. There were no policemen in sight, in fact they learned that there were no policemen anywhere anyway. Soon the whole cargo had disappeared and that night, the whole community celebrated, producing many drunks.

Awaiting Christmas, the explorers continued to meet and talk with the people and visit in their homes. The same warm welcome was forthcoming everywhere for a meal, be it dinner at noon or supper at five. The houses were very clean and warm. Usually the kitchen was the common room where visitors were received. There the big wood burning range, which was often the only stove in the house, radiated a clean heat. Some older homes still used the huge fireplaces in which cooking was done. The romance of the open hearth was going, but also was the drudgery it exacted of the women. The parlour was only used in the summer and then only on special occasions. The kitchen walls were usually papered and the window curtains were always clean and gay. The floors were covered with home hooked woolen rugs or home made braided carpets. The hooked rugs were thick and colourful, made of the best wool. There were always potted plants on the window ledges.

Visitors were given the best chair in the house and once everybody was settled, the conversation went back and forth. The women were not shy in their homes and talked away, more than the men, as they busily worked at something, carding the wool, spinning it into yarn, weaving it into heavy cloth for men's clothing, knitting socks and mittens or even quilting at the big frame by the window. They made woolen sheets and feather beds; bedding quite different from the stiff linen sheets and wool mattresses of France.

There was no electricity then but the work went on just the same at night by the feeble light of kerosene lamps. There were simply no free moments. Even the numerous children had their allotted chores and the whole household seemed to function in complete harmony.

They inspected the Spruce Gum factory, owned and run by Louis Melanson. The raw material was gum from spruce trees. It was advertised as being good for the digestion and for exciting an appetite. The newcomers didn't chew it as they felt they were famished enough on Madame Stuart's fare. Chewing gum was not done in France at the time and the widespread practice in Canada was something new to them.

The country store which was called "La Choppe" was the focal point for the men of the village. The evening passtime was to congregate at the Choppe for an evening of conversation and story telling. There were a number of captain's chairs in the main part. If all the chairs were taken, men sat on the counters, boxes or even on the floor. Bits of news were exchanged and discussed but the real gossip was about women. The jokes were invariably sex-oriented, but serious topics were also debated with some heat. They also heard old stories of shipwrecks, fishing and hunting expeditions and great feats of strength and courage. In the group were the liars, the philosophers and the oracles, all stubborn as mules never letting go of their point as they swore, in English, which was not a sin, and pounded their fists on the counter.

One of the most comical nightly visitors at the Choppe was Johnie-à-Batiste, tall and rotund with black hair and moustache. He was a Thibodeau and therefore sported the baronial swing of the St. Castins. Considering that he was the undertaker, he was the jolliest person one could meet, always with merry eyes and laughing mouth as he stuttered away his stories. His work took him to several villages and he knew everything worth knowing for miles around.

Johnie invited the new boys to visit his carpentry shop. There he made coffins and boxes and wooden crosses. He enjoyed his work as he talked to visitors. On a rainy day, more men than usual would gather and play poker. Sometimes as he worked, Johnie would smile and say; "I'll make this one a little bigger for Magitte's big ass", or spreading the excelsior in another one, he would smile and stutter; "a little more in this one to give Samy-a-'ptit-Chu (Samy little ass) a softer ride".

Christmas was approaching and Madame Stuart gave her guests the good news about Christmas dinner. She was going to have paté-à-la-rapure (rapie pie). Jean went into excited praise of this gourmet dish, so much so that they could hardly wait to taste it. Alas, when it arrived on the table on

Christmas Day, they looked at it and knew they were in for another disagreeable dish of Acadian cuisine. In a huge tureen they saw some sort of mixture, hot, brown and soft with a few pieces of meat, chicken they thought, floating around. There was no appetizing aroma coming from this sticky mixture, such as they thought should come from a good dish. They thought it a mess, tasteless and flavourless. But they were hungry, so closing their eyes, aided by some black rum, they somehow filled up on it.

It was about this time that Emile Jean set about making arrangements for his brothers Roger and Paul to enter College Sainte Anne. All three had given their father a solemn engagement to carry out his wishes. This was the condition upon which he had allowed the two younger boys to go to Canada. They would complete their education, spending holidays in the woods. However, a few days later, Father Blanche called Emile to his office, to explain that Father Morin and LeDoré, who formed his council, as laid down by the rules of the order, were strongly opposed to the enrollment of the Stehelin sons, and as Father Blanche could not argue them out of their position, he had to go their way. He was very embarrassed.

The reasons for the objection were very complex. These young men had started their education in the new type colleges in France, where there was freedom of thought. At Sainte Anne, the good fathers put the clock back to the old days, when young men were educated and regimented in the old way. The Acadian parents and students were so respectful of the priests that they were docile and easily maniable to their teachings and politics.

The young Frenchmen would be too independent, modern, in an unwanted way, certainly critical of the old fashioned discipline and old teaching objectives. Things were going so well for the Eudists that they looked forward to their order replenishing its ranks and thus resuming its growth and influence. The presence of the Stehelins would be a threat to this grand design. Furthermore, on the material side, the drab diet, the cold building, the discomfort and the strict discipline would make them dissatisfied and potential agitators.

These were all valid reasons from the council's point of view, if one accepts that they had the right to run their college as they saw fit. But there were also perhaps hidden reasons. Father Blanche was energetic, enthusiastic and full of confidence, authoritarian perhaps. He had been a good friend of his old comrade in arms. He had helped him all along the way, even to advising on the purchase of lands on the Silver River. His confreres did not like this involvement and closeness to, "a rich industrialist from Paris". Perhaps they also felt that Father Blanche's enthusiasm and leadership in social and economic matters of the community should be restrained. Unlike him, they stayed apart from the people and their problems. They saw their task as ministering to their religious needs and educating their sons. They had the colonial outlook, and they saw themselves as missionaries.

Fortunately, Father Blanche could not be undermined, because the General knew that besides being the only man who could found Sainte Anne, he was also the white hope of the Eudist Order itself. If the government edict to disband was carried out, the Eudists would have to go to a new country, a new home, and who but Father Blanche would be up to the task of finding it? Subsequent events proved clearly that he was earmarked for the task.

The family understood perfectly the decision of these men and the friendship with Father Blanche continued unhurt. Neither did the incident blemish relations with the Eudists, even with Father Morin who visited the family many times during his stay at Church Point. He was always welcome and was extended the warmest hospitality.

Roger and Paul were, of course, delighted that they would not have to enter Sainte Anne after all. Their heads were too full of thoughts of adventure to have settled down to latin and greek and a diet of dried fish and potatoes. They could not have bent to the authoritarian discipline, which had been thrown out of the French colleges with the coming of the new era.

THE FIRST WINTER

At Church Point Christmas and New Year festivities had passed. Compared with France and home, where New Year celebrations were the big event of the year, the last ten days had been dull and depressing. But that was all past now and the four brothers got on their way to the woods, at last, to Langford Lake and the timber operation.

The first stage of the trip would take them to Weymouth where they would halt for a night's rest and for supplies. General was hitched to the wagine and off they went one cold morning. As far as St. Bernard, about six miles, the road was intermittently bare with hard frozen ruts or covered with narrow snowdrifts from which the cold north wind from St. Mary's Bay blew clouds of snow. When they hit these snowdrifts, they had to get out of the carriage and walk alongside.

After they passed St. Bernard, the road was sheltered by trees that cut the wind and made the cold less biting. From here onward, the road was covered with snow and they had to walk the rest of the way to Weymouth, as General laboriously ploughed through the heavy snow at a slow walking pace. Arriving at the top of the hill above Weymouth, with Joe Muise's trotting park on the left, they saw the town for the first time, blanketed in snow with the Sissiboo River in the valley frozen hard, except for a narrow open channel snaking to the Bay about a mile down river. In the distance, they could see the tall masts of many sailing vessels, tied up for the winter. On the wharves alongside the ships, they saw huge piles of lumber neatly stacked and drying in the winter sun, awaiting spring and the resumption of shipping to the markets of the United States, the West Indies, and countries as far away as Spain, Portugal, England and South America.

The village was then known as Weymouth Bridge. Weymouth was down river at its estuary at the bay. The population was made up of English, French, Irish and some Blacks living up river at Sissiboo Falls about three miles away. Sissiboo, according to legend, is an Indian or a French name meaning "six hibous" (owls) or "Big River". The name of the village came either from Massachusetts or England. It is probable that it reminded Loyalist and English setters of the River Wey in Dorsetshire, England.

Like in Yarmouth, the houses were painted different colours but this presented a cheerful contrast to the houses at Church Point that were nearly all unpainted and well weathered. In contrast, there was a white steppled church which stood on a hill, in relief against the background of hardwoods and evergreens, stretching as far as the eye could see. One got the impression that the object of this colourful scene was to brighten up the countryside, under snow, for so long a period each year.

Weymouth Bridge in 1895, had two hotels; the Goodwin which had been in business for some years and which is still operating today, looking exactly as it did then, and the American House which later became the home of Judge Grierson and after that a convent for teaching nuns. It was after noon when the brothers arrived and went to the Goodwin for the night. They didn't see much more of Weymouth Bridge that day.

The proprietor of the hotel was Uncle John Goodwin. His wife was a very fine, distinguished looking lady. There were three daughters in the household, Carie, Annie, and Alice and one son, Olie. The family received the young men with warmth and friendliness. They said they knew Jean's brothers would be arriving soon and they were anxiously waiting to receive them. The house was warm and comfortably furnished and it had a bathroom, a convenience which did not exist at Stuart's Hotel. The evening meal was very good. The world looked a lot rosier.

After supper, not dinner as the evening meal was called in France, they sat with the family in front of the coal burning grate in the front room. They were pleased to find such lovely looking girls and although they spoke no French, all present turned themselves inside out to get some conversation going. There were signs, coy glances and other devices, urged by necessity, to get thoughts across. All agreed they had spent a very fine first evening. In years to come, the Goodwin remained headquarters for the family. For them, there was always friendliness and kind attention. That night, they went to bed happy and excited, because tomorrow they would be entering the mysterious forest.

They were awakened the next day by the bright sun of a beautiful cold winter morning. After a good breakfast, with coffee instead of boiled tea, they got into their heavy, long overcoats and knee high boots and got on their way. They left the wagine and started off in a two seater sleigh. It was locally made, with two sets of bright red bobsleighs shod with iron runners. It was really too heavy for one horse to haul and in later years, they used a span of horses on it. Today, General was alone and he gave his best with what seemed great heart and enthusiasm.

The tide was out and the river low. They noticed that along the bank as far as they could see, were quite large pads of ice, scattered about, pell mell, as if strewn by a mad giant or a terrible storm.

They noticed the stores, sitting on stilts driven into the mud. They seemed precariously perched and strange looking indeed. Looking at them from the front, however, with their brightly painted false facades, they did look quite secure.

Jean knew his way about and they went into a large store owned and operated by George Hankinson. The new brothers were introduced and warmly welcomed. This was a very interesting store. It was large, with a tall coal burning stove in the middle of the customer area and counters on three sides. On the shelves were groceries of all kinds. On the floor were barrels containing food items that were sold by the pound, such as dried beans, peas, oatmeal, dried fruit, crackers and such things. Hanging from the ceiling were harnesses for horses and oxen, horse blankets, heavy clothing for men, boots, mocassins and implements of various kinds, buck saws, cross cut saws, picks, peavies, axes and other items. In the back was a large storeroom which was called the "back shop" and which stored bulky merchandise, such as bags of animal feed, barrels of flour piled high, items of ships chandlery, rope, canvas, chains, paint and hardware. George Hankinson was also in the lumber business, operating his own logging camps and sawmill. Several brothers worked with him, some in the store, others in the woods and some on the wharves. He was the brains of the business. He was quite young at the time and the newcomers struck a lasting friendship with him.

Jean picked up the provisions and equipment he needed and they set off again. Up the hill and straight ahead to the top where four roads met. There were no signs indicating where these roads led to, because signs were not needed. Everybody knew where they went and there were few strangers travelling in these parts to be confused by the lack of signs.

The further they went, the more snow they encountered. They were enthralled by their first sight of the real woods, which started just outside Weymouth on the road to Ohio, Southville and other hamlets along the way. Everything glistened in the sun which was made brighter by the whiteness of the snow. There was a good thickness of snow everywhere and the frost, crystalized on the tips of the branches, sparkled like so many diamonds.

General trotted along on the smooth snow packed road, jingling his merry bells. Jean's dog, Jack, followed, or ran abreast or ahead, barking joyfully. Jean knew most of the people along the road. Here lived the Bobines, there the Miraults, then the black settlements of the Cromwells, the Langfords and beyond the Dugas, Porters, Steels, Fords, Sabines and many others. The houses were small and although some looked well kept and nice, most looked very poorly.

As they went along, Jean told them stories about the people. Apparently, there were many illegitimate children about but they created no problems as they were taken in by the family of the girl or by the grandparents. Wedding stories were good too. In one instance, a bride was not too enamoured of the husband she had been forced to marry because she was pregnant, although it was not certain that he was the putative father. She connived with the guests at the wedding feast, such as it was, to get her husband drunk and keep him drunk all night so she could have a last fling with all and sundry men around.

About noon, they reached the Cerino home where they would stop for dinner. This family, half French, half English, lived almost at the edge of the forest on the Queen's Road, as all main roads were called, just before the woods road took over. It was a very old two storey house, the second storey being very low with very small windows. The "front room" where guests were always received was very simply furnished with very old rocking chairs, probably home made. The ubiquitous spinning wheel and weaving loom were in the background. Rich looking woolen hooked rugs adorned the rustic, worn plank floor, which was painted yellow. There were plants in pots on the window ledges, a big crucifix on the wall and the usual wedding and baby pictures from the frames of which hung the family rosaries.

Nanon, long a widow, was an old woman at this time, but she ran the household and ruled with an iron hand. She was thin and bent over and her face was wrinkled, toothless and almost yellow. With her very pronounced hooked nose, long face and shrill voice, she well deserved her nickname, "The Parrot". She always wore a white kerchief over her head, tied under her chin, black dress and black shawl. She spoke half French and half English and she seemed to trot inside and out all day, running everything with the aid of her spicy language.

Nanon kept talking to the visitors, telling them all about her activities. She said the day started at dawn with breakfast of eggs, bread and molasses and boiled tea. She would then allot the tasks to her daughter Lisa and her sons, Raymond and Ben, all adults and unmarried. The lauguage was picturesque, pointed and sarcastic, especially when she explained how she disciplined these "children" of hers. The Stehelin boys could not get over the dirty stories that came out of this frail looking little old woman. No one could get a word in edgewise when Nanon was around.

Lisa, like her mother, was a skillful country woman, well over her twenties at the time. She performed the inside chores and in between was at the spinning wheel or the loom. She seemed to be in a continuous state of despair, because she too would have liked to talk but never had a chance to get into the conversation. Raymond, the oldest, was big and ungainly, with long black hair and flowing black moustache. They thought he was another Basque type. He was never in a hurry, as he slowly rolled along like a sailor. He was a good worker but he had to be prodded hard by Nanon. Ben, the second one in the family, was cross-eyed and had his mother's hooked nose. He was not fond of work at all. He indulged in the only pastime known to these people, playing practical jokes on people and inventing fantastic stories about sex and hunting. Ben liked big game hunting and at any time of the year, he loved to run away and for weeks, roam the woods and hunt, now and then visiting logging camps for a meal. He was a clever inventor of machinery for sawmills and a good blacksmith to produce his ideas. But he only worked when it pleased him.

At night, no doubt feeling some remorse for the talk of the day, and needing to cleanse her tongue and settle things with God, Nanon would gather the family and any strangers in the house, into the front room and on their knees, to recite the rosary. After that, it was bedtime for all. Tomorrow would be another long busy day. It was drudgery to eke out a bare living from this sad existence.

The Stehelins had dinner with the family that day. The fare was frugal enough; boiled salt pork, cabbage, potatoes, bread and the ever present molasses and boiled tea. Naturally, the questions were numerous. To these people, France was a place somewhere far away, but it was all very hazy in their minds. They knew that the Acadians had come from there but to them, it might have been fifty or three hundred years ago. Ben wanted to know if the girls in France were good with the men. That question earned him a clout on the ear from Nanon. Raymond wanted to know if the oxen were big and strong in France. To him, this was important, as a team of oxen was the most valuable possession a man could have. The Frenchmen from France, as the Stehelins were beginning to be called by everyone, naturally exaggerated about the strength of the oxen and the size of the cows. Ben wanted to know about wine and if one could get drunk easily on it. This was their criterion for a good liquor, how fast one could get drunk on it. Nanon wanted to know about the churches and she just opened her mouth wide and was silent for a few moments when they told her they were as long as from here to the field and as wide as from here to the other side of the road, all of stone and twenty times as high as her house. She knew there had been many saints in France and that pleased her. Somehow, she never expected to hear of saints around here because people were bad and didn't go to church. She was interested to know something about the kind of weaving the women of France did, what kind of pigs the mother of these boys raised, and the hens she kept. Lisa didn't have a chance to ask any questions but she seemed content making eyes at these good looking boys.

Well rested, having paid the munificent sum of twenty-five cents per meal, although Nanon didn't want to take anything, they set out once again on the way to the woods. The snow was getting deeper now and having passed the last house, the Comeaus, they found themselves, at last, into the deep forest. They had the happy thought that now the dreams of so many months would unfold right before their eyes. The scenery did not disappoint them and conjured to assure their imagination that those dreams had not been exaggerated.

The spruce trees were very tall and big, just as they had expected. They were laden with snow and the afternoon sunlight through the thick branches made delightful patches of light and shadow. The road was completely unbroken, not even a single beaten path, only a carpet of immaculate whiteness. The jingling of the sleighbells rang out on the silent air like sweet music and lingered on as the echo faded away somewhere in the deep woods. Never having seen snow, one can imagine how entranced they were before such beauty of nature. The sleigh glided along smoothly and silently and they felt as though they were travelling in a dreamland.

Dreams have a way of ending brutally and with a bang when the sleigh runner hit a boulder hidden under the carpet of snow, they were jolted back to reality. General was surprised too as the jolt seemed to stop him short and nearly unharness him. Jean told them there would be more such treacherous boulders and it was therefore decided to slow the pace. In that case, it would be nice and easier on General for everybody to walk behind the sleigh.

Coming to Canada had meant buying all sorts of clothing and equipment. Following the best advice available, they had bought high leather boots with smooth soles and heels. They soon learned that these were no good in the snow. The ice would build up on the soles and especially on the heels, forming frozen lumps that made if difficult to walk, in fact, made it dangerous, as they twisted their ankles at every step. They had to stop often and scrape the soles and heels of their boots. Besides they were wearing long and heavy woolen overcoats with capes, and, of course, carrying their new shot guns and rifles. One never knew when some wild animal might rush out of these thick woods. It was only a matter of minutes before they were sweating profusely and puffing themselves towards early exhaustion. They removed their coats and continued to stop to scrape their boots.

General too seemed to find the going hard. The deep snow was causing him to falter as he struggled to get through. Jack seemed to be the only one at ease. He would run into the woods, all the time barking joyously, sometimes he jumped playfully at General's nose, as if to encourage him in his hard work. And they still had five miles to go.

On they went. At the foot of each hill, they stopped for a breather and at the top, they stopped again. Both men and beast needed these little respites. They came to a fairly wide river, swollen wider by winter rains, which had, Jean told them, an interesting story from way back in time. It was then, as it is today, a historical landmark: the Sept-sous-et-demi or Seven pence ha-penny river. The water is always high in winter, forming a frozen pond on the right, which in the summer is a lush meadow. Here and there big boulders protruded through the ice which itself was covered with snow. Under the ice, the water was running, gurgling on its way downstream.

67

As far back as anyone can remember, travellers, hunters, fishermen and poachers have halted on the bridge, if only to take a breather and in the summertime to drink of the cool water, running clear and sparkling. The river is legendry and no one knows for certain how it got its name. There are, however, two stories about it. One is very simple; hunters resting on its banks, many years ago, found pieces of money, the value totalling seven pence ha-penny. The other story would have it that a party of hunters arriving at the river at a period of flood, found it uncrossable. The bridge had been carried away and the swollen water rushing on appeared too dangerous to ford. Instead of turning back, they decided to tarry there and wait until the water went down and it would be safe to cross. To wile away the time, they played poker, presumably they conveniently carried a deck of cards in their haversack. One fellow lost, or it might be that one fellow won seven pence ha-penny in the game.

There are many legends about this area, embellished as they were passed down by succeeding generations, to nest eventually in the folklore of the people. Some stories were told long before the Stehelins ever came to these parts, others seem to be based on the family's passage here. A very old story about this river was told by the older people and it scared many. It would seem that a lone hunter, walking out from a hunting trip in the Langford lake woods, reached the river at dusk. Rain had fallen for several days and upon reaching the bank, he found the bridge had been carried away by the rushing torrent. All that was left of it was one of the three stringers. It would be too dangerous to attempt to cross on the log or through the flooded meadow, so he wisely decided to wait until the foaming, rushing stream spent itself. In those days, people were used to such emergencies and they had lots of time. He quickly put up a lean-to and got his fire going. Nightfall came very early and as he sat in the half light, he suddenly heard, over the roar of the rushing water, the sound of a horse's hooves pounding on the rocky road on the opposite side of the river. Soon a horse and rider appeared, galloping at full tilt toward the river. The hunter got out onto the road and waved frantically to warn the man that the bridge was gone. It was to no avail as the huge black horse, shiny with sweat and foaming at the mouth, came crashing down the road and without hesitation, galloped onto the lone log over the torrent. It was not until the mount crossed to his side that the hunter examined the rider. He was bent over the horse but he was obviously a tall man. He appeared thin and old because his flowing white beard and hair were white as snow. He was dressed in a black flowing cape with a hood on its back. And that is about all he could grasp of this terrifying apparition because when he hailed the man, he and his horse just vanished into thin air and the noise of the horse's pounding hooves died in a faint echo.

On this winter day, the river was swollen too, the water running over the bridge to a depth of a few inches. They had to get on the sleigh to get across and then went back to walking. After Seven pence ha-penny, they came to the famous burntlands which extended to the Sissiboo River, at least eight miles away to the east. There are many such desolate areas in Nova Scotia which, over many years, have reproduced nothing of value and have never been reforested.

After the burntlands, they re-entered the virgin forest for the last two miles to their destination, the banks of the Silver River. They saw no wild animals and had it not been for the sleigh bells and Jack barking, the stillness would have enveloped them completely.

Towards the close of a perfect winter day, full of sunshine, after a five hour trip from Southville Corner, the team broke into a clearing at the bottom of which they saw blue smoke rising from the stovepipe of a cabin. It was a typical lumbermen's camp, snuggled in the heavily snow laden big pine trees. The roof was covered with snow and it had a verandah on the front and a lean-to on one side which was used to store firewood. The only protection from the cold and the wet was a covering of tar paper, held down by battens.

The men working at the mill had finished their day's work and came out of the cabin when they heard the sleigh bells and the barking. They welcomed the newcomers with loud hurrahs and strong handshakes. The cook was a fine Acadian woman named Fébrénie, who with her little daughter,

Marie, stood in the doorway adding her welcome and shouting over the noise, that supper was ready.

The young men fairly dropped with weariness as they entered the camp, which was to be their home until spring, when Jean's house was to be built. Inside it was warm and cozy, snug as anything, with the cast iron kettle boiling away on the old Waterloo stove, the queen of the kitchens of those days. It was a low stove sitting on four legs, with a round raised oven at the back. Along one wall was a long tressel table with long wooden benches along each side. The crew sat around this table for their meals and card games. This rough board table was covered with white oilcloth. The walls were unfinished and, of course, nothing was painted, not even the floor which was of very ordinary spruce lumber with wide cracks filled with wholesome dust.

There were ten men and two boys to sit at that table that night, but they all managed to get enough room to wield the bone handled knives and forks. That night, the meal was standard fare for lumber camps of the day; baked beans, fried potatoes, dried fish, bread and molasses for dessert, with black, boiled tea, sweetened with, yes, you guessed it, molasses. The huge dried fish was passed around and everyone tore off a piece. It was hard and salted, no doubt good for the teeth, requiring some chewing.

The meal seemed very good to the young Frenchmen. They were famished and terribly happy to be out of the deep snow and away from those huge boulders on that terrible road. As tired as they were, they learned something about these workmen. Gustin Blinn called Boss was the master carpenter-engineer, master minding the building of the water powered sawmill. Fric Thibodeau, Jean's brother-in-law was responsible for the total operation including the logging operation being carried out along Little Tusket Lake. Johnie-à-Marc was the best teamster of oxen in the whole area. Pti Jean-à-Joe-à-Henriette had the most powerful arm at one end of the cross cut saw and others, whose names they delighted to hear as something out of their world. After a short conversation at the table, while they devoured their supper, the new boys asked for nothing more than to be permitted to sleep.

They saw only one very small bedroom off the kitchen which they learned was the room where Fébrénie, her husband Jim and little Marie slept. To get to their sleeping place, they were directed to a ladder in one corner of the room. They climbed up through a small hole into the attic. The whole floor was covered with hessian straw filled palliasses. They went down on the first ones they stumbled on and wrapped in their Parisian long overcoats and two grey blankets, fell into the best sleep of their lives.

The new boys were awakened at daybreak the next morning by the voices of the men downstairs, talking as they ate breakfast. Rested and ready to get up to see what was going on, they climbed down the ladder to another surprise. They learned that morning ablutions were carried out on the verandah, in the cold! Hastily they poured some cold water from a bucket into a tin basin and splashed their faces once or twice. In two minutes flat, they were at the table for breakfast, which strangely enough resembled the supper menu of the night before. Only the dried fish was missing. They were hungry and they had to get used to this food. At last they were in the woods and that was all that mattered.

After breakfast, they followed the men to the mill, a very short walk down to the river. The sun was shining warmly, the snow glistened and the forest, sombre, mysterious but inviting was all around them. Life was indeed wonderful.

The dam had been built before the frost had set in and now they were building the mill machinery. The dam was a very ingenious and a intriguing piece of engineering. It was built of logs, laid vertically at an angle across the course of the river, supported by solid cribwork behind. The crevices between the logs were filled with earth and moss and the front was banked with gravel which was plentiful on site. This dam was designed to raise the water level by some fifteen feet. Not only did this body of water provide motive power for the mill, but it also formed a storage pond for logs awaiting to be hauled into the mill for sawing. It was a charming pool which was always well stocked with fine trout in the spring and with eels in the fall.

When the sluice gate would be opened, the water would

be channelled through a sluice way to turbines that would run the machines installed on the floor above. There were to be three turbines and by January, 1895, one had been installed. It had been built at Salmon River, at least thirty miles away towards Yarmouth, and had been hauled by two yokes of oxen. It took the teamsters four days to make the trip. The other two smaller turbines were being built on the spot. The largest turbine was five feet in diameter and six feet high, attached on its end in a deep trough. This larger turbine developed enough power to run the gang saw and the haul-up, the ramp on which the logs were hauled from the water into the mill. The other two turbines set up in series behind the big one were three feet in diameter by four feet high. They would run the trimmer, the edger, the planner and special machines to make finishing lumber for doors, window framing, and wood trim, to make tongued and grooved hardwood flooring, sheathing for walls and ceilings and shingles.

These turbines were intricately constructed. The iron paddles were fixed around the wooden drum with iron hoops that could be tightened if necessary with wooden wedges. The turbine rested and turned on a pivot holding in place the hardwood shaft. Various belts connected the turbines to the machines. The size of the wooden pulleys determined the correct power to be delivered to each one.

The up and down gang saw was simply conceived and simply built. Eight six foot long saws were affixed vertically in a large wooden frame four feet wide. The entire frame moved up and down as several logs at a time, held together by iron dogs, passed through the frame on the slow moving carriage. The saws could be moved varying distances one from another to produce the thickness of lumber wanted. This was done by moving wooden pegs that held each saw in place. The planks then went to the edger, then to the trimmer. The mill would have a sawing capacity of fifteen thousand board feet per nine hour day.

The whole factory was engineered, designed and built by men who could neither read nor write. Every part, except belts, and some iron wheels was made of wood or fashioned of iron at the forge. Standing underneath, where the heart of the mill was, amongst wheels of varying sizes, connected by belts, these Europeans wondered and marvelled. How did these men make the intricate calculations required to deliver the right amount of power to each machine? How did they put together this maze of belts and pulleys into a perfectly functioning whole. The Mill Boss somehow had figured all these things in his head and drawn working diagrams on pieces of wood. By way of tools, all he had was a rule and the basic tools of a carpenter.

That winter of 1895 was a very busy one for the four brothers. Jean was the directing force. He had been in the country four years, spoke English and knew the people and their ways of doing things. Everybody admitted that he had turned out to be a good business man. By spring, the mill would be ready to saw the winter's cut which would produce about three hundred thousand feet of lumber. Life was rustic, devoid of the comfort they had been used to, but once equipped with lumbermen's rubbers, heavy woolen socks, mitts and caps and the wonderful Canadian mackinaw coat, these young men still thought being a pioneer was thrilling adventure.

They learned a lot too. They could never be carpenters, a trade that seemed to be in the bones of the Acadians, but they could learn to be woodsmen. They learned to plan and carry out a logging operation, select mature trees to cut, with an eye for conservation. The work day was nine hours and the work week was six days. The morning stint was from seven o'clock to noon. After dinner and a rest, work resumed at one o'clock and ended at five. The workforce worked steadily and conscientiously, for wages ranging from twelve dollars to eighteen dollars for the boss per month.

The workmen were nearly all Acadians from along Ste. Mary's Bay. It was the custom to hire the bosses and they, in turn, hired the men they thought best suited for the job. Living very closely with these men, the Frenchmen learned to know and respect them.

The history of the Acadian people was little known in France. It was, therefore, a revelation to learn that this small group of people, descendants of the first settlers of Canada, had suffered so much through the wars between England and France, finally to be abandoned by France and brutally expelled from their lands and the only country they knew. This Expulsion had taken place in 1755, but somehow, miraculously, they had survived as a race and gradually many had returned to their native land to begin life over again. They made progress very slowly at first, but by 1827, with the abolition of the Test Act, they got the same civic and political rights as all other inhabitants of the colony.

In that little cabin by the Silver River, during the winter of 1895, by the feeble light of the kerosene lamp, these Acadians told their story of the past, the hardships and exploits of their ancestors and sang the old ballads, some very sad, of their people. The hardships suffered were not very far behind and they were still timid, afraid of L'Anglais.

Boss Blinn was nearly venerated by his men. He was their uncontested leader in everything. He was a fine man, with a frank and pleasing countenance, couched in his well kept grey beard and blue eyes always dancing with mirth. He was respected as a master craftman meticulously precise in the work he bossed. He was the guiding spirit of all the construction work.

Boss Blinn had travelled widely in the United States and the West Indies. Going to the West Indies on a sailing ship was considered a "must" in the training of the better young men. The Acadians knew and loved the sea and they were superb designers and builders of schooners. Justin (Boss Blinn) was an authority on the history of his people. He knew about the American War of Independence and how the Acadians had rallied to the support of the British while much of the English population had sided with the rebels in spirit and nearly joined them in fact. It troubled him that the Acadians got nothing for their loyalty, not even some better land, while the Loyalists were welcomed and given the best lands and large grants of money.

These men loved stories and legends and they were very superstitious. Ghost stories, tales about haunted houses, shipwrecks, and, of course, Indian legends, fascinated them. The Mic Mac Indians were quite numerous in the area and got along very well with the Acadians. Abbé Sigogne had considered them part of his flock and responsibility, and had treated them with kindness, as human beings, which was perhaps more compassionate consideration than they had received from the missionaries before him. As a mark of esteem and veneration, they called him the Patriarch.

One night by the dim light of the little lamp on the big table, Boss Blinn told a sad Indian legend, made more interesting because it took place on this very site. The poignant drama took place many years ago when the Governor of Port Royal wanted to send a very important message to the French settled at Cap de Sable (the Pubnico area). For this long and dangerous mission, the Governor chose a young Indian Brave. This young Indian was madly in love with an Indian maid and he persuaded her to accompany him. She was very happy to follow her lover and on the day set, the two started off in his birch bark canoe. The Indians knew the water route and could cover enormous distances in their canoes. The mission was so secret that they left the fort by night. Paddling down the Annapolis Basin, they went up the Hebert River (Bear River) through many lakes (now known as Munroe, Jolly, Uniake, Grand, Sissiboo) portaging over rapids and difficult parts of rivers.

It was in the summertime. The moon shone in all its brilliance and it was in its silvery light that the canoe carrying the lovers glided softly down Long Tusket, Little Tusket and along the Silver River to the very spot where the mill was being built. The maiden, lying at the feet of her hero was as happy as a bird, trying out its wings for the first time. She gazed at the young brave, naked to the waist, with the eagle plume, symbol of his tribe, held in a leather band around his long black hair. Softly, she sang a beautiful Indian lament, breaking the stillness of the night. The deep quiet of the forest was only interrupted now and then by the prolonged cry of the loon, seeking its mate. Indeed a night of love and delight.

At this spot, they decided to make camp for the night. A shelter of spruce branches was soon erected, a soft couch of sweet scented fir boughs was made and the fire was lighted, sending a glow into the woods around and a fresh scent of burning pine resin into the air. The young maiden started preparing food, while her mate went to the river for water.

Now this youth had a rival, madly in love with the young squaw. He had followed the pair secretly and this night, watching everything from his hiding place, he could contain his hatred and jealousy no longer. As the brave was stooped drawing water, his enemy sprang from the darkness and with a single blow of his tomahawk, struck him down dead. With one foot on his fallen foe, the killer rent the stillness with the war cry of his tribe. Hearing the dreadful cry, the maiden rushed to the river. For a long time, she held the head of her lover in her arms and for the last time, she kissed his forehead. Then rising slowly, with an air of majestic disdain for her enemy, she threw her arms towards heaven, uttered her last cry of sorrow, and threw herself into the river, to disappear forever. Legend has it that every summer, at the time of the full moon, the Indian maiden comes down alone in her birch bark canoe, making the forest and the waters echo with the haunting cries of her grief. Down through the years, older people who knew the story would never spend a night in the summertime near the site of the old Stehelin mill. Some people said they had heard and seen the drama and they were terrified.

The Acadians were very devout Catholics, and they had carried into these woods, the old family custom of reciting the rosary. This exercise was piously carried out in common every Sunday morning, by these rough men, kneeling on the cabin floor.

After a time, an interesting character joined the crew. He was Bill Barr, a big strong man with only one seeing eye. He was a practical joker and one of his specialties was eating ants and inviting or rather daring the young Frenchmen to eat a few live ones too.

Charles-à-Paul, another character, had the features of an Eskimo. He had a red face, at least that part of it that could be seen in his black beard and his lively little eyes made him look happy all the time. He chewed tobacco and he seemed to spit long streaks of juice at the right point in his stories, to produce effect and emphasis. His job was teaming the oxen, but his heart was really in hunting and fishing. He fancied himself the best hunter around and to the Frenchmen, after witnessing some of his hunting exploits, he certainly was that, without a doubt. They had all faith in his knowledge of the woods and his ability to teach them the arts of his favorite sport. He guided them on their first hunting trips, teaching them as they went along. They learned how to set moose snares, which was illegal, dead falls for small animals and metal traps for bears, foxes, wildcats and beavers.

On Sundays, the young men roamed the forest, with their new guns and Charles-à-Paul with his very old long barrelled rifle and an old tin can hanging from his neck to make tea when they stopped to eat their lunch. Dressed in very old clothes, and a wide brimmed black hat, he looked the part of the woodsman in Wild Bill Buffalo's shows that the Stehelins had seen in Paris. Charles-à-Paul certainly earned his twelve dollars a month teaming the oxen and putting fresh venison on the table.

Fébrénie, the cook, aided by her little daughter Marie, was the wife of Jim McLaughlin who worked at the mill. He was not an expert at anything and he liked to get drunk. Many men of those days would start drinking and continue in a state of drunkenness for several days. Then they would dry out and not take another drink maybe for months, until the thirst for liquor hit them again. Jim was like that and when his rum ran out and he was on a bender, he would resort to drinking lemon extract, a supply of which he always kept hidden in the woods.

Poor little Fébrénie never got a day off. The men had to be fed Sundays like any other days. Fortunately there was little housework to do. The rough floor had to be broomed once a day and that was about it. There were not many dishes to wash either. Each cover consisted of a tin plate, a tin mug and a knife, fork and spoon. Little Marie did the dishes and served on the table. Jim was responsible for the water and the firewood.

Some men went home for the weekend. Those who stayed in, did some washing, some even shaved, some went fishing or hunting or amused themselves talking, as they whittled at some little piece of art. Some were real artists. They were good at building models of sailing ships, windmills, and water mills, and they amused themselves sailing their little boats on the mill pond and running their miniature mills in a rivulet.

The mail was always awaited with great excitement. There were local newspapers, and some from France. There were letters from home, from Emile the father who already was taking hold of things and telling his sons what to do. He insisted on being kept accurately informed and it was up to Emile Junior to write all details and appreciations of the situation.

The Stehelins soon moved on to learn other skills. Their father instructed them to look into the matter of aquiring more timberland. This was not an easy assignment, as it meant learning to appraise land, evaluate the timber standing on it, in order to arrive at an estimate of its market value. It was not difficult to find land for sale. Crown lands were available and could be granted for less than one dollar an acre. They granted as much as they could in the vicinity of the main operation. It was not easy to determine value of lands offered for sale by individuals. Although eager to sell, they natually hiked prices as high as they thought the inexperienced Frenchmen might pay. The Stehelins paid as much as seven dollars and fifty cents per acre for some parcels, a price which was considered high at the time.

It was necessary for at least one brother to become a surveyor, and the lot fell on Emile. Jean stayed with the woods and mill operations and Paul and Roger, could help Emile. There was no surveyors' school nearby so they hired a surveyor to teach them the art. Mr. Parker, from Bear River, came and spent the rest of that winter and most of the next summer with them.

To these men, working and living in the woods in wintertime, was pleasant and exciting. There was so much beauty to be admired at every turn. The venerable trees of the virgin forest, crowned with tufts of dark green, covered in a dark brown bark, standing straight in the glittering snow presented them with a beautiful spectacle in colour and very slight movement. At another place, the small pines and spruce were thick and their needles, tipped with droplets of ice, sparkled in the bright sunshine, like numberless diamonds, rubies, emeralds and topazes.

As one moved about, everywhere the same patches of light and shadow invested the vast underbrush with beauty and mystery. Not a sound was heard, except perhaps the song of a bird or the chirping of a squirrel. Here the majesty of nature in all its primitive beauty, as it came out of the hand of the Creator, lay undisturbed. As for the presence of man, it only created the "swish, swish" of snowshoes, gliding over the carpet of snow. Man brought life to this profound solitude. It is easy to understand his inner feelings when it comes so naturally for him to pray in this, the greatest of cathedrals. No doubt it is a prayer of love, joy and thanksgiving.

The snowshoe was a contraption to be mastered. Adept users seemed to walk along effortlessly and without tiring. At first, they tried using them with ordinary mocassins. The gear did not seem to hold the snowshoes on, especially when they travelled over rough country. They fell all over the place and once in the course of their acrobatics, they broke the surveying compass. Their first day had been killing, and they returned to camp, so tired they could not stay awake long enough to eat supper.

The next morning, they consulted with their mentor in all woods matters, Charles-à-Paul, and borrowed his special snowshoe gear. They were called carristoes and they were made from the green hide of the knee joint of the moose. The lower end was sewn in a long point. This stocking-like boot was quite soft and tight fitting. Outside the toes, on each boot, crosswise, was tied a peg of wood about three inches long. A strap or a lace also of green hide, was looped around the piece of wood and tightly tied to the snowshoe. This gear left the heel free to play as one walked. Wearing two pairs of heavy homemade wool stockings up to the knees, they felt warm and comfortable and could walk all day without tiring. They learned that in the woods there usually is a simple solution to any problem.

During January and February, they could not travel too far afield, because it was too cold to camp outside. With March and the warmer weather, they went away for days, living outside quite comfortably. They carried a piece of canvas about five feet by eight feet, blankets and provisions. They would erect a shelter by setting the sheet of canvas on a ridge pole, between two trees, tying the sides down, and filling the open ends with small spruce trees and branches. They soon learned to make camp facing the rising sun. They learned to make comfortable beds on the ground with tender young fir boughs.

They felt more comfortable than in the attic of the small cabin and sitting by their big fire, which they kept going all night, they savoured fully the romance of the forest, far from Paris, in the depth of the somber and beningly enveloping scented trees. As the moon came up and the stars brightened, casting a dreamy light upon the scene, tired but hardy, they were happy just to dream with their eyes open. Their souls filled with inexpressible pleasure and peace, they would fall into the slumber of the just, in this their paradise, so glorious in its shining simplicity. In their hours of work, away from the world, its pleasures and its cares, they often thanked God for having privileged them to taste of this abundance of His bounty. They were moved to silent thought by little things, even by the crystal pure air slightly scented by the smoke of a burning birch log, a perfume which they felt mounted towards Heaven, like insence in a delicate taper-like billow of white smoke.

And so, the winter which had been unusually severe, went by very quickly. The work had been hard, the comforts few and the fare very frugal indeed. It was incredible how they developed physically. They faced spring healthier than six months ago, and all on potatoes, venison, dried fish, beans, bread and molasses. They were happy and content and the future looked as promising as ever.

One should not gather that this first winter was all work and no play. On the contrary, the pleasures were learning about the sports of fishing and hunting. They had shotguns and rifles and fishing gear. All they needed was to learn how to use them, and there was lots of game to practice on, moose, rabbits and birds, and trout under the ice. They had good teachers and they learned quickly.

Hunting in France, mostly on horseback over open country and in thinned forests, with dogs, was quite a different experience than hunting in the dense woods of Canada, and they marvelled at some simple but effective ways employed by the natives. They were very ingenious at setting snares and building deadfalls for moose and small game. To catch fur bearing animals, which could be profitable, they used bought steel traps.

Their method of snaring a partridge deserves special mention. Timmy Sullivan, a great hunter of that day, taught young Paul and Roger how to bag a partridge with a piece of string. One cold afternoon, towards dusk, they came upon eight partridges roosting in one spruce tree, with heads stretched straight upwards, perfectly immobile as they slept. They looked like so many bottles, just hanging on the branches. Timmy told the two boys to be very still, as he went back along the road a little way to cut an alder. To the small end of this pole, he attached his string, which was now a snare. Ever so slowly, he approached the tree, and very patiently, slipped the noose around the neck of the partridge on the lowest branch. The partridges above did not fly away and Timmy just went on picking them off until he had bagged all eight of them.

Many visitors came to the camp that winter. Most of them were hunters, or rather, they were poachers, because they came after moose which the law forbade to kill at that time of year. The open season was in the fall and early winter. But no one seemed to pay any attention to game laws here.

These inveterate poachers came with their bulldogs, some weighing a hundred pounds, especially trained to hunt moose in the snow. Hunting with dogs was also forbidden by law, but again, no attention was paid to this law either, not even by the game warden who was the worst poacher of all.

These hunts were competitive, as a hunter and his dogs matched himself against another team. Many bets were placed before the hunting began. Charles-à-Paul was known to have a good dog for this sport. He was mostly bulldog, weighed about sixty pounds, with a good nose and a very tenacious temperament.

The parties got under way, and when the dogs picked up the scent of a moose, they never let go, and, in most cases, from that point the animal was doomed, but the long hunt provided the excitement and competition. Eventually, when a dog got near the exhausted moose, he jumped at its face, sank its teeth into its nose and hung on, if he could, until the hunters arrived and tried their skill at shooting the moose and not the dogs, in this wild mêlée. Some dogs went for the animal's hocks but this was not considered the way a good dog should go about it.

Moose yard in herds in the wintertime, and when the snow is falling, they keep a trail open by going around and around over the wide circle, perhaps a mile in circumference. They feed on the small branches of spruce and hemlock along this trail. They also dig up ground hemlock which is more tender. In this winter habitat when dogs attacked the herd, the scared animals were forced to leave the beaten trail for the deep snow where they became easy prey. But even in such a hopeless situation, the bull moose especially, but also the cow, would defend itself to the bitter end with great ferocity and skill. Sometimes, the enraged animal would kill the dog hanging at its mouth by battering it against a big tree. The dog let go or was smashed to pieces. Then the hunters were in danger of being charged by an infuriated bull moose. To cope with such a possible situation, the hunters always had more than one dog in the battle.

Sometimes one would witness epic battles, with danger for the hunters, not only from bullets flying in the whirlwind of snow, stirred up by the scuffing of moose and dogs, but also from the dogs, turned wild that would turn on their masters if they tried to get near the moose. Ned Sullivan had a particularly nasty bulldog named Tim. Even when the moose was dead, Tim would jump at the face of anyone, including his master, who tried to come near it. To cope with this situation, Ned always carried a good length of rope with which to lasso Tim after the kill. Throwing one end of the rope over a strong branch of a tree nearby, in no time Tim's neck was in the noose and two men hoisted him up as fast as they could. Tim, nearly strangled, soon quieted down.

During those months, these boys had been well initiated

into the art of the rugged existence of the woodsman, the trapper and the coureur-des-bois. They developed physically too, especially the younger ones, Paul and Roger and they were now confident they could endure and compete with the old timers, Big Jim, Charles-à-Paul, Bill Barr, Timmy and others.

With the going of the snow and the frost, in March, the Stehelins began building the first house. It was to be Jean and Katie's home. It would have a large living room and a kitchen downstairs and three bedrooms upstairs. There would be no inside plumbing and, of course, it would be heated by wood burning stoves and a fireplace. The Queen's Road, so called because it belonged to the govenment, ran alongside the house. On the other side of this so-called road, which was nothing more than a woods track, they started building a house for about forty-five workmen. It was called the "Cookhouse". It consisted of a very large room downstairs where the men ate and sat around. Upstairs there were bunks in the one common dormitory. At one end of the house, they built an ell, for a kitchen and an adjoining bedroom for the woman cook and her husband. A single female cook was never hired. At the far end of the kitchen, they built a large brick and mortar oven, which would supply the bread for the entire settlement. This was the custom in France when an entire village was owned by one man.

Back in France, the father was receiving enthusiastic letters from his sons. He had followed the operation and directed it as much as was possible from that distance. It was early in March that Emile Jean, in the little cabin, received a letter from his father announcing his decision to come out with his wife in June. The news fairly shook the whole camp and as one can imagine, the building of the little house and the cookhouse moved in real earnest. The sons had to try to make things nice and that would be difficult they feared, considering the life-style of their parents at St. Charles. If their father were disappointed with the enterprise, he would quickly fold the tents and bring the boys home, or look for something else for them in Canada.

A BEAUTIFUL SPRING

Since the beginning of man, the arrival of spring has been greeted with joy and faith expressed in so many rituals, in ceremonials to dieties. Spring inspires a personal thought in every man, working in his most secret inner self, as he contemplates the miraculous renewal, and sees the hope of his own resurrection. Each bud of the silky, tender shoot is a promise of his own better future. The robin tells him this, as he adds his praise, in the early morning after his return.

This first spring in the woods in Nova Scotia, for men of another climate and country, was more especially awaited with great impatience. Spring in the cities is to a great extent shaped by man, but here in the forest, man would not break the harmony of nature by changing the order of things with a ravaging hand.

Early in March, for the first time since their arrival in these woods, the newcomers began to see patches of earth, as the snow melted away, very slowly at first, then very quickly as the sun rose higher in the clear blue sky. With longer days and more warmth, the ice on the lakes melted, raising the level of the water of the lakes and rivers.

With early April, the rivers were in full flood and the dam at the mill held the water back filling the pond in readiness for the sawing operation. They saw the first flight of geese, homing northward to their mating grounds. A few flocks landed on Langford Lake and as they rested and fed, their honking awakened the camp early in the morning. To the

Acadians, these wedgelike formations passing high overhead that early were a sure and happy omen of an early spring and a fruitful summer.

The geese were soon followed by smaller birds, that returned to the thickets and made music once again. The smaller animals were busy too, and seemed not afraid of men. The squirrel chatted happily and the drumming of the partridge was heard among the firs and the spruce. The woodpecker, with his tuft of red on his head, rattled away industriously at a dead spruce. The bluejay and the moose bird added their song to the concert of welcome to all in nature.

The forest began to garb itself in its spring and summer verdure. Small, tender green buds on the maples, the birches and the beeches, soon broke open, releasing soft green leaves that filled out quickly to spread over the whole woods, investing it with shadows and giving it cool refreshing shade.

On the trunks of the spruce, the pines and the fir trees, swellings appeared under the bark and soon burst under the pressure of the new and perfumed running sap. The good smell of the steaming earth mingled with the scent of the resin and the balsam.

The pink and white Mayflower, the emblem flower of Nova Scotia, couched in its dark green leaves, thrust up everywhere. In crevices, in the huge granite boulders, tender moss came to life again as it turned green. The tops of these granites were also adorned with the miniature fernlike lungworth, pushing up cheerfully, as if from the very stone itself. In the swamps, the ferns sprang up from sticky stems and burst out of their heads into big spreading leaves. The loon returned to the waters and early in the morning and in the evening, their mournful but friendly cry, echoed through the forest from lake to lake.

Each in his own way was deeply impressed by the awakening he was part of. The whole of nature, animals, birds, trees, plants and waters seemed to awaken at the same time, each bringing its share in a ceremonial salutation to the Great Sun of March, which to the Indians, was the manifestation of the return to man of the Creator himself. The marvellous and the sublime was full of meaning. If this mysterious rebirth brings freedom to everything, surely it is intended to bring a grander freedom, a new life of joy, to man, and an urge to live at peace with his environment. Easter is for Man wherever he may be. If this world is ever to be perfect, man must understand that every part of the universe is precious, that he himself is no more precious than the other parts, and that all together must move in evolution towards perfect harmony to attain one entity, one Being. Perhaps, thusly shall "Earth pass away and Heaven take its place".

While perhaps keeping these thoughts in their hearts, the young men were eager to engage in the sport, new to them, of fly-fishing. They tackled it with their usual enthusiasm and entrain, confident that they would master it like all the other challenges to the pioneer. Most natives fished with an ordinary worm on a hook, tied to a line which was fed over the brook by a long alder pole. There seemed nothing sporting in this way of fishing. In May, fly-fishing was more appealing, requiring movement and skill. They discovered that nothing could prove more deceptive to the novice. Charles-à-Paul, a fly fisherman, seemed to catch all the trout he wanted, but the new boys tired themselves casting their line and lost every fish that rose to their flies. Big fish would just roll over and disappear underwater, as if playing a game with them. After instruction from Charles-à-Paul and much practice, suddenly it seemed, their luck changed, as they mastered the professional twist of the wrist and they could strike the fish as it jumped for the fly.

The river between the dam at the mill and the head of Langford Lake was the best place to catch eels. They were caught at night with the aid of a lantern or a little fire on the river bank, which attracted them to the baited lines. The boys were taught to use no hooks. Instead they tied a lump of earth worms to a line which hung in the water from an alder pole. It was simply a matter of holding the pole until they felt a steady pull on the line. The eel was then pulled out of the water quickly and as soon as its tail hit the ground, it would let go of the lump of worms, quite intact, ready for the next cast. If the fisherman was too slow, the eel would swallow the worms, and that necessitated an operation and the messing up of that beautiful bunch of worms.

In Europe, eels are considered a delicacy, but served in the camp, cut in three inch chunks and fried, they were absolutely tasteless. It must be the sauce that makes the dish palatable. The men said that the male eel was better tasting than the female.

When they caught more eels than they could eat just then, they salted them for winter in an empty flour barrel. Similarly, when the trout were running in abundance, they salted and smoked some and hung them out to dry. What fisherman would not dream of smoked trout, bread and wine, served by the flaming fireplace!

Sometimes, in the depth of the woods, they would unexpectedly come upon signs that some humans had been there before them. In a letter is related such a finding:

"In the course of my fishing trips along the Silver River, I discovered an Indian hut, built between two boulders, on the slope of a hill overlooking the river. The roof of bark and moss was built over spruce poles placed across the tops of the two boulders. There was a small opening at the centre of the roof to let out the smoke from a fireplace built of rocks at the centre of the earthen floor. The inside walls, formed by the boulders were covered with tapestries of woven fir branches, well dried and brown, still giving out a scent of woodsy perfume. There was room for two persons inside, one on either side of the fireplace. There stretched out on a bed of fresh sweet smelling fir boughs, lulled by the music of the fast running rapids, I spent exquisite nights, listening to the voices of the forest, as I gazed at the sky with its galaxy of stars twinkling over the tops of the majestic hemlocks. In the morning, I would catch my trout for breakfast and there in the splendour of the rising sun, I thought myself the happiest man in all the world. In after years, I often slipped away, down Langford Lake in my birch bark canoe, to spend the night in my special little Indian home."

As soon as the frost was out of the ground, they started breaking up and clearing a few acres of land that would be the site of the settlement. This proved to be a long and laborious job. Felling the trees was simple enough, but pulling out the stumps with oxen was hard work. Besides, the land was generously strewn with big granite boulders that had to be removed. The stumps were burned and the boulders that could not be pulled away had to be blasted. Making holes in the rock for the dynamite was a job in itself. They only had chissels and sledge hammers. After long days of hard work, they were rewarded by the sight of fine sandy soil, which enriched with manure, which was plentiful, produced a good crop of potatoes that very year.

When the beautiful month of May arrived, everything was ready. A beautiful site had been cleared. They cut the trees to the river and to Langford lake further down. The mill sat astride the river and the green forest provided a backdrop on two sides. The little house, charming in its simplicity and colourful in its grey paint with maroon trim, varnished hardwood floors and pine walls and ceilings, stood ready for Katie, its chatelaine. Katie was proud of her home and in her travels around the square and to the mill, she showed her happiness by accentuating the swag of her ancestor, the Baron de St. Castin.

In anticipation of the extra demands for transportation, it was decided to get another horse, a white mare which they named Lady. To get the mail a little quicker, the boys took turns to ride into Weymouth twice a week. Southville had a post office, but only got mail once a week. Besides the boys had now begun to enjoy their visits to Weymouth, with the change in atmosphere it brought and the contacts they made with an every growing circle of friends. The road to the Corner (sometimes called Severin's Corner, sometimes Comeau's Corner) was very bad. It is a government road but hardly any money had even been spent on it.

Weymouth Bridge was not without interest to the newcomers who were strangers to the way of life in the new world. They enjoyed especially the characters they met in the stores and on the wharves, places where there was much activity. There was a little old grey bearded postmaster who was known as the meanest miser in the village. He ran the post office as an adjunct to his general store.

In those days, tobacco was sold in plugs. Some were for

chewing, and these were black and soft. Others were light brown and very hard for pipe smoking. Cigarette smoking was not too common but cigarette tobacco was sold in cans. Pipe smokers carried a pocket knife for many uses, one of which was to slice little pieces off the plug, they crushed them by rubbing the chips between the palms of their hands. The chewer hauled the plug out of his back pocket, where it was kept moist and bit a piece off and began to chew and spit. It was common knowledge that the postmaster got his tobacco for nothing by neatly cutting a thin slice off every plug.

Another interesting place was the blacksmith shop. It was centrally located and had become, long ago, the rendezvous for all the men, miles around. It was a very busy place. There were always many horses and oxen to be shod and there was ironwork of all sorts to be fashioned. People made appointments to have their animals shod. In fact, this was the only place where it was wise to make an appointment for service. Even the doctor did not require appointments.

The blacksmith was the man who had all the news fresh, especially the juicy gossip. Men from miles around kept him well stocked with the latest and the best. The shop was the most entertaining place in the village, especially when liquor flowed. It seemed no frequenter of the place was an abstainer. Passersby were discussed and jokes were made about some of them. If a woman, known to be of easy virtue, passed by, she was hailed with some ribald remark or suggestion. Usually, she returned the fire in kind with obvious saucy pleasure. Everybody would laugh.

The Sissiboo River cut the village in two. On the north side lived the rich people, the merchants, the lumber barons who were English, Irish or Scottish. The bank and the Goodwin Hotel were on that side. On the south side, lived the not so well to-do and the few Acadians who lived in the village. One doctor and the lawyer lived on this side. The stores were about evenly divided between the two sides. The Weymouth Times and L'Evangeline newspapers were on the south side. A small band of Indians lived on the outskirts along the railway track near the road leading from St. Bernard to Ohio.

Along the steep banks of the river, above the falls, lived

a good number of Black people. Some were the descendants of slaves brought to the country by the Loyalists and subsequently affranchised. Others had come on their own, mostly from the U.S.A. and some on vessels trading with the West Indies. They were very poor and uneducated. The men were employed as labourers and the women as house servants. They were not artisans but they were good workers, loyal and friendly. Many Black men and women worked for the Stehelins over the years, in mutual respect and trust.

Weymouth Bridge was a place of great activity. The stores were well stocked, the road was busy with carts moving to and fro, from the wharves to the mills, carrying lumber. It was a captivating sight to stand on the bridge and see the forest of masts, rising from the many wooden ships lying at the many wharves, piled high with lumber. At the time, most vessels were square riggers. They were better and faster than the schooners that followed them, but they were more expensive to build. Certainly they were more beautiful, with their myriads of lines and dozens of yards and sails. The flags of so many countries flying from the mastheads was indicative of the extent of the trade and the prosperity of the entire area. There were Spaniards, Yankees, Portuguese, English and others. The large crews of these ships mingled with the villagers, in the bars, in the streets and in the homes. In fact, some progeny around the village bore traits of foreign blood, but these accidents were well accepted as things that happen in the best regulated societies.

Early in April, the long awaited cablegram arrived. The young men's father and mother would be arriving early in June. Everything was ready and there was time enough to attend to the final preparations.

THE SUMMER OF DECISION

All through the winter, the household of St. Charles had been in a state of excitement and feverish preparation. It was something for young men to venture to strange countries, but it was something else for a lady from France to undertake a trip into the woods of Nova Scotia. A special wardrobe had to be selected, but of what should it consist? In the end, this lady came in the clothes she wore in France with a few extras, woolens and warm coats and boots. The children were left in charge of their eldest sister, Therese, and an aunt. The parents would be gone the summer, returning in October.
 At Havre towards the end of May, they boarded the *Normandie*, having received from the sons, such glowing reports of its comfort and fine cuisine. Alas, Madame Stehelin enjoyed very little of these niceties, as she was kept down by seasickness most of the voyage. Emile on the other hand, enjoyed the voyage immensely and landed in New York feeling like he had never felt before, ready and impatient for the adventure ahead.
 Neither spoke a word of English, but somehow they made their way to the Fall River boat, retracing the route their three sons had travelled only six months before. Arriving at Boston, they were more than delighted to be met by Daly Hogan, a young man from Weymouth who was studying dentistry there. Daly got them safely through the city and aboard the Yarmouth boat.
 The uncomfortable trip on the *Yarmouth* was the first

inconvenience they encountered. They had expected a standard of comfort somewhat akin to that of the *Normandie*, but the cabins were small and smelly, the whole ship was badly kept and the food was very inferior. They never forgot the fried steak and fried potatoes for dinner, and for breakfast, eggs floating in bacon fat. On the other hand, the weather was good and they stayed outside as late as possible.

Arriving in Yarmouth very early the next morning, they got on the train and went as far as Church Point where they spent the rest of the day and night with their old friend, Father Blanche. The Stuart Hotel put on its best cuisine and service and many people called to meet the Monsieur de France. Everybody wanted to be helpful. Most of the time was spent by the two old companions talking and discussing each other's problems. Father Blanche had not had it easy, and his friend had apprehensions about the venture of his sons in the woods.

The parents were naturally very anxious to be reunited with their four sons, and the next morning, they took Vitale's mail team to the station and the train to Weymouth. Like their sons before them, they marvelled at the beauty of the countryside, especially the dense forest through which the comfortable train travelled the entire distance to Weymouth. Passing through the reservation near St. Bernard, they saw their first Indians, which interested them greatly, although they were disappointed because they did not look like the picturesque Redskins in Jules Verne's books. They looked poorly, standing by their tarpaper shacks. At Weymouth, they were warmly received by Uncle John. Jean was there to meet them. He had planned that they would spend the night at the hotel and start out for the woods early the next day.

During the rest of that day, they visited the village and in the evening, people called on them and welcomed them very warmly. Thus began many friendships. There were the Kemps, manager of the bank, the Campbells who also had a large family, mostly boys. There were the two Burrill brothers and Squire Hogan whose son, Daly, had met them in Boston, and others.

The next day was a beautiful day to set out for the woods. They got into the family wagine which looked a bit flimsy and certainly very dirty by comparison with the polished landeau of St. Charles. They were dressed suitably they thought, but very differently than people dressed here. Emile wore what was called in France, the Costume de chasse, with breeches and high riding boots. The lady wore a long dress with ruffles and carried the parasol, the companion of the fashionable lady of Paris.

They enjoyed the drive and were interested in the commentary and information they were given by Jean as they went along. At the Corner, which became le Coin from then onwards, they called on Mr. and Mrs. Comeau, to begin a friendship that was to last through two generations. Here they embraced their other three sons, who had come out to meet them. They were pleased to see that they all looked in perfect health and that the two younger ones had grown so much.

Here they left the carriage. The problem of conveying their mother to the Silver River habitation had preoccupied the boys, but ingenious Boss Blinn had soon built the transport that, he was sure, she would enjoy and find very comfortable. It was a sleigh about ten feet long with wide hardwood runners. The platform was about six feet long and was covered with a carpet. In the middle of the floor, he had fastened the best arm chair in the little house. There was a nice railing about two feet high around the platform, with an opening at the back. The conveyance looked very comfortable and picturesque in the extreme. One yoke of oxen was hitched to the sleigh and the teamster was none other than Johnie-à-Marc.

The lady was a bit frightened when she saw the little bearded man chewing something; she thought he looked more like some bandit from the mountains of her native southern France. He approached her and with his best toothless smile, welcomed her in his most polite language. "Hello la Vielle" (Old Lady), adding in a French that she hardly understood, that she would be very comfortable on the sleigh. It was plain to all that this language was intended as a warm and most cordial welcome, but to a lady of forty-five, it was hardly considered complimentary. However, she quickly recovered her equilibre and joined her husband and her sons in a hearty laugh. Similarily, the father was welcomed as the Old Man (le

Vieux), but he didn't mind that at all. He did, however, use the incident to joke that indeed they were in a mission country, which in Europe was a term used to say that one was in an uncivilized country.

The mother on the sleigh and the father on General, the convey moved off. Over the atrocious road, the sleigh made slow headway, bouncing from boulder to boulder and plunging here and there in great big muddy puddles. Johnie seemed nimble as a cat, jumping from rock to rock, as he prodded the oxen and talked to them, or so it seemed. The six mile trip took five hours.

At first the lady was very frightened. The sleigh lurching and bumping along what they called the road was upsetting, but when it had to go through a narrow river, because it was too wide for the bridge, she was sure she was going to drown, in spite of Johnie's reassuring words. Besides, she imagined she saw bears and other wild animals at every turn. She remembered the letters about wild animals everywhere.

After a while, fear gave way to curiosity and then to excitement as they, like their sons before them, began to fall under the magical spell of the forest, its multi-coloured trees and its wild shrubbery, all in the fairest sunlight and the purest air. Even the road became exciting as each bend presented something new, something different. If they did compare with their mode of travel in France, in fine carriages, over good roads, with liveried coachmen, they never looked back or talked about it. They enjoyed everything and felt this to be a fantastic expedition.

The trip was enlivened by the conversation she tried to have with Johnie. She asked questions but could hardly make out his patois. He probably had just as much trouble understanding her language, but with a lot of goodwill and lots of oui, oui here and there, everybody laughed with her, and everybody seemed happy.

Here and there she would ask to stop and would send Johnie or one of the boys to pick certain wild flowers or shrubs that she fancied. And so in this atmosphere of gaiety and great joy, the sleigh, laden with flowers, branches and ferns, towards the end of a beautiful June afternoon, pulled into the square, overlooking the lake on one side with the deep forest around and the roof of the mill straight ahead. It must have been a moment filled with thought and some emotion as the sleigh silently made its way to the front of the new home. After all these years of thinking, planning and hoping, this was it.

The little house looked so new and clean in its grey and maroon paint. The door was at the side, entering into the living room which had arched windows and a big fireplace at one side. At the back was a stairway leading to the rooms upstairs. The kitchen was at the back and the dining area was at the end of the big room. The hardwood floors and the pine walls and ceiling produced a pleasing relief. The furniture was ever so simple. Rocking chairs, which had disappeared from France by this time, were the main pieces. There was an American couch by the fireplace and a few side tables by arm chairs around the room. The stairs wound up to the bedrooms which were small and furnished with beds that looked small and unstable, compared with the heavy beds on tracks that were the fashion at St. Charles. Gay coloured cotton curtains decorated each window.

Katie, very proud of the new home, received her father and mother-in-law with all the charm she could muster. In fact, she made a very good impression and she endeared herself to them. In the years ahead, she was accepted and loved in a manner that was unaffected and genuine.

In anticipation of the arrival of their parents, the sons had hired a young girl, Rosie Babin from Corberrie. She was the maid and she hustled about to make her new masters comfortable and at home. In the background appeared Smith, whose job it was to keep the house clean, get the water and the firewood and generally do all the odd jobs. He was a very happy little man, not too brilliant, but a twenty-four hour worker.

The family now consisted of seven members, all happy to be reunited in this little home. Compared with St. Charles, this environment might have appeared very modest, but in the depth of this beautiful, quiet forest, it was joy and luxury enough. After a meal which no doubt seemed very frugal, they slept the sleep of the just in the perfectly happy assurance that tomorrow would be even more exciting and wonderful. At the cookhouse, Johnie-à-Marc had a lot to tell his fellow workers about le vieux and la vielle from France. His report was good and that night, the fledgling settlement slept in complete peace and contentment.

The next day, Emile went to inspect the mill. He knew something about water driven machinery because his felt factory had been run by water power. Boss Blinn took him under the mill, in the water pen, where he could examine the very heart of the system. He could not help but marvel at the intricate works and balancing of the pulleys and drums which synchronized the whole mill into one operating unit. They then opened the water gates and he saw the logs begin their way at the haulup and end as lumber at the other end, at the trimmer where the final marking indicated the cubic content of every piece. There were planks, scantlings, deals and boards coming out in perfect order and precision.

It didn't take long to visit the improvised blacksmith shop, the lean-to barn and the new cookhouse which seemed to be a very good building. His days were very busy, looking and talking with his sons and the workmen. No doubt in his mind he was evaluating everything with the view of making the final decision, sometime before returning home in the fall.

At the house, life was changing as the new mistress began to organize a new way. The first encounter with local cuisine had been unenthusiastic to say the least. The new lady did not intend to get along on beans, dried fish, and salt meat. They could get along without wine but she could see no reason to live on such an unappetizing diet. The boys kept the larder well stocked with small game, moose meat and trout but still there was not enough variety for people used to their French cuisine. Madame was not an expert cook, but she had wisely brought a cookbook with her and armed with it, in full confidence, she tackled the kitchen. In no time, she managed to turn out excellent meals.

The mother caused problems for her sons, however, because she asked for all sorts of foods and spices that were hard to find in Weymouth. And so each trip to the village became a veritable foraging expedition. They had to spend so much time looking for odd things that they had no time left to visit and do their other errands. They always returned with saddlebags full of parcels. Hanging from the saddle horn, they would bring carcasses of veal or lamb or quarters of beef. There was often no room left for the rider and he would have to walk the last six miles. They were kept so busy, they had to start making the trip in one day, leaving before dawn and returning late at night. For regular supplies, they had to get another horse to replace the ox team, which was too slow. Building started and added hardware and supplies were urgently needed. Soon three trips to Weymouth per week were required, plus the two trips by one of the sons on horseback.

In August, Emile must have decided to develop the enterprise and immerse himself into it completely. During the winter past, back in his St. Charles, he had prepared plans very carefully, just in case he decided to go ahead. He had given his approval for the building of the house, the cookhouse and the mill. Beyond that, further building would await his arrival. After all, he was paying and he felt he had to restrain the enthusiasm of his sons.

Building a family home large enough to accommodate eleven children, the parents and Katie started then. It would embody some architectural features of St. Charles and it would be finished by the coming fall before Emile Senior returned to France. The new little house would become a part of the bigger one. Its downstairs would become the dining room and its upstair bedrooms would be suitable for the unmarried sons. The house would stand at the bottom of the square, facing the incoming road with the mill and the river behind, and Langford Lake on its left, a location which would give it an air of dominance over the entire settlement.

The main entrance was at the center of the front of the house. Its double doors were flanked with narrow windows to the floor. Upon entering into the main hall, the whole depth of the house, one would have recognized, on a smaller scale, the double landing staircase of St. Charles with the two windows at the first landing.

On the right of the hall through double doors, one entered the salon (living room). It took the entire half of the house about twenty-four by thirty feet, with windows on three sides and a fireplace at the far end. The view was very beautiful. On the front, a view of the busy square, on one end, the lake, and on the back, the river.

To the left of the hall were two smaller rooms. One was the bedroom of the father and mother, with its own door to the verandah, which extended the full length of the front of the house, and the other a dressing room. The room was furnished with a double bed for the wife and a single bed for the husband. The dining room had to be big enough to seat at least sixteen people so it took the entire ground floor of the first house which now formed an ell of the big house. It had a fireplace on the outside wall and a large window looking onto the mill pond and Little Tusket in the distance. The kitchen was across the hall from the dining room and was an addition to the new house. It was rather unpretentious, not well lighted and equipped with a large cast iron wood burning cook stove and a black iron sink. The walls were of planed spruce boards from which hung cast iron pots and pans.

Upstairs there were several bedrooms, each with its own wood stove. The servants lived on the third floor in rooms that had slanted ceilings but were quite comfortable.

Throughout the house, the walls were finished in sheating, varnished to a high gloss. The hall was in white pine with a red border at floor and ceiling. The stairs were of hardwood, also highly varnished. The living and dining rooms had walls and ceiling finished in hardwood sheating. The varnished doors were of the period, with four panels. The finish around the windows and the doors was rather ornate but common in those days. The rooms upstairs were all finished in pine. It was the cheapest wood of those days. The chimneys were of poured concrete. They made forms of wood and when the cement was cured, they stripped the outside wooden forms, and set fire to the inside wood. These chimneys were practically indestructible. All the buildings were painted a light grey with maroon trim and shutters.

To Europeans, the speed at which the house was built

seemed fantastic. In about two months, four carpenters and a few handy men had all but completed it. Some furniture was added to that already in the first house, and Smith was established in his routine in the new house. He was the general handyman, but his first jobs were to keep the water tank in the attic filled and the fires going whenever they were required. Later they installed a force pump at which Smith worked a good part of the day.

The barn was tackled next and took less time to complete. There was not the same urgency, but it was completed in the fall. It was fifty feet square and fifty feet high with a sharp pitched roof. On one side, a sliding door opened into the horse stalls and harness room. The walls were covered with planed spruce boards painted light blue. There were stalls for six horses and the stanchions between stalls were of heavy stained hardwood. On the other side of the building, with a similar sliding door, was the stable for the oxen and the cows. Unlike the space for the horses, it was very plain, and the walls were not covered and painted. It was obvious that horses were favoured animals. The sons, having been brought up with them, spent hours grooming them and polishing saddles and harness. None even tried to learn the art of teaming the lowly oxen.

In the middle, between the two smaller doors of the stables, were very large double sliding doors, opening onto the barn floor. Here the hay carts were brought in and the hay was lifted by huge forks into the lofts above. Carriages and sleighs were kept here and against the back wall were large feed boxes. Three sets of stairs led to a loft in the peak of the back of the barn, to a dove cote housing a large flock of white pigeons.

Clearing more land for agricultural use continued throughout the summer. A crew of men and a yoke of oxen did nothing else. They started along Langford Lake, behind the barn and continued pushing outward along the road, thus enlarging the square more and more. Emile wanted to clear along the lake, perhaps because he dreamed of building homes there for his sons. He seemed to want to keep the family together forever, he himself remaining the father, running everything in the best interests of all.

There was never an end to clearing land. As the lumber operations grew, more oxen were needed requiring more fodder. One ox ate a ton of hay per year. As the number of mouths to feed increased, more cows and more produce were required. Over the years about fifty acres were cleared. Today one would have difficulty finding the locations of these fields. The square remains, but it is gradually shrinking and the lake cannot be seen from it any more.

Purchasing more land was also given top priority. Emile felt the cost was low compared to prices in Europe and, therefore, he was convinced it was a good investment. He kept the survey crew, led by his son Emile, going all that summer and he granted or purchased what were considered good lands. The better parcels were acquired through Crown Grants.

Early that summer, the crew explored further down the Silver River, where they found the Caribou Plains. It was a flat, clear piece of land extending about one mile down the west side of the Caribou River and several hundred yards westward to a hill and a fine stand of spruce. Further down this river they came upon a very substantial beaver dam on which they crossed to a slope on the other side, where they found a stand of pine. Just above the dam, they found a large pond with ducks in it. Over the years, summer and winter, hunters always found ducks here.

The Plain itself was of sandy soil, bare except for quantities of blueberry bushes that produced in profusion year after year. There were also low lying wildflowers of varied colours. It was indeed an enchanting and unexpected sight in the middle of the forest.

According to legend, very old in the county, not only the Plains but the entire area, is associated with the caribou that, many years ago, roamed the province in large herds. This must have been a resting place, or perhaps a winter herding area. Many years before, huge piles of caribou bones had been found here. It was speculated that either some disease of epidemic proportion had overtaken very large herds, or this was the place where old caribou came to die. The name Caribou, given to the plains and the river and the lake, can be seen on very old maps so it must have been very long ago that the name was given to the area.

They looked at this land very carefully and concluded it might make good farm land. It was practically cleared, was well irrigated and only about five miles from the settlement. They obtained a Crown Grant that summer and commenced working the land.

They decided to make this a station on the way to further exploration, and that summer, they improved an old woods road sufficiently to get a yoke of oxen with a cart through. This old road was called MacMahon's trail. The Stehelins built a bridge across the Silver River and from it, a road to the Plain, about one mile east. Four men and two yokes of oxen took twelve days to build this road.

The discovery created an air of exploration and great excitement back at home, and on a beautiful early August day, Emile Sr. saddled General and rode to see this romantic corner of his fast growing domain. He was so enthused about the possibilities, that he decided to develop a large farm there. They would start by building a house for workmen and one son would supervise the work. He selected the site for the house on a little wooded hill, just on the edge of the plain. The view of the river and the little lake below and the plains in the background was termed "exquiste".

The lumber and the shingles and the hardware were brought in by ox cart, and the carpenters started building. They finished the house in early September. It consisted of one fairly large room downstairs, perhaps twenty-five by twenty feet, with two smaller rooms on one side, and a common sleeping room upstairs. It was shingled all around and finished inside with ordinary planed spruce boards. It had a wide covered verandah all along the front. A small lean-to type barn was built at the back. It was something new in this country to build houses in the woods, that looked permanent. Mills and logging camps of those days were built of scrubb lumber, covered with tar paper, to last only the duration of an operation.

Over the next fifty years, the little house stood, the rendez-vous of hundreds of hunters and fishermen. One could spend hours reading names, written on the walls, of men who had spent a night or days there. They left little notes, poems, dates, recording successful moose hunts, happy fishing expeditions or simply good drunks or good poker games. All these names and dates, pencilled so long ago on these rough boards, reminded one of the passage of time and the pilgrimage of men on the face of this earth.

On the back of the door, hundreds of hunters read the lines penned by one Edmund F. Jenner in the year 1902. Mr. Jenner was the pharmacist at Digby and he loved the woods so much that he was made the Game Warden for the County. Here are his moving lines:

> Away from the racket and noise of the city,
> Five leagues from a phone, ten from a train
> Midst the moose and the wild cat, the fox and the otter,
> You will find the old camp on the Cariboo Plains.
>
> It has sheltered the game warden, poacher and tourist
> The sportsman, the game hog, the nigger and tramp.
> The lumberman, angler and Indian can tell you
> Of the night they passed in the Caribou camp.
>
> Well, long may it stand here, here's luck to the sportsman
> May the game never fail while this shanty remains:
> Come, fill up your glasses, here's Health to the Stehelins
> Who built the snug camp on the Caribou Plains.
>
> Edmund F.L. Jenner

While the work was going on at Caribou, the survey team had moved to other areas, this time looking for natural fodder for the animals. There were already three yokes of oxen and three horses to feed and cows were to be added before next spring. If they could find some grass nearby, that much less hay would have to be grown or carted from Southville or Weymouth next winter.

They found some grass on the lowlands along the rivers. In some places they found blue grass and in others some kind of white-yellowish grass, both with long and slender blades. The blue grass was considered the best and they cut and dried some, stocking it in high piles around a center pole, with other poles hanging over the hay from the top end of this center pole. They built these piles wherever they found the grass which they carted home later when it was needed.

Sime's Meadow contained five acres and produced more than other meadows, because it could be kept flooded until June. For this purpose, a little dam was built where the road crossed the brook at the lower edge of the meadow. In Nova Scotia, all dams had to be opened by June. This was the law, to allow the free flow of water to supply all the riparian owners along the course of rivers and lakes to operate their drives. After the drives, dams could be closed again, but had to be opened for some time each day, to give water powered mills downstream the water they needed to operate.

Looking further afield for more lands to acquire, it was decided to send the cruising party in search of the Blue Mountains, which supposedly lay further inland from the Caribou River. Charles-à-Paul was added to the party as a guide. He was considered the best guide in the whole county.

During the long winter evenings just past, the workmen recounted and discussed many legends. One which interested everybody was that of the Blue Mountains. There were many stories and much mystery about them. No one had ever found them but everybody was sure they existed, somewhere between St. Mary's Bay and the Atlantic Ocean, probably in the vicinity of the junction point of the counties of Annapolis, Digby, Queens, Shelburne and Yarmouth. At the foot of the mountain, so legend said, was the Great Prairie.

Careful preparations were made, food was packed, equipment was checked, fishing gear and guns were readied. On the day fixed, Emile, Paul, Roger and Charles-à-Paul got into the loaded canoe and headed down Langford lake. At the foot of the lake, instead of following the Silver River, which they knew very well, they left the canoe and with their gear on their backs, set out on a trail going eastward, which was to take them to new territory, behind the headwaters of the Caribou and other rivers.*

The first two miles along the trail were atrocious, going through thick brush country and swamps. Loaded down with

* See map in picture section.

their gear and the awkward survey equipment, they found the going slow and very hard. They were relieved to reach better terrain at Judge Ridge, below which flows Judge Brook. This was a beautiful little river flowing strongly, with little cascades here and there and many beaver dams and ponds. The fishing was excellent, and they ate well that day.

Along the ridge, they saw spruce and pine timber, the size of which they had never seen before. These and maple trees appeared gigantic. Here and there were colourful wild cherry trees. It was a magnificent sight. Untouched by man, the picture was an eerie one, of nature as it was made and had remained through time.

Carrying on, they found the going much easier. The terrain was more uniform, free of thick underbrush, broken here and there by enormous outcroppings of granite boulders, but more open, as is the case in virgin forests. They found many bear dens, with all the signs that they had been occupied during the past winter. The smaller trees around them had been cropped of their branches to a height of about seven feet, which indicated that the bears were a good size. The spot was noted, of course, for future bear hunts of which there were many successful ones.

As they went along, they sketched a map, took bearings and kept notes. Part of the report reads as follows:

"The leaves of the big hardwoods were in all their freshness. Here and there the sombre green foliage of the spruce, cast shadows across which played the rays of the bright sun. The dark green of the little plants along the ground and the lungworth ferns on the big rocks, blended with the grey granite. The going was easy, and we did not hurry. Every few minutes we stopped to examine, now a tree, now a plant in the hollow of a rock, now a beautiful flower. There was nothing to hurry us, we were on a trip of discovery and this whole section of the country was new to us and fascinating.

"Descending the slope of this hill (Judge Ridge), we came to a section which we christened "The Chain Bogs" because it was low ground, broken by patches of little knolls wooded with young fir and spruce. On all sides we saw signs of moose. In fact, judging by the dung around, one would have said that a large number of moose had wintered here. Needless to say, this discovery was not lost on us, and in later years, when meat was needed, we would go and spend a night lying in wait in the Chain Bogs. We never returned empty handed.

"In the middle of the Chain Bogs, set deep in a nest of greenery, we found a small lake which we christened Bear Lake because we found many bear dens along its shoreline. One den in particular attracted our attention, because it was so well situated under a huge boulder. Later it became one of our favorite hideouts for hunting. It might well have been built by Indians long ago. Birch logs, set side by side, the cracks filled with moss, formed two sides. Inside the natural rock formed a chimney, in which one could build a grand fire. One could see the open country sloping to the lake. It was an ideal place for hunting. On moonlight nights stretched out on a bed of sweet scented fir branches, with our ear intent for the slightest noise, and our rifles at the ready, we spent the kinds of hours that are unforgettable to hunters anywhere. We would hear the slight crackle of trampled branches, and then the head of the bull moose would appear, raised above the line of the trees, perfectly motionless as he took stock of the situation, sniffing the odours of the night. Then when he seemed satisfied that nothing would disturb him, he would cautiously descend towards the lake to bathe and drink, while eating the white water lilies that adorned the waters. I especially remember one night when the moon was full and Paul, Roger and I were in the den lying in wait. It was in the fall of the year during the mating season. With the aid of a birch bark horn, we imitated the long drawn out, mournful call of the cow moose. Soon in the distance we heard the answering call of a bull. He was coming towards us very slowly, his progress punctuated by a hoarse, sonorous cry. Coming slowly, we could hear the crackling of the branches, which by now he tramped impatiently and wrecklessly. After a long and even more languishing call from our homemade horn, he sprang out of the woods and onto the shore of the lake. At that moment, it so happened that the moon shone low on the horizon, and as the animal stood still, his head with immense antlers was silhouetted against the huge yellow moon and his body was reflected in the water. Thus, with his head held high, he made a magnificent picture of savage grandeur.

"But hunters are pitiless. The antlers, the Massacre as the Acadians called it, had ten points and measured fifty-five inches across. His hide was nearly jet black, and made a fine rug for the living room floor at the big house. The head and antlers, mounted, were presented to the Lieutenant Governor of Nova Scotia, the Honourable Duncan Fraser who was a frequent hunting visitor to the "Stehelin Place".

"The den at Bear Lake remains a vivid memory of the free life. Probably no one todays know of it, but it probably shelters bears as it did then, the descendants of those we saw there years ago.

"After passing the Chain Bogs, we came upon a steep rise covered with fine spruce, another beautiful sight of virgin timber. Descending the next two miles we reached the source of the Caribou River. Here we made camp under big trees at the top of a rapid, whose singing waters had captured our imagination. While we set up the lean-to, our faithful Charles-à-Paul went fishing in the rapids. He soon returned with a fine catch of speckled trout, which, rolled in corn meal, and placed on slices of salt pork, soon began to cook giving off that delectable odor known only to fishermen. With coffee mingling its aroma with that of the frying trout, we became very hungry, and under the last rays of the dying sun, we had a supper fit for the gods. Stretched out on a bed of soft fir boughs, before a big fire of birch logs, which gave off a special perfume, in absolute peace and calm, we lit our pipes, exchanged a few words, until little by little drowsiness overtook us and we fell into the sleep of the just. I shall never forget the moon shining through the branches of the big trees above our heads, lightning the forest with its soft radiance and giving off the scent of the woods, floating on the gentle breeze.

"At daybreak, the sun awakened us, and after a plunge in the cool waters and our breakfast of bacon, tea and tea biscuits, we were ready for another day. Charles-à-Paul only then told us that while fishing the night before, he had found, near the river, a big canoe, hollowed out of a huge pine tree. It looked very old, but seemed in perfect condition. It was water tight, and a pair of paddles were in it. No doubt, it had been left there by Indians long ago. It was big enough to carry our party, our gear and provisions. We decided to paddle up river, which would take us further north in the direction of Rocky Lake. Before setting out, on the spot where we had found the canoe, we left a piece of wood which we shaped like an arrow, pointed in the direction we were taking. That is the unwritten law of the forest. You may borrow but you may never steal. Later on we returned the canoe where we had found it."

Going in an easterly direction from Rocky Lake, the expedition continued. They found little forested areas, only bogs, swamps, dwarfed trees and shrubbery. They saw herons, and shot ducks which they broiled on the open fire.

They then veered into an easterly direction again and came upon burnt lands. Fire must have passed here many years before, because small birches and dwarfed pines were visible in a large meadow. From there they went on to Stillwater lake, which according to their calculations, would have been about nineteen miles from the junction point of the four counties at latitude 44'25 and longitude 65'20.

Through their binoculars, they only saw rolling country. This high ground must have been the Blue Mountains. In due time, they reached the junction point of the four counties. The marker is a huge granite in the middle of a burntland. On the rock are marked the county lines and the names of the counties. It was in the area of the watershed of the Shelburne and the Sissiboo Rivers.

Feeling they had cleared up the legend surrounding the Blue Mountains, they started out on their return trip. They went to Lake Rosignol, thence to Silver Lake, and East Jordan Lake. They went to Long Lake, Stoney Lake and Moose Lake. From Moose Lake, they went on to Lake Wallace, which strangely enough, is a few miles from a lake called Blue Mountain Lake! From there they reached Dexter Brook, old familiar ground, and upon reaching Caribou River, they set up camp on the Plain and rested for two days, living luxuriously off the country on ducks, trout and blueberries. They came home from Caribou on the south side of the Silver River where they found more blue grass meadows and more very fine timberland.

The expedition never did find the grandiose Blue Mountains nor the Grand Prairie they were looking for, but as a result of it, grants were taken out for about one thousand acres of magnificent timberland.

When the party returned to the settlement, they found furious activity going on. Further buildings were being planned and their location laid out on the ground. The father was a man who knew what he wanted and seemed in a hurry to get things done.

The most exciting undertaking was the setting up of a plant to generate electricity. In 1895, in the woods, this was something new indeed. Weymouth did not get electricity until 1926.

The dynamo was to be water run and incorporated into the mill. A small extension was added to the mill building. A separate water pen and water wheel were installed. The small water gate could be opened at night when the main gate to the mill machinery was closed. It would be left open until a curfew hour, around eleven o'clock. This would economize on the flow of water and provide a luxury to the houses.

The system was bought from Canadian General Electric Co. Ltd. The dynamo had a capacity of two hundred lights at any given time, which meant they could install about three hundred light outlets as they would never all be burning at the same time.

With the dynamo and wiring equipment, an expert arrived in late August. He only stayed one day, during which he showed Boss Blinn not only how to set up the plant but also how to wire the houses and the outside poles. By the end of that summer, the mill, the big house, the cookhouse and the barn were lighted by electricity. As well, the settlement was lighted from poles with lights in reflectors all around the square. At night, the whole place was ablaze with light.

The dynamo cost four hundred dollars, and the wire and outlets to wire all the houses, building and outdoors cost about three hundred dollars. Not an insignificant sum in those days.

It was during this first summer that the settlement got

its name. It was only natural that eventually the place would have to be given some identity.

Emile Stehelin had not really had time to think of a name for his domain. Had he thought about it, he probably would have called it St. Charles, as he was devoted to that name, being an admirer of the Emperor Chalesmagne and it was the name of his father whom he had not known well, but whose memory he revered. However, the name adopted was given it quite by accident.

Father Blanche was invited to come and visit during the late summer, before Emile was to return to France. To commemorate a new enterprise and get it well under way, it was the custom to hold a public religious ceremony of formal blessing. Father Blanche would officiate at such a ceremony.

The planned affair had been well advertised and a warm invitation to attend was passed on to all for miles around, by word of mouth. On the appointed Sunday, a large crowd of people from the surrounding villages began to arrive very early, in carts, on horseback and by water. The Indian chief, Peter Paul, with a band of his Micmacs, had arrived the night before and set up camp on the sand beach just below the house. They had come down the lakes and portages by canoe from the reservation at Bear River.

Father Blanche had arrived on horseback on the Friday afternoon before. On Saturday night, there was a big dinner at the new house. The old friend was the guest of honour, seated to the right of the lady of the house. Opposite and to the right of Emile sat his daughter-in-law, Katie. The sons were seated around, the youngest, Paul, at the foot of the table. The fare that night was trout followed by a Gigot a L'ail. The wine was not a vintage one, but the best they could find in Weymouth. The conversation carried long into the night, in the living room, with coffee and rum. These men, far away from home, were happy in the feeling that they could continue their way of life here in the forest of Canada.

Sunday morning was bright and calm. At ten o'clock, Father Blanche appeared at the doorway of the big house, resplendent in the green vestments of that day. He was tall and his big shaggy head with pinch nose glasses, radiated grace, friendliness and charm. They had erected an altar on the verandah, covered with a white tablecloth and adorned with wildflowers of many colours. Paul and Roger served as acolytes. No offering in the greatest of cathedrals mounted towards Heaven with more devotion and thought of the Creator, than the humble prayers of these simple and devout people.

The homily was simple and warm, suggesting that in each heart, there be a prayer for the success of the enterprise and the well being of all present. Father Blanche spoke in French and in English, a feat of self-confidence in a man who had been in the country only five years.

After Mass, the procession was formed and behind a hurriedly shaped cross, the whole assembly followed the tall leader around the village square and down to the mill. On its return, the procession had to pass a haystack. From a distance could clearly be seen a rather well painted sign atop it which read "New France". Nobody knew who put up the sign. With the approval of his friend, Father Blanche raised his long arm in blessing of this, the name of the village, chosen by the people. "So be it, amen" murmured the Alsatian. In later years, the dazzling sight of the hamlet at night, lit up in all its brilliance, inspired the Blacks and the Acadians to rechristen New France; The Electric City, a name still heard amont their descendants.

Dinner was served on improvised tables in the open air. Naturally, the fare was venison, trout and birds. The air of merriment increased in tempo as more whiskey and rum bottles, brought by the visitors, were uncorked and passed around. The afternoon and early evening were spent around a bonfire, telling stories, singing songs and dancing.

Father Blanche enjoyed himself too, moving about from group to group talking, even in his broken English. There were many Acadians but there were also the Wagoners, the Steeles, the Sullivans, the Hills and, of course, Nanon, her two sons and her daughter. From Southville were the black people, the Cromwells, the Langfords, the Jarvis' and many others. Peter Paul, with his squaw, both dressed in their regalia, looked splendid. From Weymouth, came the Beatons, the

Rices, and, of course, Uncle John Goodwin, and many others.

At dusk, the horses were gathered and harnessed and the departure of the crowd began in the midst of handshakes and the farewell hurrah. The teams gradually disappeared into the night, but the jingle of the harness bells lingered a while longer, on the still air of a perfect night, until silence enveloped well christened New France. That night at the big house, it was a time for relaxation and perhaps meditation. It is a blessing that man has dreams to soften the hard realities of life.

The next day, planning for the exploitation of the property, resumed with ever greater enthusiasm and vigour. Projecting an annual cut of three million board feet, the problem of getting the finished lumber to ships'-side at Weymouth presented a real problem. The road was bad, even from the Corner. Ox teams were slow. A thousand board feet was a good load.

At first, they thought of fixing the last six miles of the road, but even a good road would not speed traffic very much. Animal power would still be very slow, but with a better road, they could give out contracts to many local teams to haul the lumber. They approached the government at Halifax, pointing out the economic boost a good road would bring to the entire area. But apparently there was no road building policy. The people in the government promised to look into the matter, but that was the end of it. Even in those days, development assistance went to the eastern part of the province.

Emile and Jean visited Halifax, Amherst, New Glasgow, and Cape Breton. Somewhere they saw a railroad run on log tracks, which seemed to give good service. They decided such a system might work at New France, and they brought back a small boiler, some wheels and other parts to get started on a railway. Boss Blinn took charge of this project and put together a small engine which was named La Mouche à Feu (Firefly). It was extremely simple; the boiler and engine were set up on a small truck on four wheels with a tender to hold cordwood for fuel. He also built a few flat cars and commenced construction of the roadbed and track. Thus was born "The New France and Weymouth Railway".

September arrived and after a full summer with much accomplished, it was time for Emile and his wife to return to France. He was indeed well satisfied with the progress of the enterprise and leaving instructions and plans, they were on the way back to Le Havre. The four sons were to carry out the next stage of development, until his return in the spring of 1896. The die was cast.

The route for the railway had been traced on the map before Emile Sr. left and now began the tedious task of surveying it, and acquiring the necessary rights of way. The line would take the shortest route to Weymouth Bridge. Starting at New France, it would go to Lake Doyle, thence to Riverdale, skirting Provost Lake, thence to Danvers, then descending to the Sissiboo River at Yarmouth Corner, and finally skirting the river down to the Main Road at Weymouth Bridge.*

The acquisition of parcels of land for the right of way proved somewhat difficult and slow. The Stehelins owned only as far as Lake Doyle beyond which many parcels would have to be bought from individuals.

Within the village of Weymouth, the acquisition of land, by contrast, went very smoothly. The Wharf was purchased. Lands adjacent to it in the marsh were bought to provide more space to stack lumber and build a barn to store tools and provide shelter for the animals that would be needed to load ships. To get the right of way from the main road to his Wharf, Emile had to buy two large stores. Having no present use for them, he rented one as a furniture store downstairs and a club upstairs. The other store, the Stehelins rented as a grocery store and next to it, they owned and rented the famous Weymouth blacksmith shop. All these buildings were destroyed by fire in 1929. Most of the land is presently occupied by Weymouth Motors Ltd., and a gasoline station. The wharf behind the new buildings, has practically disappeared.

By November, three miles of the way had been cleared to a width of thirty feet when the survey work stopped. With December and the first snow, they began to fell the trees along the way. These would be used to build the track next spring. Hemlock trees would be used to build bridges, crib work over

* See map in picture section.

gullies and the sleeper bed under the track.

To close this momentous summer, nothing describes the enthusiasm and hopes of the family better than two letters written to Mathilde, the younger sister of Emile, who was living in Paris.

5 August 1895

My Dear Mathilde:

Thank you for your good letter and for the good wishes you formulated for me. I hope that all will go well here and that I will be repaid for all my labours by the happiness and comfortable life, even perhaps wealth, for my wife and my children.

That is the object of all my work, because as for myself, I am satisfied anywhere and my wants can be reduced to very little. Here one is forced to limit oneself to the strict necessities as one cannot always procure the extras.

Upon arrival, we found our property well advanced (construction). The mill is already in full operation, but we have not so far sold any lumber, because we need it to build our buildings which will, happily, be completed soon.

The country is really very beautiful and for me, as I do not look for social life with my fellowmen, I find this solitude and quiet in the forest filled with charm.

Our homestead was cut right out of the forest, that is to say, the land we opened to form a yard of about three hectars was forest one year ago. We already have a mill, our house, a house for the workmen, and we are about to build a barn for twenty animals, horses, oxen, etc., and homes for my sons, Emile, Paul and Roger. This makes already quite a few houses, all of wood covered with wooden shingles.

In about a month's time, we will begin sawing lumber for the market. The mill produces a lot, and we will soon have caught up the time taken in building which was, of course, indispensible.

I also bought a plain next to my lands (Cariboo) which Emile and the young ones are now plowing, to seed with hay this fall and next spring with oats and potatoes, etc. I will start a farm there in the spring and begin the raising of cattle, horses, sheep and pigs. Everything will be functioning early next year. Here everything goes fast and buildings of wood seem to go up as by magic.

You must have received a letter my wife wrote you recently. Why do letters take fifteen days to arrive? It is annoying and makes news scarce. We go or send someone every week for the mail, otherwise, we are without communication with the world. As for myself, I find this very agreeable, but my wife would like to talk (with someone). However, she will catch up on our return (to France), I think around the end of September.

My kiss and regards to everyone, Max (Mathilde's husband), Alice, the children. To M. de Clery, my best regards, Emile.

Second letter: Marie Therese to Mathilde (the first part is missing).

"Frau Gilm:

....all this time they have been readying lumber and Monday (probably in June) they started building the house which should take ten days. The workmen here are strong and soon our four carpenters will start building the barn which means that by August, everything will be done and well finished. As you can see, Dear Mathilde, everything goes well here and once the younger ones are here, we will be the happiest people in the world, God willing and we pray for it every day.

The mill is working and saws one hundred and ninety-eight logs per day, each fifteen to eighteen meters long. All the work, building, is steady and well done. The natural grain of the woods makes nice designs (refers to the finishing in the little home). The bedrooms are also finished in wood. My husband's is in maple, mine in pine varnished and with red trim, which is very cheerful and produces a pleasing effect. Jean and Katie also have a room of varnished wood and red trim. The boys' rooms, as well as the rooms downstairs, hall and stairway are all in spruce. At the moment, we are a bit squeezed and Emile had an extension built onto the kitchen which will provide a pantry downstairs plus two rooms upstairs. The maids will have their own stairway to their rooms (on the third floor).

We plan to return (to France) in September unless we have to change dates for business reasons, to return for good in May, 1896.

We have chosen a nice site on the lake to build a very fine building (this refers to a club-cum-boathouse-bathing house, later named the Casino). Its location is the best we could have chosen, on a hill, wooded with big trees, a beach on the edge of the lake, and a cover where boats will be moored. The one we have now (sailboat) sails very well. We just returned from a trip from one lake to the other, the two sons (Paul and Roger), my husband, Katie and Mily (Emile son) and two dogs. The boys manoeuvered well but I was very scared. The older sons were surprised to learn of this adventure because they know of my fear of the water, which I did not hide. The water frightens me.

I had a large yard built, with chicken and ducks. Emile, father, has been lucky at hunting lately. He shot an enormous porcupine which weighed two hundred pounds? The meat is very good, and they use the fat for the guns, then last Sunday, a richepone, a bird like a wild goose with beautiful plumage and hard to kill because it is very cunning. We are having it stuffed in Yarmouth, to take back to France.

Give our kisses to the children and grandchildren and our remembrance to the others, not forgetting your husband, M. de Clery and Marie Therese. She would go very well here, French girls are much appreciated."

After the departure of the parents, one momentous event took place before the close of that memorable year of 1895. Emile Jean, who had arrived in Canada less than one year ago, married in November.

He was twenty-five years old, and all through that summer, in the solitude of the forest, on the trails, with his gun, his fishing rod and his dog, he spent many thoughtful hours, some at the new Caribou house, some at the Indian hut he had found in the spring, along the Silver River. Secretly, he began to muse about bringing a woman into his life. Sometime during the summer, he had approached his father and mother and told them of his great desire to make Anne Baldwin, of Tamworth, England, his wife, if she would have him as her husband. Miss Baldwin was well known to the family. She had gone to France to learn French, a practice which was much in vogue in English families of that time. By pure coincidence, she had enrolled at the Sacred Heart Convent at Beauvais, not far from Gisors. She was the youngest of three children. Her brother Will and her sister, Lizie, lived with her widowed mother. Her father had been a newspaper publisher.

At the school, she met the two Stehelin daughters, Therese and Germaine and in time, was invited to visit at St. Charles. Emile Stehelin was anxious for his children to learn English, and it was, therefore, natural that he should ask the English girl to spend a summer in the home as a tutoress for his daughters. There she met the young man who was now dreaming of asking her hand in marriage. There had been no sweeping courtship, nothing but evenings dancing in the homes around Gisors. In those days, young ladies were chaperoned, and anyway, young people were careful not to divulge their feelings. Marriage was for the parents to arrange and it was a complicated matter of negotiation between the fathers. After that summer, the two young people forgot about each other, or so it would have appeared.

Emile Stehelin, Sr., wrote to Mrs. Baldwin, formally asking for the hand of her daughter on behalf of his son. No doubt the letter was written in French, well knowing that it would be understood with the help of Anne herself. To the young suitor, waiting in the forest of Nova Scotia, the reply seemed terribly slow in coming.

In the Baldwin family, the proposal caused an upheaval and an initial refusal on the part of Anne's mother. It seemed too much to ask, to let her daughter go to Canada, so far away, perhaps never to see her again. She had never met the young man in question and, of course, he was a Frenchman. There were arguments, tears and even threats of rejection. The whole idea was too heart-rendering to be seriously contemplated, so argued the mother and the sister.

But Miss Baldwin was very determined and when all means of persuasion had failed, she announced that she would return to France and become a nun, never to return to England. To this family of Methodist background, this was much worse than anything that could ever befall the young woman in Canada. The day was carried by the petite lady of twenty-two years and, in due course, Mrs. Baldwin's answer, couched in most cordial and flowing terms, accepting the proposal on behalf of her daughter, arrived at New France. And so the engagement was sealed by mail in September, 1895.

Plans for the wedding were discussed by letter back and forth across the Atlantic, and it was decided that all the Stehelins would go to England for the wedding which was projected for November. Unfortunately, it seemed impossible for the future groom to leave the business at New France for two months. It was then suggested that the marriage be postponed until the next spring. But, of course, there was always the choice, left to Miss Baldwin to make, to come to Canada on her own and be married here. Needless to say, the young woman hesitated not one second and feverish preparations were begun for her to sail for Halifax in early November.

The most time taking task was to assemble the trouseau, a sacred institution in those days. Boxes and trunks were filled with all the household supplies a bride had to have. There were the clothes to be made and that took time. When November arrived, the sad leave taking took place at Southhampton. Anne was not allowed to travel on her own. A lady companion had been hired to accompany her and return after the marriage.

Eight days on the sea in the fall of the year was not a pleasant experience for anyone, let alone an excited young girl who had never been on a ship, except the Channel boat between France and England. She was seasick and was terribly relieved to see land and the dock at Halifax.

At the ship to meet her were her future husband, with Jean and Katie. The wedding had to take place as soon as possible, because the companion lady had to return by the same boat. On that very afternoon, after obtaining special dispensation, with Jean and Katie and two Halifax friends of Jean's as witnesses, they were married at the Eudist Seminary on Quinpool Road.

The wedding dinner that night was at the Queen Hotel. The party was joined by three or four more friends. The Queen was the best hotel in the old city and indeed it had an atmosphere all its own which they liked. And so they spent their short honeymoon there, visiting the places of interest and getting to know one another, not having seen each other in two years.

They took the Dominion Atlantic Railway to Weymouth. It was a very interesting trip that lasted from early morning until mid-afternoon. The train was very comfortable and they enjoyed the sights. The names of the towns they passed reminded the young bride of towns and cities in England.

At Weymouth, they stopped a couple of days at the Goodwin, where they met many people of the village. There was better communication now that a member of the family spoke English.

The trip to New France was disconcerting, to say the least, to a young woman from England. She had been told what it would be like, but she now realized that it had not sunken in. Here she was, bouncing about on a sleigh pulled by a yoke of oxen, goaded along ever so slowly by Johnie-à-Marc. The November rains had flooded the road and between the deep holes full of water, the mud, and the big rocks, she didn't know what to think. It was not the beautiful June trip of her mother-in-law, amid greenery and sunshine. December would be here tomorrow, the trees were bare and the snow would soon cover the ground.

It was late afternoon when the sleigh finally pulled into the Square where the big house seemed to welcome her. From the mens' house, appeared the workmen, waving their caps and shouting their loud hurrahs in welcome to the new bride. One by one they came forward, tipped their caps and bid the happy couple many years of marital bliss and of course, many children. The bride felt better now as she straightened her tiny hat and adjusted her long skirts as she stepped off the sleigh.

Even General seemed to sense the occasion as he waved his mane and pawed the ground as the groom dismounted.

In the front hall of the home, Katie, Jean, Paul and Roger were there to welcome their new sister-in-law. Rosie Babin, the young maid was also there to add her word of warm welcome, "soyez la bienvenue icite".

Rosie served tea in the living room in front of the fire with molasses cookies, something new indeed, but very much appreciated. As darkness came, the whole settlement seemed to come alive with the switching on of the electric lights everywhere. Every bulb in every building came alight, and outside, the lights on the poles cast a cheerful glow on the whole square. Who would have imagined that such a charming home existed at the end of such an atrocious road? so mused the girl from Tamworth.

Dinner was served late in the evening as was the custom in Europe. The dining room was simply furnished with a sideboard and a very long table with many chairs. A hardwood fire was blazing cheerfully in the fireplace. The aroma from the kitchen was different than that of roast beef, chicken or lamb. It was to be a surprise. After a potage, Rosie entered triumphantly carrying a large platter of steaks, dark steaks, moose steaks. They were delicious, as moose meet is at its best in the fall of the year. The dessert was another surprise, thick blueberry pie topped with whipped cream; all produced on the property.

It was not difficult to get wine but the choice was limited and the quality was indifferent. Jean had managed to get two bottles of champagne, which to Frenchmen anywhere, is indispensible to toast special occasions. There were six Stehelins at the table and the glasses were raised and clinked to the happiness of the bride and the groom, to the absent ones in France and England, and to the future prosperity of New France.

In the living room, in front of another warming fire, the men sipped their coffee and rum as they talked, while the two ladies, as was the custom then, remained behind at the table to chat about things of interest to them. The young men must have thought of the changes in the year since they had arrived at the little cabin in which they spent the first winter. On its site now stood this large comfortable house with thick moose skins on every floor. That night as they took a last glance outside, the moonlight danced on the still lake and a light snow began to cover the ground. The first snow that Anne saw. They were all immensely happy, but what did the future hold in store for these adventurers, they wondered.

The most exciting time for the new bride, was when she accompanied her husband to the woods to shoot partridge and rabbits. The trails, through the dense forest carpeted with multi-coloured fallen leaves, were so romantic and mysterious.

There was snow on the ground a foot deep and the roofs and trees were covered as Christmas Day approached. There was no midnight mass, but the reveillon, which normally follows it, was the occasion for the beginning of the celebrations. The four Stehelins and the wives of two of them, seated around the table in the dining room, now gayly decorated with bows of fir and pine, garlands of evergreens and red berries, lived the tradition of their homeland in their attempt to recreate its customs and atmosphere.

There was no turkey for Christmas dinner, but there were other meats which, to these new Canadians, were even better. Venison, partridges and rabbits. As they talked of those at home, they imagined the scene at St. Charles, their mother and father and seven remaining children. As they drank to their good health, they imagined that the parents at home would be drinking to the health of their sons in Canada.

Thus came to a happy end the first Year of a full life and a rewarding one in the New World.

THE FAMILY SETTLES IN THE WILD

When Emile left Canada in September of 1895, his health was completely restored and full of enthusiasm, he was busy planning the future of New France. He attended to matters connected with the sale of his factory, and he turned his attention to preparing for the move of the remainder of his family to Nova Scotia.

The children who had remained in France, three girls and the four boys, were told of the plans to move to the New World. They heard with great excitement of New France, the home that awaited them and they listened excitedly to the wild tales of the forest with its animals and its dangers. Departure was projected for March of 1896.

St. Charles was to be retained fully furnished, except for some pieces to be taken to New France. The property was to be cared for by Leon and his wife who lived in the coachhouse, faithful servants for many years. All through the long years that the property remained vacant, Mère Leontine kept fresh flowers in their usual places around the house, as though the masters might come back any moment. From these arrangements, one gains the impression that the object of the project at New France was to create an enterprise that would give the sons a livelihood. Once the sons were settled, Emile and his wife would return to St. Charles.

The future of the daughters did present some problems. Therese, was already twenty-four years old and no ardent suitor had rushed to seek her hand in marriage. In those days, a girl past twenty-four had to be considered difficult to marry off. The other two girls were so young, Germaine 16 and Simone 12, there seemed no cause to worry about their future yet. But in the final decision, it was the future of the sons that mattered. If a father could not get his daughters married off, he could leave them enough to live on. In those days, there was never any thought given to the idea that a single girl might work to earn her living.

The family home, St. Charles, was built by Emile in 1886, on land adjoining his felt factory, on the main Dieppe-Paris road, just outside Gisors and next to the picturesque village of Eragny. The river Epte, flowing at the bottom of the garden, provided the motive power for the factory.

This particular corner of Normandy is very interesting historcially. On the way to England in the eleventh century, the Romans founded Gisors. It was at Gisors that it was decided that the French crusaders would adopt the red cross on a white background and the English a white cross on a red background. Richard the Lion Hearted left from Gisors, only to be imprisoned by the German Emperor, a fellow crusader. Taking advantage of Richard's misfortune, his cousin, Louis VIIth took Normandy. Richard retook it after his release, and so it was traded back and forth over the centuries.

Another interesting bit of history, is the presence of a number of dolmens of the ancient druids, on the wooded hill just outside the town. A big flat stone with a large hole in the middle, resting on four large three to four feet high stones, stands as an altar, used to offer human sacrifices to the gods. The unfortunate man chosen as the victim had his head put through the hole from underneath and from the top, the priest severed it from the body with some sort of cutlass. The assembly through its priest thusly sought the benevolence of their gods, after which they read the future from the entrails of the victim.

All the family's time during that fall and early winter was taken up preparing for the migration and visiting friends. They bought the linen, bedding, silver and dishes for the new home. As they liked the furniture they had seen in Canada, lighter and inexpensive, they decided to furnish the home from the stores in Halifax and Weymouth. They brought out only a few special pieces. There was the piano, a Pleyel, an oak desk which was very dear to Emile, having been made by one of his Alsatian craftman of wood from a Roman cider press. They took several leather chairs, a few comfortable beds, Emile Jean's cello and a lute. A number of books were taken as well as song books, personal effects and special articles.

That last Christmas was a happy one with the house full of relations, some from Alsace, come for a final reveillon and New Year celebration. New Year is the important feast in France. It is the time for the exchange of good wishes in the midst of great merriment and the endless toasts in Champagne.

Emile attended especially to the procurement and the shipping of wines and Champagne and for future supplies. The red wine was shipped in forty gallon casks and would be bottled at New France. The Champagne was in cases of twenty-four bottles. One could buy champagne bearing one's own label. The Stehelin brand was Stehelin-Eperney. This was a bit of snobbery, because it might imply that the family owned their own vineyard and winery, which was not so.

At last the day of departure arrived, February 24, 1896. From the train speeding towards Le Havre, the family looked for the last time at their home now silent. That night, they boarded the Bretagne for New York. There were six children; Therese, twenty-four years old; Louis, twenty-one; Germaine, seventeen; Maurice, fourteen; Simone, eleven; and Bernard, ten. Accompanying them was their favorite dog, a little bull-terrier, named Stop. Charles stayed behind to finish his contract with the Army. After finishing his one year of compulsory service, he had enlisted for a further period, thinking he would like to make the Army his career. The sudden change of orientation of the family changed his plans and he followed the family to Canada later that year.

Crossing the Atlantic in the winter time is always a test of intestinal fortitude, even for the most seasoned travellers. Although the Bretagne was the last word in comfort, stability and speed, seasickness was the common lot of the children and their mother. She suffered terribly and was unable to take hardly any food. She vowed by all the saints that she would never set foot on a ship again. The father experienced no ill effects and enjoyed the trip. The sea air felt good, sharpening the appetite for the varied and excellent French cuisine, eased down by good wine, followed by black coffee laced with strong Cognac. There was nothing much to do aboard ship in those days, a few games on deck and an orchestra at night in the grand salon. The most important event of the day was reading the latest news received by wireless and pinned onto a notice board in the main hall.

After seven days of tossing about in a rough sea, suddenly land appeared in the distance. For the children, the Statue of Liberty was the first lesson in American history. The huge lady, holding a torch on high, symbolized Liberty illuminating the World. It was the work of Bartholdi, the great sculptor of the day and also an Alsatian from Colmar. Erected in 1886, it was the gift of France to the United States. To the children, the sight of the city was awe inspiring by the height of its buildings, its huge bridge and the ships all over its waterfront.

The family disembarked directly into the train waiting on the pier. They would be taken to Boston instead of taking the Fall River Boat. The porters on the train were all Black men and one can imagine the amazement and curiosity of the children who had never seen black people, especially black men dressed in immaculate white jackets and gold braided peak caps that were not unlike in shape of the kepi of the French soldier. Noting that this family spoke no English, these Black men looked after them throughout the train trip with solicitude and great dignity. From that day, every Black man was the friend of the children.

At Boston, they were met by Jean, who had come to help on the last leg of the journey. He took them to the United States Hotel, which, to the children, was palatial. Here they discovered another marvel; the elevator. They had to stay in Boston a day or so because the boat to Yarmouth made only two crossings per week.

The trip on the *Yarmouth* was terribly rough, taking twenty-four hours instead of the usual twelve. After the luxury of the *Bretagne*, this was a dirty, uncomfortable tramp steamer. The cabins were very small, dingy and cold. The lounge, an area with fixed uncomfortable hard seats, where they saw their first spitoons, was crowded with passengers who had not taken cabins. Some were sleeping, others were smoking or spitting tobacco juice and missing the spitoons and some were inebriated within an hour of leaving port. Some women were obviously having an uncomfortable time of it.

The crew were a motley looking bunch, dirty, poorly dressed, no uniforms. On their heads, anything from bowler hats to fur caps.

All night the old ship rolled and pitched in the storm. The engines had to be stopped for hours to pump the ship. Somehow she made port at Yarmouth with most of the passengers in a sorry state. Madame Stehelin was deathly sick and on the dock, she could find no place just to sit while waiting for the train. A little restaurant a short distance along the wharf had no washroom. Surely the parents must have asked themselves what they were doing in this miserable country.

When the train backed onto the wharf, with bell ringing, they climbed aboard where they found comfort at last. It was warm in the coach and there were washrooms at both ends.

The trip to Weymouth was agreeable, especially to the younger children. There was something to look at all the way. Mostly forest and lakes. The company ran a good train and the coaches were clean inside and out. The steam engine was jet black and its brass trim was well polished.

The train blew its whistle as it crossed narrow snow packed roads on which they saw oxen pulling logs on sleighs. As they approached Weymouth, near another crossing, the parents pointed out some Indians standing by their small and poor looking little shacks as they waved at the train. In a few minutes, the train broke into open country and from the high ground, they got their first view of the town in the distance. They saw the houses built on either side of the river. Here and there they noticed church steeples. The fact that there was more than one church caught their attention, because in France, there was only one church in each village. The train moved very slowly onto the bridge and the children were scared when it leaned on one side, as it negotiated the curve. From the train, they had a magnificent view of the village, cut in two by an iron road bridge. The tide was out, and on both sides of a stretch of open water, they saw very large brownish ice packs. They also saw the tall masts of several vessels, lying at the wharves on both sides of the river.

Emile explained to his children that these wooden ships took lumber to far away places, some to Portgual, some to Spain, and others to England. They could see activity alongside the ships and were told that they were loading lumber, some perhaps from New France.

The railway station at Weymouth was indeed more inspiring than the ones they had seen on the way, and its station master wore a uniform. They were to discover later on, however, that he wore his uniform very seldom. Unlike in France, people here seemed to dislike uniforms. Unlike in France also, here the station master did all the different jobs around the place. He sold tickets, moved freight, helped passengers and once in a while tapped some message on the Morse telegraph, which seemed to be ticking away continuously. There were two trains each day, one in the morning from Yarmouth and the other in the afternoon from Halifax. They carried the mail and express parcels as well as many passengers. There were always a number of people at the station at train time. They came to see who boarded and who got off, to have a look at the people who didn't get off and generally to have a visit with friends and neighbours.

Early the next morning, the family got aboard three sleighs and started on the last leg of their long journey to New France, their new home. It was a nice cold early March day. There was plenty of snow on the ground except when they reached wind swept section of the road at Ohio, where they encountered bare patches, and they had to get off and walk short distances here and there.

At the Corner, the snow was deep and the road was narrow but in the morning sun, the woods looked beautiful. My grandmother recognized her special sleigh, the one she had travelled on the summer before, and its little driver, Johnie-à-Marc. A second sleigh, much larger, was teamed by an equally scary looking individual. The children were a bit afraid, especially when they saw these men spitting long streaks of yellow spittle into the snow. These teamsters carried short rods which had iron pins in the end. They would stick these into the skin of the oxen and uttering strange words of command, kept the beasts moving. The oxen were very slow but they could plod along at the same gait all day without tiring. The parents, with the confidence and abandon of seasoned dwellers of the forest, reassured their children and everybody settled down to enjoy the long trip.

The trees were covered with snow and the branches of the dark spruce hung low under its weight. The sun was shining brightly, and the effect on the snow was dazzling. This was fairyland for certain, where it was easy for these children to dream and imagine all sorts of stories, all sorts of adventures. The parents had not seen the snow before, and they too were enchanted with the scene and felt certain in their own minds that they had found the paradise of any human being's wildest dream.

After a long while, gliding very slowly over this carpet of whiteness in silence except for the jingle of the ox bells, they were suddenly frightened by the firing of guns and the appearance in the distance of strange looking bearded fellows. But they were soon overjoyed as they recognized their two brothers, Paul and Roger, coming towards them on their snowshoes. They were dressed strangely, in checkered mackinawas, fur hats, with guns on their shoulders and wicked looking knives hanging from their wide belts. They were not the same brothers who had left home a year ago. The ox teams stopped and amid the barking of the dogs and the cries of joy, a family was being reunited in the depth of the forest, on an old woods road in Nova Scotia. In all the excitement, everybody talked at the same time, kissed one another and asked questions. One can imagine the dreams of adventure that must have been fired in the minds of the younger boys, Maurice and Bernard, as they admired the gear and ways of their older brothers. The two younger girls were excited too, but the reaction of Therese was less enthusiastic. After all, this was very nice but where would she find a husband here?

On the way again, by midafternoon of that beautiful day, the convoy glided slowly into the clearing with its new buildings in grey and maroon, neatly ranged on either side of the square and the big house at the bottom, securely seated in the snow, which looked so big, so warm and inviting with wood scented smoke curling gently from its chimneys.

There was complete silence as they moved along towards the big house. There was so much to look at. On the right was the big barn and beyond it they got a first look at Langford Lake, frozen and white. On the left were the office, the forge, and the Cookhouse. Further away and beyond the big house was the huge mill covered with snow.

As they approached their new home, they got their first look at woodsmen. About twenty of them came towards the sleighs to welcome the Old Man, the Old Lady, and the rest of their family. They were strange looking men, some with beards, some with long hair, either smoking a pipe or chewing tobacco. They spoke half French and half English but somehow everybody seemed to get along and communicate.

The ox teams were led to the barn, the sound of the bells died away and there was only the sound of laughter and talking as the family entered their home. At the door they were met by Katie and my mother, Anne (Baldwin), who was now completing her first winter away from England. They knew Anne, of course, and heard from her of the wonderful, happy winter spent in the forest in such complete abandon.

In the hall and in the living room, fires were burning brightly and after the long trip, they enjoyed the warmth and comfort they provided. At dusk, the whole colony suddenly came ablaze with light. Every window of every building shed its light, blending with the lights outside to give a special lustre to the snow everywhere. St. Charles did not have electric lights.

That evening, they sat, fourteen, around the big dining room table. They were hungry children who savoured for the first time, the venison of the forest, enriched by the wines of the homeland. The parents must have been happy that evening as they enjoyed the talk, the laughter and the noisy joy of their children. In those days, a large family was regarded as a great

The author's grandfather's felt factory.

i

The family at St. Charles, 1880, with three more still to be born.

The landeau of St. Charles.

The ship on which the family crossed the ocean in 1894.

Emile Charles Adolphe Stehelin

Marie Therese Buissons Stehelin

Major E. J. Stehelin, 1916

Author's mother, Anne Baldwin Stehelin, 1894

Anne Baldwin

Jacqueline at the little Camp—foot of Longford Lake around 1923.

Bernadette and Jacqueline, New France 1905.

Jean Jacques Stehelin, 1891

Charles Stehelin (circled in photo).

Therese Stehelin

Louis Stehelin around 1925, a bachelor, lived in Weymouth until around 1928 when he returned to St. Charles, France. He taught English in colleges in Brittany and Normandy. Died at St. Charles.

Roger Stehelin, 1904

Emile III (Mitte)

Paul Stehelin, 1914

Germaine Stehelin, married Captain Nevius Kay and sailed in wooden schooners for 17 years. They were shipwrecked in a big storm. Later lived in Briooklyn, then Ontario where she died.

Maurice Stehelin   Jacqueline

Grandfather, Emile Charles A. Stehelin, and Maurice (Mo) Stehelin during war.

Simone, 1924

Bernard Stehelin, 1915

Father Blanche, later Bishop of Sicca

Germaine, Mother, Therese, Grandmother, Simone, Bernadette

Emile Sr., going for war news, The Western Union, 1914-18

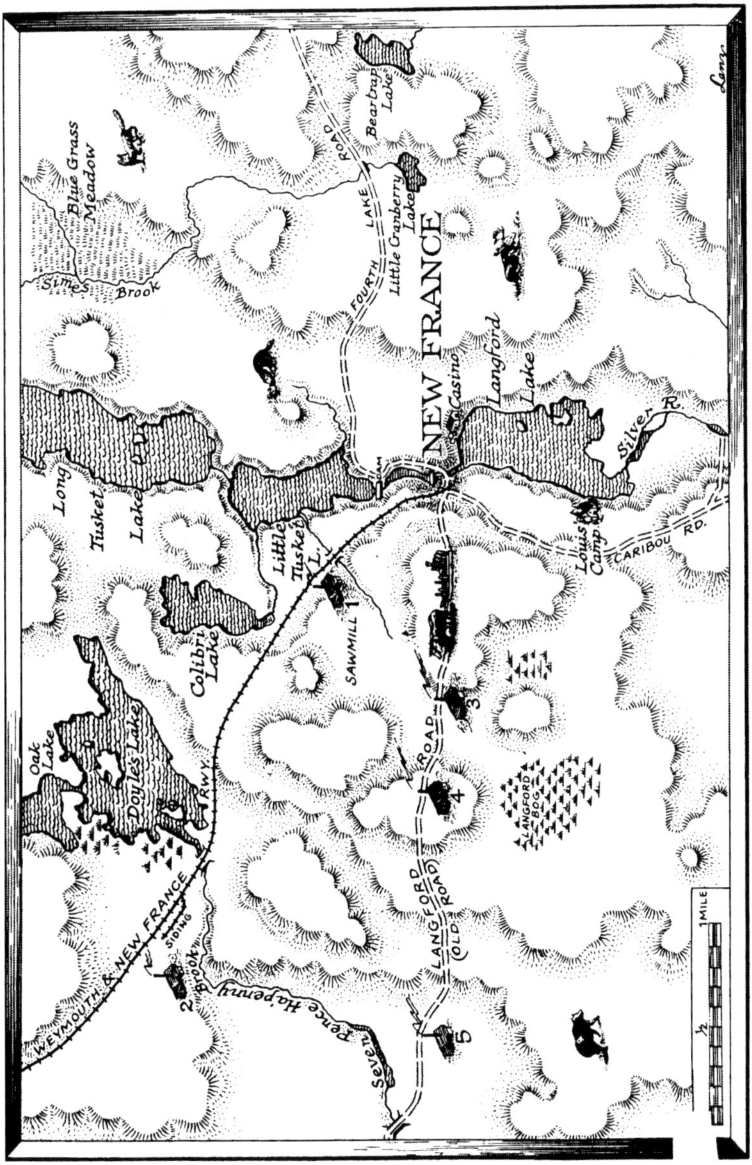

Blue Grass Meadow
Simes Brook
Beartrap Lake
Fourth Lake Road
Little Cranberry Lake
NEW FRANCE
Casino
Langford Lake
Silver R.
Long Tusket Lake
Little Tusket L.
DAM
Louis' Camp
Caribou Rd.
Colibri Lake
Sawmill
Oak Lake
Doyle's Lake
Rwy.
Road
Langford Bog
Weymouth & New France
Siding
Langford Road
(Old Road)
Seven Pence Ha'penny Brook
1
2
3
4
5
½
1 Mile
Lenz

xviii

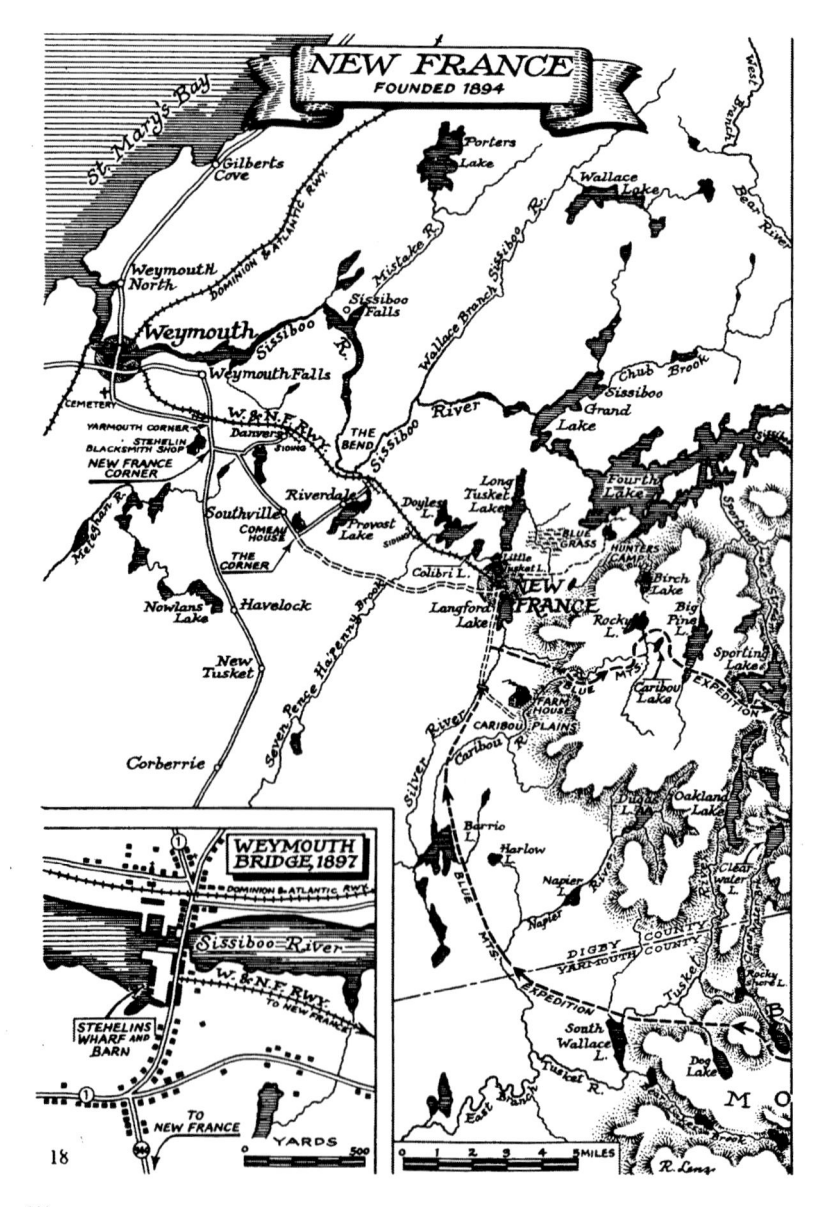

xix

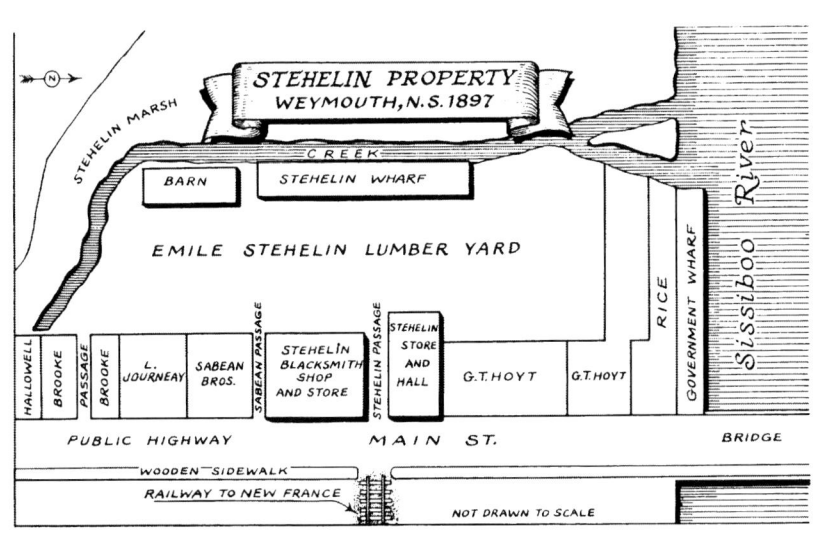

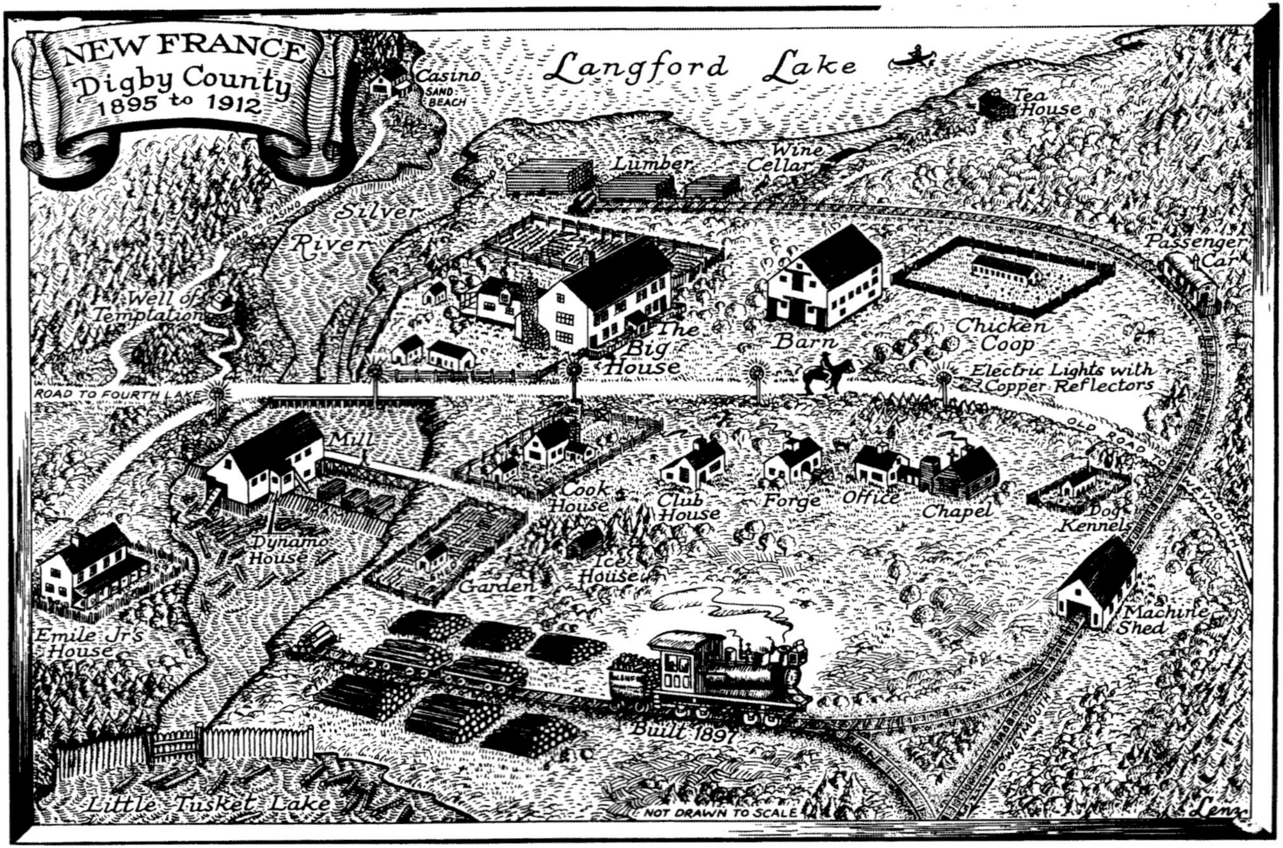
NEW FRANCE
Digby County
1895 to 1912
Casino
SAND BEACH
Langford Lake
Tea House
Lumber
Wine Cellar
Silver River
ROAD TO CASINO
Passenger Car
Well of Temptation
The Big House
Barn
Chicken Coop
Electric Lights with Copper Reflectors
ROAD TO FOURTH LAKE
OLD ROAD TO WEYMOUTH
Mill
Cook House
Club House
Forge
Office
Chapel
Dog Kennels
Dynamo House
Ice House
Garden
Machine Shed
Emile Jr's House
Built 1897
TO WEYMOUTH
Little Tusket Lake
NOT DRAWN TO SCALE
Lenz

The wedding, October 1900 (Courtesy Mrs. Eddie Dionne). Front row, left to right—Therese, Dr. Fred Hogan, Germaine, Nevius, Anne Stehelin, Emile and Marie Therese (Father and mother of the bride), Father Sullivan, Simone, Dr. Sanborne, Roger.

Back view of barn, house and cookhouse

The cookhouse

Left to right: Teamster, Paul, Roger, Katie, Madame, Emile Jean, Monsieur, Jean Jacques

The sawmill.

Inside the mill. Boss Blinn (in foreground), Jean, Emile, Roger (at right).

Transportation vehicle for Madame Stehelin

The Maria Therese, 1897

New France, Emile Jean's house

The house at Caribou Plains

Simone and Germain

Ice boat, Langford Lake

Hunting party

Fishing party

Logging crew

The Caribou, W. & N. F. Ry.

Chief Peter Paul

Chief Peter Paul and Mi'kmaw tribe

xxxi

Mathilde

Formerly a hotel, the last Stehelin home in Weymouth (Courtesy Earl Sabine).

blessing, to be cherished and enjoyed, in spite of all the anxieties they invariably caused the parents.

The days that followed were very busy ones for everyone. The father and the older sons attended to the running of the business, visited the logging camps up Long Tusket Lake, got everything ready for the drive and the sawing to commence in early April. Everything seemed in order and soon the whole enterprise would awaken with bustling activity. At the house, the new mistress took over and made plans for the orderly running of the household.

Supplying the whole house with water was one of Smith's jobs. Each bedroom and there were nine of them, had a washing set which had to be kept supplied. The kitchen pails had to be kept well filled, but his big job was supplying the big hogshead in the attic. Smith, or Smitty as he was affectionately called, was a faithful servant boy, not very bright but always very happy. He worked all day long and as he moved about the house, he whistled, "not to surprise the girls" he would say with a wink. In the winter, he was also responsible for keeping all the woodboxes, upstairs and downstairs, filled. For fourteen years, he carried water and firewood, always happy in his job and its twelve dollars per month pay. In fact, he was so happy that at first he refused to take any pay, but a bank account was opened for him and every month his pay was deposited. Needless to say, Smitty was loved by all.

The younger children, Maurice, Bernard and Simone, were quite content to play in the snow, visit the mill, the forge and the cookhouse, always accompanied by dogs. They were not completely free. A school program was organized and Louis was given the job of master. Therese was to help, but she was too impatient and soon had to be relieved of her duties, occupying herself in other pursuits, such as looking after the hen house. Anne Stehelin taught English and piano.

Lumbering activities were in full swing. That year, the target cut had been set at three million board feet of spruce in various finished dimensions. All that winter, logging operations had been going on along Little Tusket Lake, on the road to Fourth Lake and on the south side of Long Tusket, about opposite the two little islands.

Logging operations were uncomplicated in those days, the accent being on manpower and animal power instead of machine power. In the fall of the year, camps were built on site. Second grade lumber was used and the walls and roof were covered with tarpaper held down by battens. To keep out the cold from underneath, small trees were stacked all around the base. The snow would fill in the spaces between the trees, thus making the banking quite tight and windproof. The stove was always an old Waterloo. The pots and pans were very ordinary of cast iron. Perhaps the most important item was the cast iron tea kettle. Tea was the main beverage and it was boiled in large tin tea pots. These were wide at the bottom and narrow at the top so they would heat more quickly. The men slept in the loft on straw palliasses with any kind of covering from wool blankets to home made quilts. A man's coat and clothing was always part of his bed covering. If the cook was a woman, they built an ell to the camp as a bedroom for herself and her husband. If the cook was a man, he simply slept behind the stove on a rough bed he made for himself.

The food was very simple but good. There was always a barrel of salt beef, often fresh moose meat, and a barrel of salted eels in the camp. Potatoes were in abundance and were always served in their skins to economize. There was dried salt cod, dried beans, flour, cabbage, turnips and a puncheon of molasses, to replace sugar and jams. One can imagine the quantities of food these healthy men could consume, regardless of whether they worked or not. Their wages were good for the time. A foreman got twenty dollars a month, found and an ordinary workman got fourteen, found. In today's management concept, this was not a good system because the amount of food a man ate bore no relation to the yield of his work. Before coming to the modern system of piece work, lumber operators tried making the men pay for their board, at least on days they didn't work. This was very unpopular and often termed "yankee sharp practice" because it was introduced by an American operation.

The tools were very simple. The cross cut saw and the double edged axe were the cutting tools. The peavy was the tool used to roll the logs. Once the logs were cut and limbed, they were hauled by yokes of oxen onto the ice on the lake. The oxen stayed on site all winter, sheltered at night under rough lean-tos. Horses were not practical because they were not sure footed like the slow oxen and sometimes broke a limb. Also they required oats and hay, while the oxen seemed to get along well mostly on hay and very little feed.

The winter, the first for most of the family, had been a very beautiful one. Everyone had enjoyed the sports in the snow and on the lakes, frozen crystal clear. But all hands had been very busy too.

There was no longing for spring, but when the season for its arrival came, there awakened instinctively an expectation for it. Of all the seasons, spring is the most joyful and the most hopeful one. Awakening from the lethargy of winter, all nature participated in the miracle of renewal. It didn't burst out suddenly. Rather, it was ushered in like an orchestration. Now the water began to gurgle under the breaking ice, then set free, it thundered over and around the rocks in the swollen river. The vegetation timidly pushed its head through the last snow. The songs of the birds, back in their thickets, joined in. The loon gave its echoing call. The whole orchestra is then giving its all. It is the time of the reaffirmation of love, the time when the young of the animals of the forest are born, and when the birds hatch their young. The children, with great excitement, ran everywhere in search of brightly coloured Easter eggs, whilst their elders, in the midst of this spectacle of sight and sound reflected on the meaning of this great triumph of life.

At break-up time, the drives took up all the time and work of the timber crews. The operation consisted of driving the logs, cut during the winter, through the lakes and rivers down to the mill.

When the lakes were free of ice, the drive began and every man available was engaged in it. The logs floating on Long Tusket had to be driven through the pass between it and Little Tusket. Drivers, equipped with long poles with spikes in one end of them, kept the flow of logs going. They worked from the banks, but often they had to run on the logs like nimble cats to untangle a stoppage.

For the run down to the Little Tusket Lake, quantities of logs were herded in a mass, held together by other logs chained together to form a boom. There was no towing power other than the strong arms of men at the oars of a punt, aided by a feeble downstream current.

When the first boom arrived at the foot of Little Tusket, the two gates of the dam were opened and the logs were carried away in the torrent into the river below. For the newcomers, especially the children, this was the exciting part of the drive. The men, always wet to the skin, had to work very quickly with their only tools, the peavies and the long pikes, to keep the flow of logs going and prevent jams. It was a back breaking job, as they pushed and tugged, running here and there on the floating logs. In spite of all the art of these men, log jams were inevitable and when they could not be opened by sheer human strength, they used dynamite.

At that time, there were several other mill operators below New France on the water system used by the family. They had a legal right to drive their logs through New France, down to their mills, at Barrio Lakes and beyond. There were, therefore, hundreds of men going through New France on the drives, some stopping at the cookhouse for a meal or a night's rest. These visits enlivened the place and the children especially liked to listen to the stories they told and hear their songs and ballads telling of their lives and work in the forest and on the rivers. Watching the logs rushing down the sluices, into the foaming, roaring water of the river below, watching these men run on the rolling logs in all directions, shouting as they handled their long pikes, was very exciting and thrilling.

After the last drive had gone through, all the sluice gates of both dams were closed to build up the head of water again to run the mill. Sawing would begin as soon as possible, ten hours per day, build the water level at night and go on as long as the water lasted. Usually until June, when it had to shut down and wait for the September rains to start up again.

The finished lumber was neatly piled to dry before being hauled to the Weymouth Bridge family wharf. The lumber was hauled to Weymouth by ox teams. Owners of these teams hauled for a set amount per thousand board feet.

Sometimes there were as many as twenty teams hauling at one time. It was a slow affair, one team hauling at most, about fifteen hundred feet per load, if the wood was fairly dry.

It was time to celebrate the first Easter at New France. The snow was gone and it was with great joy that Father Blanche and his assistant, Father Morin, were received to officiate at the paschal ceremonies. They had come the last six miles on horseback which was no chore for the old soldier, but must have been an excrutiating experience for Father Morin, who was no accomplished rider.

The services of Easter week were held in the living room of the big house. With the family and the workmen, the room was crowded and the overflow listened from the hall. A complete set of vestments and communion silver plate had been brought from France. These sets were sold packaged and ready for the "missions".

The visitors stayed for a few days after Easter, which gave time for old friends to discuss current events and talk over plans for the future. They were concerned over the troubled state of Europe and of France in particular. Under rapidly succeeding governments, democracy was trying to establish itself, steadily opposed by the privileged classes that showed remarkable vitality and resource in fighting back. The Republique was fragile, because it had mostly the poor and the uneducated on its side. The loses of Alsace and Lorraine was a deep wound in the heart of the Homeland and gradually but surely Frenchmen everywhere began to prepare for La Revanche. Revenge against the German and the return of French lands.

My grandfather was a republican, although he despaired of the Republique as it operated. He was a liberal, wishing the development of education, technology and industry. Father Blanche, in his position as a man of the Church, had to be a Royalist, if a mild one, because he knew the days of the monarchy were past forever. He wished that the old wounds could be healed. It was true that the Church had fought democracy to maintain its special privileges under the Monarchy. Unfortunarely, its opposition had pushed the struggling Republique to take strong anti-clerical measures, the most drastic being the edict to disband religious orders and the imposition of military service for young clerics. But there was hope that time would heal the breach, caused by excesses on both sides.

On one thing, these three men agreed; it was good to be in Canada, living in peace in the reign of the great Queen Victoria. One was trying to set up his children in business and the others were trying to get a college going, without means except what the poor Acadians offered so generously. Added to the problems, they had to work without the support expected of the hierarchy in Halifax, who still felt that assimilation with the Irish was the best solution to the Acadian problem. No significant financial support came from that quarter except some government funds allotted for education.

This chapter can end in no better way than to quote a letter written during this first winter.

(Translation) 14 March, 1896.

My Dear Mathilde,

We are beginning to get settled in our new home, which is very pleasant when one looks out the windows and sees the snow that falls all day long. We are warm, even too warm at times. Each one has a nice bedroom, furnished with American furniture, which is not massive, is pretty and is not expensive. I assure you that I enjoy life here more than I would in France, (I enjoy) this comfort more when I realize that we are in the midst of the virgin forest and very far from any habitation. My children, especially the younger ones, are in ecstasy at this absolutely free life. They run all day in the snow with the dogs and the teams all of which gives life to our solitude.

Our crossing to New York was very bad. My wife, Therese, Germaine and Maurice were sick all the way. The others including myself were never sick and we did honour to the fine cuisine of the *Bretagne*. It was at New York that my problems began, with eight of us, trying to make our way in my English which is rudimentary. We had a horrible crossing from Boston to Yarmouth. The storm tossed us for twenty-four hours, and during the night, the ship took so much water that we had to stop and pump it out. I was very relieved when I saw land again, where we landed around noon. The voyage was practically ended as the trip from Yarmouth to Weymouth is only a matter of two hours on the train. So here we are quietly awaiting the end of winter that will not delay beyond another month. Until then, we dress like Laplanders when we go outside and we spend our evenings talking of you all whom we have left so far away.

With spring, the work outside will begin and all my sons will be fully occupied as we have hauled many logs to the sawmill and this year we will produce a good quantity of lumber. Also already our agriculature is important (a substantial enterprise) and will keep us busy when the weather is right. Thus no one will have time to be lonesome. I assure you that I do not regret having determined to live my way and free, with all my children around me.

My wife wrote you all from the hotel in Boston, but her letters were picked up before we put stamps on them. You may not have received them.

Au Revoir, my dear and good sister. Thank you for your (expression of) good affection and even if far away, I love you just as always. I kiss you tenderly. Kiss your husband and children for us. My friendly regards to Mr. de Clery. Write me sometime.

E.S.

NEW HOME, OLD WAYS

This was the time of endless exploration and discovery. Early in the mornings, they heard the drumming of the partridge and the hammering of the red-headed little woodpecker. They saw the hardwoods clothing the forest with their tender little green leaves shooting out of the tips of thousands of branches. They imagined the bears coming out of their winter dens, hungry and lean, their coats mangy, roaming the meadows in search of new vegetation. The moose would be caring for their calves. Somehow the urge to hunt went away, as if this was the time of truce and communion between man, nature and beast. If the guns were put away, the fishing rods were readied and soon trout were in abundance on the family table.

The mill sent out its many sounds. Now the dull thumping noise of the chains running on the haulup ramp as the logs were hauled from the pond onto the mill floor. The strident notes of the gang saw would come in and then the sharp, short high notes of the trimmer saws. From another corner, the planner furnished its stacato low toned sounds. Finally the edger gave forth its dull low steady sound. All these sounds were mixed, yet with a little listening experience they were distinguishable one from another.

Perhaps, at this time, the biggest effort was put into the task of establishing the gardens and building the farm at Caribou Plain. The fall before, after a road had been opened the full distance of six miles deeper into the forest, some breaking up of land had been done. This spring, hay would be planted and next year potatoes and vegetables. More land was being cleared around New France. Along the road out, several fields were readied for planting. The founder, a solicitous father, wanted his children always near him. Projecting ahead, he imagined their homes along Langford Lake and their families living happily under the protecting shadow of the Big House, always the family home, where all the important decisions would be made.

As a special project for himself, my grandfather had left instructions the previous fall to till a special piece of land between the cookhouse and the mill pond, manure it well and build a wire fence around it. This would be his own kitchen garden. He believed in keeping everyone busy at all times. Every morning the day was laid out for each one. The evenings were spent quietly at home, like at St. Charles. Even the pure evening air of New France was not good for one's health and bedroom windows were not opened at night. The rooms were aired during the day, if the weather was dry. However, the custom of hanging heavy curtains around the bed was not introduced in the new home.

Reading was the accepted pasttime during the long evenings, with music and singing at times. The Pleyel piano and a few instruments had been given very high priority in planning what would be taken from St. Charles. All Jules Verne's books, the rage at the time, novels, reference books, newspapers and magazines, local and from France, provided ample reading material. In the living room, there was a good chair for each member of the family. Small tables with a lamp and a chair on each side provided comfort for two people. These sets were arranged around the living room. The sons smoked the pipe, producing a pleasant aroma. My grandfather smoked cigarettes and a cigar now and then. He made his own cigarettes from imported tobacco and special rice paper. Every morning after breakfast, which was very frugal, consisting of bread, preserves, cheese and Turkish coffee, using his little machine, he made his twenty cigarettes, his ration for the day. In the evening, when he finished his supply, he knew it was ten o'clock and time to retire. His routine was upset, however, if his last cigarette was gone by nine o'clock. Had he discovered that young Maurice and Bernard had swiped a few during the day, there would have been tears flowing as he administered two good spankings. Somewhat perplexed, he retraced his day, usually ending with the conclusion that he had probably been distracted by something and had smoked more than usual. He would never roll a few more to take him to the usual ten o'clock.

The entire family had to give some time to the kitchen garden and that first year, the results were rewarding indeed. The tilling, the weeding and the carrying of water in buckets from the mill pond paid off handsomely. In the fields, vegetables, cabbages, turnips, and potatoes and carrots were grown for the cookhouse as well as for the big house.

Being Alsatians, they were very fond of sauerkraut with ham, sausages, and other pork products. They would have to set up their own Charcuterie (pork preparation shop) and it was not too early to build the smoke house. Several piglets were bought and they were being fattened in the new pigsty behind the barn. After the butchering in the fall, the process would begin. The sausage machine would be busy, the smoke house would send out its scented whisps of smoke and the kraut would be "making" in the puncheons of brine. But the smokehouse would be used now to smoke trout which were eaten raw in the manner smoked salmon was eaten in France. They were delighted to find that smoked trout was just as tasty as unobtainable smoked salmon.

Flowers were not forgotten. Nasturtiums grew in profusion along the wire fence of the kitchen garden. Their flowers went into the summer salads and their capers were pickled to go in the fish sauces. Between the house and the river, blue and red flowers covered the slope.

The poultry run seemed to be developing well. The Plymouth Rock hens, favourites in France, supplied the full needs of the home, until one day when Therese, who had been given the job of running this aspect of the enterprise, returned to the house, exasperated with the conduct of her hens. Some would simply not get off the few nests to give a chance to the other hens to lay their eggs. Those who could not find a place to lay were obviously furious. Therese tried to restore the routine, feathers flew, all to no avail. The hens had just become stubborn, all of them, at the same time. Therese was very excited and very annoyed as she resigned from the job.

The problem was that all the hens had decided to brood at the same time and there were not enough nests to accommodate them all. My grandmother consulted with Boss Blinn and as usual, he came up with a simple solution.

In those days, flour was bought in large wooden barrels. Considering the number of hungry mouths being fed, there were always lots of empty barrels around. Under the direction of Boss Blinn, men cut square holes in the sides of these barrels and stood them on end. With some hay or shavings from the mill in the bottom, each hen had her own cozy nest. Even the rooster seemed to sense that they were all very happy again, because now he seemed to crow more loudly at sunrise, so joked my grandfather.

In France, much of the women's apparel and the men's clothing were made in the home by seamstresses and tailors who came every year and stayed for the time they were needed. This custom the family transplanted to New France and during that summer, a seamstress from Ohio came for about a month. She made skirts, blouses and hats for the girls and shirts and cotton trousers for the men. A person doing this kind of work was considered highly skilled and was not to be treated as a servant. She was treated as part of the family.

This particular young woman was skilled and very pleasant around the house. My grandmother was very pleased with her work and hired her again in succeeding years, until the relationship was terminated by a faux-pas on the part of the young lady. When my grandmother got the bill one year, she noticed that she was charged for a lot of overtime. At the same time, she discovered that Roger had been particularly attentive to the lady. Feeling somewhat duped on two accounts, she refused to pay for "all the time the 'coquette' had spent in the woods with my son".

Marie Therese de Buisson Stehelin was born at Lorques, a shepherds' village outside Marseilles, the daughter of Jean Ambroise and Clothilde Sidonie Caret. Her father was a notary at Marseilles and was interested in real estate as well as practising his profession. At Lorques, the family had its country home.

The south of France is very different than the colder Alsace of the north and its people are of a different temperament. The land is grey and dry under a hot sun in the Mediterranean blue sky. The climate seems to make the people more easy living, given to romantic dreaming and feasting with much singing, laughing and dancing. Life under the sun always seems easier. The needs are fewer, the days are freer and tomorrow will look after itself. My grandmother displayed this whimsical, changeable temperament and when the future looked uncertain, she could dismiss it with the favourite old saying, "Apres nous le Deluge" (After us the Deluge).

Southern women are beautiful as a rule, and she was no exception. She was vivacious, gay and loved people around her. She was accomplished in the art of running her household. She had always had servants who were well trained in the various duties to be performed in a large family. At New France, she found no such trained servants and so, cheerfully, armed with a good French cookbook she learned to cook so she could teach them the French cuisine.

It was at her father's country home, Mont Roch de la Descalys, that on the 28th day of July, 1869, at the stroke of midnight, she married my grandfather. It was the anniversary of his birth and he was thirty-two years old and she was twenty. Coming from hilly, wooded and industrial Alsace, he was of a different temperament. He came from a long line of businessmen and was, therefore, calm and careful in every move he made. His Latin blood, if he had any, his ancestry having been Swiss, had been diluted with Frank and Germanic strains. Husband and wife were compatible, even if they handled crisis differently. In such situations, he would reflect on the problem, whereas she would simply faint. Perhaps when she recovered the problem had gone away. The marriage was by contract, executed before the mayor of the village. The religious blessing took place immediately following.

Theirs was a very fruitful union. By 1886, sixteen years after their marriage, twelve children had been born, of which eleven were still living. Thus, by the time Marie Therese reached thirty-six years of age, she had completed her family, and was still young and beautiful.

Such a high rate of births may seem too accelerated, if not unhealthy, for the mother. Childbearing and giving birth had been very easy for her, just as it should be for any young and healthy woman. In those days, it was looked upon simply as a very natural and not overly taxing process. When a child was born, it was handed over to the care of a "nourice" (wet nurse) who breast fed it and cared for it completely.

Wet nursing was a recognized occupation. It relieved the mother of all the work connected with child raising and it was a status symbol for the family, to be able to afford this luxury. The nourices were usually women from the farms around the countryside. Most of them were married women who had given birth around the same time as the child they were hired to suckle and care for. Their own offspring went on the bottle and cow's milk. Sometimes a girl who had had an illegitimate child hired herself out as a nourice but in either case, a nourice had to be selected with great care. The doctor was closely involved in such a decision. Not only the physical aspect had to be checked but also the psychological traits had to be studied to ensure compatibility between the nourice and baby. If a child developed a bad temper, as one son of the family did, it was blamed on the nourice because, in this case, it was said she withdrew her breast when he was still hungry. Another son was sickly, because, it was said, the nourice dried up too soon and a new one had to take over. These women lived in the home and received specially good treatment, lest any work or emotional upset might cause them to lose their milk or leave the job.

Saint Roch had a special place in my grandmother's devotions and she brought a statue of him to New France. The reason for such a sustained attachment to one whose sainthood was lost in the misty legends of the past was a good one, to her at least. St Roch had appeared to her. She was twelve years old at the time. She was at St. Roch de la Descalys, on a hot afternoon at the hour of the siesta, reclining in the shade of an olive tree. It was a very quiet time, when nature itself seemed to rest. There was no sound, except perhaps the occasional song of the cricket or the cooing of a dove. She was dozing peacefully, when suddenly the two sheep dogs at her side jumped to their feet and motionless, on the alert, fixed their watchful gaze on a stranger shepherd coming through the gate. The dogs did not run after him nor did they bark at him.

The stranger wore an old brown shepherd's coat and his large black felt hat was thrown at the back of his head. In his right hand, he carried his shepherd's crook and at his side, walked his big dog. He moved like a shadow as his noiseless steps took him towards the little chapel of St. Roch, nestled in a corner of the outside wall of the courtyard. As he passed Marie Therese, who sat erect and motionless, he turned his head towards her and smiled. His face was that of a young man with bright blue eyes. As he made his way towards the chapel, the door opened by itself and he and his dog entered and disappeared inside. After a long time, the stranger, not having come out, the young girl went to see where he was. As she opened the door, she saw no one inside, but upon looking up at the statue, she was convinced the young man she had seen was St. Roch himself.

St. Roch had lived centuries before and he was known for having healed people affected by the bubonic plague. He tended the sick and saved many lives. The little statue at New France was a reminder that the saint was not far away should some dreaded plague come this way.

As a good wife and mother, she took charge of the household with a sure hand. The husband was not involved in the running of the home. This was her responsibility.

The kitchen routine was the first priority. Rosie, the young cook was willing, but she had to be taught a new way of cooking. After a reasonable time, gone was the fugal fare of the Acadians and the family was eating "à la Française" again.

For the housework, there were three girls and, of course, the inimitable Smitty. The girls stayed for long times and they were dependable. When they left, it was to help at home, get married or in a few cases, because they had gotten pregnant.

Of course, there were behavioural problems, usually moral ones to do with sex. In such a healthy atmosphere, many men, good food, fresh air and freedom, there were bound to be lapses. There was not much to do, in a communal life setting such as this, and indeed it would have been a dull existence without some living "as it is".

My grandfather understood this and my grandmother too, but only to a point. When she thought things got out of hand and to her way of thinking, excessivly permissive, she would call all the girls, those in the big house, those in the cookhouse, and the one at my father's house, to a "presence". Sitting in her chair in the living room, the girls stood in line in front of her as they listened to her little remonstrances which they called sermons. Nothing strong enough to make some of them quit, but just enough to remind them of basic norms. As we would say today, "cool it". At one of these sessions, the self-appointed leader of the girls, a buxom and frank wench, asked to say something. Of course, she must be heard and with her fists on her haunches, she said, "Madame, it's alright for you to preach to us this way. You have a fine home, a fine husband and a piano to amuse yourself, but all we have is our "derrières". My grandmother fainted dead away and someone had to run to the office to get my grandfather or one of the sons. Needless to add that my grandfather derived some secret amusement out of these situations and he would console his wife by explaining that this is the reason for sending all the wonderful missionaries to the missions. They probably never changed things very much but at least they themselves acquired merit, perhaps sainthood through their self-exile, dedication and hard work.

Late in the summer, and every summer thereafter, children and the maids, went to Caribou Plain to pick blueberries. They went by ox team armed with pails, barrels and large canning utensils. It was a nice outing and they rode very comfortably in a hayrack half filled with hay. The group lived in the little house on the brow of the hill overlooking the Caribou River. They lived and worked in a room downstairs and slept in the large common room upstairs. My grandmother organized these forays but did not go herself, neither did she allow any of her grown sons to go. The only man allowed was Johnie-à-Marc, the teamster, who slept in the little barn with the oxen or under the stars.

The berries were so plentiful that in one week six girls could pick and bottle enough blueberries for the whole colony's winter needs. They would see moose grazing over the plain and Johnie would get plenty of trout to enliven their frugal rations.

It would get very hot in the woods from the middle of June to the middle of August. The founder tried to introduce the siesta between noon and two o'clock in the afternoon. He tried to convince the men that it would be easier on themselves and the animals and the only change would be that they would work until six o'clock to make up the time. The system was tried but the men never accepted it. They would rather work hard and sweat through the heat in order to be through at five o'clock and have a long cool evening to go fishing, to talk and perhaps even take a "cookie" out for a walk, to pick wild strawberries, or take her out in a boat. And so winter and summer, it was seven to five with one hour's rest at noon.

One sport, probably introduced by the Stehelins was cockfighting. These took place well away from the big house because the roosters came from the lady's henhouse and had she found out what was going on, there would have been no more cockfighting.

That summer, the office was built and next to it, the old forge was torn down and a new one was put up in its place. The office was a low building, about thirty feet long by about twenty feet wide. It faced south and having two very large windows in the front, it was full of sunshine all day. There were also two smaller windows at each end which gave sunshine from the east in the morning and from the west in late afternoon. The roof was low pitched and with the three foot eaves all around, it looked like a Swiss type mountain cottage. The door was at the back, on the north side. Inside there was a corridor the full length of the back, from which one door led to the founder's private office and another to the general office. Further down this hall, was a wicket with leaded glass which was lifted to pass the pay packets to the men each Saturday night.

The private office was a small room finished in

varnished hardwood sheathing. One of the two front windows was in this room and the ceiling vaulted, taking the pitch of the roof. It had two windows on the east wall and with its bright varnished hardwood floor and its black stove, it looked very comfortable. The desk was between the two windows on the east wall and faced the door leading into the general office.

This general office was much larger and was finished in varnished spruce sheathing and hardwood floors. There were a few desks around and big shelves at the back to hold the account books, papers and materials usually found in an office, but there was no typewriter. Against the end wall between the two west windows, was a long high slanted top desk which served to hold the big account books when someone was working on them, either standing or sitting on a high stool.

The office was the place where my grandfather spent most of his days. He would shut himself up for long hours and everyone wondered what he was doing. Of course, no one dared ask, but the sons seemed to think he was writing. If he was in fact writing, no one ever saw his work. It was rumoured in the family that Louis had destroyed his father's writings. However, a more likely story is that the papers were burnt with surplus furniture that had been stored in one of the family stores in Weymouth, at the time of the great fire around 1929. The boys spent time at the office when they were not in the woods. Louis became the office man and later he was joined by Bernard. On rainy days, one can imagine the discussions between them. No doubt, there were heated arguments about many things.

Next to the office, the old blacksmith shop looked out of place. It was the log barn, put up in a hurry in 1894 by Jean. It didn't even have a chimney, only a hole in the roof. The new one was in the style of the other buildings. It had a proper chimney, a new hearth and a new set of bellows. Shingled and painted grey with large red doors that opened practically the whole front wall, it was a fine building. Even a new butt had been made out of a molasses puncheon cut in half. The blacksmith was a very important worker, an artist really. He was busy all day, mostly shoeing oxen and horses but there were always pieces of machinery to be repaired or made.

They had to have suitable cool places to store produce, wine and meats. There were cellars under the big house and the cookhouse. These, however, would not provide enough space. At the head of Langford Lake, there is a very steep bank, mostly gravel. They built large cellars here by digging into the bank, lining the walls with granit rocks and building a roof of logs which they covered with gravel and earth. The doors were at the lower side of the slope. They were not far from the house and they discovered an added use for them; growing mushrooms. (See map)

The ice house was still the best meat keeper. They built two large ones, filled them in the winter and buried the meat in the ice and sawdust. Wrapped in cloth, soaked in vinegar, meat kept very well. Venison could be dried in a cool breeze, free from flies.

And so summer was a busy time for everybody including the children. Even they had allotted daily chores but still there was ample time to play and explore. There were wild berries to be picked, strawberries in the summer, blueberries in August, and cranberries after the first frost. There was also swimming, fishing and playing in the boats and canoes. On Sundays, picnics were popular. Up the lakes in the sail boat to a nice place to land to eat and rest. Sometimes one of the brothers would catch trout and they cooked it on a small fire built between two rocks on a beach.

As the summer wound to its end, the founder was well pleased with the progress made. The roots were well sunk into a new homeland. New France was alive, joyful and full of hope and enthusiasm for the future. The parents enjoyed peace of mind, surrounded by their many children, removed and shielded from the harmful and ill-omened way of life in France.

Autumn was beautiful, as it always is in Nova Scotia. The sun is still warm but the nights gradually get cooler. The passion to grow, flower and mature, had seemed to push nature all through spring and summer. But now the fury ceased and the green all around began to dull. Soon the leaves would fall, the maples redden, the birches yellow and the spruce take on a darker hue. It is a time to be happy as nature comes to man, with its hands full of produce, as a reward for all his labor and sweat. It is the time to be thankful.

There was much to be thankful for at the little colony. The first harvest of potatoes and vegetables had been good. The animals would have hay and there would be plenty of wood for the fires. As the evenings lengthened, there was more time to read by the fire in the large room at the big house. There was more time to linger and talk at late dinner.

Everything in nature seemed to move faster. The ducks and the geese made their stages in the lakes but were soon on the way again to their winter havens. The smaller birds here today were gone tomorrow. The heavy rains quickly stripped the hardwoods bare and overnight filled the lakes and swelled the rivers once again. The logging crews suddenly left for their winter camps and the village was quiet. One morning early, one was awakened by the sound of rifle shots reverberating through the silent forest. The big game hunt was on.

Beginning in the fall and continuing through the winter, all the sons went hunting, but Paul and Roger were the most dedicated. They loved to roam the woods and they enjoyed the job of keeping the large family and the cookhouse well supplied with venison. Every day was different, every excursion after a moose was a challenge. They found it fascinating to set and run their own trap line. Beavers were plentiful in the waters along the Silver River. The mink, the otter and other small fur bearing animals were found in swampy lands near all the rivers. The wildcat and the fox usually lived in the hardwood lands. Partridges were also plentiful and were to be found where red berries grew and where beech nuts fell from the trees. Rabbits were found in marshy lands. The wildcats and the foxes brought little return, but they had to be kept down in number to protect the small game. The bears lived off berries and roots, hibernating in the winter. They did not molest small game, but they did come near the houses and caused damage as they rummaged around for food. Bear meat was not at all popular with the men, but the family liked the hams cooked in the manner they coooked wild boar meat in France and Germany. Bear meat was only good in the fall of the year. Bears were fat then, prepared for the long foodless winter hibernation. The fur was also at its best in the fall. It was a big job to skin a bear because there was a thick layer of fat just under the skin. Tanning the hide was not difficult. After a good salting, it was stretched on the barn door where it was treated with alum and all traces of meat and fat were scraped off with any rough but not sharp, tool. As the skin dried, even a rough brick would do this work well. Alum and special soap brought out the beauty and sheen of the thick black hair. To make the hide pliable, olive oil was rubbed into it. The finished product was a beautiful thick rug about seven or eight feet long and between four and five feet wide. Every room downstairs had its bear rugs along with some moose rugs that had been tanned in the same way. In the bedrooms, there were smaller skins such as beaver, fox and wildcat. No other covering was ever placed on these varnished hardwood floors.

In the early days Paul and Roger, encountered the problem of dealing with trap raiders. These thieves would run the line ahead of them and steal the animals. They felt sure one man was involved and they tried to catch him. One day, they were in luck when they came upon a man ahead of them on the trail, leaning down at a trap, taking an animal out of it. Very carefully, they aimed, one on either side of his head, so that a bullet would zing past each ear. They fired in unison and the man fell to the ground, but only from fright as he had not been hit. The brothers stayed hidden in the woods and watched the man get up, raise both hands, and walk away without looking back. They recognized him as the one they had suspected. He well knew who had fired at him and he never bothered trap lines again. In fact, he left the area.

Learning from the natives and the poachers, the young men soon got hunting dogs that were a match for even Ned Sullivan's bulldogs. There were so many dogs at New France, that they had to build kennels. There were all sorts of dogs and they were everywhere, inside and out. Of course, there were always some outside the run at night. They were useful to keep the scavening bears away. But they caused problems when visitors, hunters and fishermen arrived. When the barking started, someone had to go out and rescue the stranger. Many a man was frightened by the dogs, but no one was ever harmed. The worst the dogs did was to keep a man at bay until someone came out.

Early in September of 1896, the education of the younger children had to receive some attention. The two boys, would go to Ste. Anne College and the three girls would go to the Sacred Heart Convent in Halifax.

The three daughters, Therese, Germaine and Simone, went to Halifax with their mother and father, to be settled at the Sacred Heart. At that time, there were French sisters at this convent and the parents were delighted to meet someone from "home" and to learn that the courses were much the same as those given in their convents in France. Therese was twenty-four at the time and she was sent to learn English. Being above school age, she was given special treatment. She had her own bedroom and received private lessons. She did not persevere long, and was soon back home. She had never wanted to come to Canada and she never learned English well. Understanding human nature, her father would not fret too much and simply say, "It is not my fault if I can't find her a husband." It would have been quite natural for him to wish that either a husband or a convent would have taken her, for her own good of course. He would have gladly given either a handsome dot.

Louis had completed his education in France, and wanting to become a priest, was sent to the Eudist Seminary in Halifax. His health was not robust, although he did continue his studies until 1898 when his father took him home. This sudden action was taken on the eve of ordination, when the Archbishop, fearing a breakdown in Louis' health in years to come, asked for a written undertaking by his father that he would take him back in the event of such an occurrence. My grandfather refused on the ground that to remove him from his priestly life and yet have him bound to his vows, would be a cruel thing to do.

In September, my grandfather took the boat at Halifax for Southhampton and Le Havre. Fearing the dreaded seasickness, my grandmother would not accompany him. At St. Charles, he felt home again, attending to the last business matters connected with the sale of his factory. He stayed until the last son remaining in France, Charles, finished his period of enlistment in the Army, when both left for "home" in Canada.

They arrived at New France on December 24th, just in time for the Christmas celebrations.

The first Christmas at New France found the family complete, fifteen in all, the parents, eleven children and two daughters-in-law. There was joy and enthusiasm among such a large family as they rose to toast to their future in this wonderful land, in the peace and quiet of a new home, deep in the silent forest. There was no Christmas tree that first year, because they didn't know about this custom. But the customs of the homeland, a mixture from Alsace and Normandy, were observed in plenty of champagne. There was the Reveillon after midnight and the big dinner on the evening of Christmas day. There was no exchange of gifts, because it was not the custom in France. Only the children received something from "Le Père Noël" (Father Christmas).

Holiday feasting, however, took on its grander aspect at New Year. There were no greeting cards, except the ones family members made for each other and for relatives. However, it was the custom to write letters of good wishes to relatives far away. The Epiphany was especially celebrated with the special cake, "La galette des Rois". This was a sort of puff pastry cake in which were hidden different little fetishes, such a ring, a coin, a bean and other trinkets, each representing something. The person finding the coin in his piece would have financial success next year. The ring indicated marriage; the bean, prosperity. There was a good omen for each.

Two letters written that year by my grandfather to his sister are enlightening.

(Translation from French)

8 June 1896

My Dear Mathilde:

I think of you often and your last letter revived memories of you. We are far away, it is true, and sometimes I wonder if it is really me here in the depth of the forest, working very simply at colonization, which seems fabulous to all those who visit my colony. As for life in France, it remains not much more than a memory. If I thought I had definitely forgotten that homeland which has nothing very attractive at present, I find myself shedding a tear when I speak of France.

We are all in good health except for a few little sores. Therese was bitten by a fly and her hand and arm are swollen half way up. She is better today, otherwise I would have sent her to the doctor. This type of accident is common in this country but the natives don't pay much attention to it and I can see now that they are right. My wife chases fleas day and night. There are over nine dogs, two captured foxes and all sorts of animals that the younger children gather. The other children are also very well and are growing amazingly.

As for myself, I come and go, managing my projects. I have started a farm which looks promising already. The only inconvenience is that it is located six kilometers from here through the woods, so that a trip there is tiring enough, but that does not bother me, after a night's rest, all fatique has disappeared.

Our piano arrived last Saturday night without the least damage. Everybody was delighted. The servant girls stood before it, mouths open like wise dogs. It will entertain us during the evenings, something we were missing. Of late, the children have been dancing to Louis' singing, accompanied by the zither, like in Germany. It was horrible but they all laughed like crazy.

Last week I took Therese (wife) on a moose hunting expedition and I killed a superb animal, the meat of which we are now enjoying. It is a fine meat tasting somewhat like that of the red deer but coarser. It is an animal large enough to feed us all winter at no cost.

My business looks promising. I am going to build a railway for our use as well as that of the public and I hope that it will pay. I don't manage my effort, and God will help me I hope.

A fond embrace. I don't forget you.

E.S.

14 August 1896

My Dear Mathilde: 14 August. 1896

    Your good letter received July 29th, on the first day of my 59th year, which tells me that you remember (birthday) in spite of my being far away. Thank you for your good wishes. I hope the Good Lord will conserve my strength long enough to finish this work and assure the future of those I love so much.

    My wife is at Church point, by the sea, these last three weeks with our daughters and the two younger sons. They are very comfortable at the hotel (Stuart's) at seventeen francs per head per week (about seven dollars). We have so many mosquitoes that the girls had no skin left from scratching the bites, so I found it necessary to send them out of the woods. They amuse themselves on the beach, fishing, walking around and talking with the natives. They can stay as long as they want to, as the cost is not ruinous.

    You ask what we eat. In summer, very little beef, because we can't keep it in spite of the fact that we have an ice house which is very cold. We buy delicious lamb alive at ten francs each (about two dollars then) and we eat it until it is gone — one week. The following week we have a calf at fifteen francs, and so on.

    We also have beautiful poultry roaming about freely which is of superior quality (Plymouth Rocks).

    My garden, tended by myself and my sons, is a marvel and gives us vegetables in abundance. The lakes give us trout and eels and in about a month, the game in the woods will be ready for shooting.

    You can see that our fare is as varied as in France and our table is really succulent.

    In fact our days go by very quickly and by night everyone is sleepy. I am building my railway as quickly as possible. I build about one kilometer per week but there are eighteen to build and I want to use if before winter. It is strange how little difficulty natural obstacles present when one is left to his own resources and is free to do anything he wishes (refers no doubt to dynamite blasting of rocks and stumps). At this moment, I hear a dynamite charge explode. It is a rock which I am breaking up because it is in the way of the track. My men handle with ease this material which in Europe is used so often to do evil things.

My kisses and do not forget me.

E.S.

These letters show that the founder is happy in his work. He is enthused about the country and the future prospects for his enterprise. He is at peace in the knowledge that this is a good life for his family and that he will build a future for them.

THE WEYMOUTH AND NEW FRANCE RAILWAY

Following Christmas and New Year festivities, each year the colony returned to work. The family eagerly pursued the activities of winter in Canada. Like the natives, they did not dread the cold and the snow. To them, they were not inconveniences, but rather they brought new experiences in a healthy and pleasant environment. The snow was everywhere in abundance, but there was with it a warm sun that stimulated everyone to activity, at work or at sports. There were sleigh rides for all on Sunday afternoons and on bright moonlit evenings. There were horse races on frozen Long Tusket Lake. For the more daring, there were the ice boats, with their ballon sails racing on Langford Lake at incredible speeds.

Paul and Roger led the hunting parties on snowshoes, unrestricted by any game laws. A moose weighed anything from nine hundred to two thousand pounds, a lot of meat even after a dressing loss of 30 percent. The best moose heads became trophies, decorating the walls of the houses and some being given to visiting relations and friends. It was not long before Maurice and Bernard were on their own in the woods in the vicinity of the home, setting and tending their rabbit snares. They were quite successful and were very proud to bring home their share of game. My grandfather went hunting too and was quite lucky, bagging his moose and birds. My grandmother often accompanied him on these hunting excursions, although she never handled a gun.

Ice fishing for trout was also a profitable as well as an enjoyable pastime. The best time was during February and

March, when the fish were in the lakes. Through holes in the ice, they lowered hooks, baited with bacon or salt pork, and just waited for the trout to bite. The best places were at the foot of the lakes and the best times were the early morning before the sun got too warm, up to around ten o'clock, and in the afternoon after the sun began to cool, around three o'clock.

Very early in 1897, a house was built for Emile Jean. It was situated on the high ground on the other side of the river, above the mill. It was a beautiful location, overlooking the colony, with a view of Langford Lake to the south and to the north, a view of the mill pond and beyond it, the foot of Little Tusket Lake. It had a verandah on the front and on the south side. Downstairs there was a kitchen and a large room which served as a living and dining room. Upstairs there were two bedrooms, one large and the other smaller. The house was finished inside in pine and birch sheathing, hardwood floors and had electric lights. The outside was painted grey with maroon trim, like all the other buildings of the settlement. In the front, an area was cleared for a garden and a small paddock for Lady, my father's white mare. My parents were very pleased to move into their own home. Living at the big house had become somewhat of a strain, especially for my mother, who had to spend more time in the home than my father. Living with one's mother-in-law and three sisters-in-law had to be trying at times. Another compelling reason to move was the approaching birth of their first child.

Very early, it seemed, the drives were on and the mill was sawing again. It was time to resume the building of the track for the railroad. One mile had been completed before the winter just past, the Mouche a feu (Firefly) had been built as well as a few flat cars. Logs had been cut during the winter along the way, ready to build in the spring.

The prospects of opening up the country behind Weymouth Bridge fired the imagination of the people in the county of Digby. Access to the virgin forest would give a great boost to the economy. There were several sawmills operating between Southville and the Yarmouth Corner and a rail line through their properties would be of immense help in getting their lumber to the wharves at Weymouth.

After long thought and planning, my grandfather was ready to put his proposal to the government of the Province. Supported by the two members of the Legislature for the county, Mr. A.H. Comeau and Mr. Angus Gidney, he went to Halifax. His proposition was simple and obviously sound. He would build his railway at his expense and risk. When completed, it would serve the people and the lumber operators along the line.

The second part of the proposal he presented was a plan worked out with many interests in the county. It was based on twin objectives that would immensely benefit the area, namely, opening up the interior and developing the forestry and agriculture now and possibly mining in the future. The railway was a good beginning, but it would not be able to provide year round service. It was, therefore, important to build a new road, to complement the railway. My grandfather offered to give the land necessary for such a road alongside his track. The existing road ended at Riverdale which was about the limit of forest resources exploitation possible. The proposed railway with a road alongside would cut through timber lands, until now inaccessible, and would cut the distance to New France, a new hub from which development could radiate, to twelve miles.

One of the staunchest supporters of the project was none other than Father Blanche. While he had his own troubles, as he struggled to get Ste. Anne on its feet, he always had time to give his support to projects that he felt would promote the development of social and economic betterment of the people, not only the Acadians, but also all the people of the county. On his visits to New France, he had familiarized himself with the plans for the development of the colony, the building of a farm at Caribou, and the building of the railway. He talked to people about it, including the two members of the Legislature and he wrote about it in the L'Evangeline. He counselled the people to get behind the project, because it would help the community.

Father Blanche's presentation of the situation and the logic of his conclusions were as always, clear and convincing. The Stehelins were engaged in a program of development which was costly and which no one else would have undertaken. They were now firmly established in the country, having become Canadian citizens and British subjects. They would not abandon their development and who could tell what would come of it by way of benefits to all. If one was to forecast the future from what had been accomplished in the first two years, New France might well have been the beginning of a large village or town. Settlement of the area had, so far, concentrated too much on the fringe along the ocean and the bays. While fishing was an important industry, the lumber business seemed to open vast perspectives. One had only to look at the dozens of ships' masts at the wharves in Weymouth to visualize a rich future for the industry. The possibilities for the development of agriculture further in the interior, where the climate was warmer, should not be overlooked either and who knows what mining possibilities existed in this unexplored territory. Why not widen one's horizons and look forward with confidence to a richer country for more people and more business enterprises.

What was needed now was the building of a road alongside the Stehelin Railway, not only to serve the people on the line, but also to foster more aggressive exploitation of those lands around the New France property and hopefully some day well beyond New France. For the present, New France could be the staging point, the railhead for development further inland.

Such a business-like approach to the venture could not help but mobilize public opinion. There was great enthusiasm for the project and the more people thought about it, the more they felt the government should do its part to help bring it about to a working conclusion. Perhaps people got carried away with a vision of a rich and prosperous future for all the people. From there, it was not too far fetched to suggest that the government build a proper steel railway and connect it with the Dominion Atlantic Railway at Weymouth.

Strong support came from the business sector, especially from the Sissiboo Falls Pulp Company Ltd. It was a new industry for the area, the company having been organized in January of 1894. It was capitalized at thirty thousand dollars and most of the shares were held in the U.S.A. by a parent company, a newspaper publisher. It used up, in raw material, one and one half to two million board feet of timber per year. It was capable of producing forty thousand pounds of wet pulp every twenty-four hours.

The Government of Nova Scotia listened with interest to all these presentations, and promised to consider the proposal very seriously. The Premier of the Province visited New France and said he was in favour of development aid for the area and that the proposed plan in its general concept seemed a good one. Of course the Premier also consulted with the local supporters of his administration. The Municipal Councillors were divided on political lines. In those days, partisanship was strong and sometimes very bitter at that lowly level. The two county members of the Legislature assured everyone of their full support and their continued representations on behalf of the project.

Time went on and nothing was decided. Perhaps the presure for assistance was not as sustained as that from bigger industries and the people depending on them in other parts of the Province.

My grandfather became very frustrated and it was when he was in this mood, that he was approached with the suggestion that a little money to the coffers of the party in power and some little more to individuals who wielded the influence would help. These suggestions made him very angry. He felt that everybody was out to rob him and the government was toying with the whole question. His reaction was prompt. He dismissed the crew working on the railway, about fifty men, and announced he was shutting down his lumber operation and would concentrate on developing a farm, only large enough to help support his family. He had left France because the government was corrupt and this experience made him wonder if things were much different in Nova Scotia. Still, he considered that he was fortunate to be living under the British Crown, to which he and his family had sworn allegiance. Discouraged he was, but not about to pack up and return to France.

When the two local newspapers reported the turn of

events, there was disappointment, if not consternation, reigning in the surrounding area. Not only were fifty jobs lost, but the great development envisaged with such enthusiasm was arrested, perhaps for a long time. Father Blanche was disappointed also, having kept alive a great vision for the future development of his people. But he was not discouraged and he continued to boost the project. He talked about it in English and in French. What had been done at New France was an example of what could be done in the interior of the county. Breaking new ground would be better for the country than practically forcing young people to move to the U.S.A. for work and a better living. The Acadians could become a great people, grouped together on their own lands. Foresight, vigour, tact and logic were all working together, to power this uncommon style of leadership.

Naturally the government in Halifax was quickly apprised of the turn of events and they were soon in contact with my grandfather through the local members of the Legislature. There were further discussions in Halifax. What decisions were reached, if any, is not clear. In any event, nothing happened for some time, except that the land owners who had contributed to the holding up of the building of the railway by asking exorbitant prices for the small pieces of land for a right of way, seemed to become very reasonable. The need for government expropriation seemed unnecessary now, and therefore, the railway part of the project could go ahead. There seems no doubt that my grandfather continued to press the government for the building of the road alongside his track. Whatever the arrangements were, he certainly seemed to think it was agreed that the government would, in fact, build it. It is doubtful, however, that there was any written commitment on the part of government.

When my grandfather and Jean returned from Halifax the last time, they resumed negotiations for the right of way. Apparently, agreement was possible with all the owners and in a month or so, the building of the track was on again. The men were back at the cookhouse and the mill was sawing lumber again. New France was full of people once more, ringing with the sounds of familiar activity.

Work on the track was progressing well enough for some thought to be given to acquiring rolling stock. My grandfather, accompanied by Jean, went to Amherst to discuss the building of a locomotive with Robb Engineering Co. Ltd. and Rhodes Curry Ltd. They came back to New France very satisfied with their trip, having made arrangements for the building of a locomotive at Robb Engineering Ltd. and the building of a small passenger coach at Rhodes Curry Ltd. They brought back sufficient wheels and machinery to build flat cars. Boss Blinn was certainly able to look after this part of the construction.

It will be recalled that the building of a railway had been decided upon during my grandfather's visit in the summer of 1895, and that the survey for the track had been started that same year. Now the building of the track as far as Lake Doyle was underway, as well as the survey of the line from there onward. To determine who the owners of the lands were, from whom rights of way would have to be obtained, proved a long tedious job. The survey had to come first, then the title searches and finally the negotiations.

On June 15th, in the new house on the hill, above the mill, the first child was born at New France. Bernardette, the daughter of Emile Jean and Anne Baldwin. There was great rejoicing throughout the colony, especially at the big house, because she was the first grandchild in the family.

In those days, midwives attended the birth of babies. In most cases, a doctor was not consulted, even through the pregnancy. The midwife learned her skills through practical experience. She was nearly always an older woman, who had given birth herself a number of times. Mrs. Steele, from Southville, came to attend at the birth several days before it was due to occur. She was a very fine and competent woman and she brought the delivery through successfully, even though it was a long and a difficult one. There were no anesthetics then, but they gave my mother cognac which was reputed to be a very good substitute. In those days, the possibility of death of the mother was never very far away, which must have been a terrible strain on her.

The track had to be as level as possible, only a ten

percent gradient was allowable. It took time to trace the best course through the jungle of underbrush and trees, marshes and around huge boulders. After the survey work, the land had to be cleared to a width of thirty feet. Whatever timber became available on the spot they cleared, helped speed up construction. Preparing the roadbed was the most time consuming part of the job. The general topography of the area is a mixture of sandy soil, rocky land, swamps, hills and a few small rivers. Swamps were stabilized by placing hardwood logs down as a foundation and lots of sand over them. There were some cuttings through hills, the most notable one being the Turnpike or Hogs Back Ridge which runs through the whole area. This ridge provided lots of gravel. In the deep valleys, to bring the road level up, they built crib works. These piers, filled with rocks, did the job well, but, of course, being made of wood, had a limited life span. The bridges over the rivers were rather simple to build of wood. The objective was grades of not more than six percent, preferably three percent wherever possible.

    The rails were made of logs twenty to thirty feet long. They were squared on three sides and laid with the remaining rounded side up. The finished rails were eight inches on three sides with the rounded top side on which fitted the concave wheels of the rolling stock.

    The sleepers were hemlock logs about ten feet long, laid on sand about two feet apart. The rails were laid on the sleepers and nailed through from the top with square wharf spikes, which held very well. The butting of the rails was square on the level, and bevelled and fitted on the grades. Square joints on grades would have pulled apart.

    The wheels of the rolling stock were quite large, of cast iron, with concave flanged running rims about ten inches wide, which fitted onto the rounded top of the wooden rails. It was practically impossible to build the track perfectly and keep it exactly to the required guage. Some axel play had to be allowed for, so that the wheels would not ride hard on the edges of the track. The wheels were put together in sets or trucks of two wheels each. The flat cars were twenty feet long and made of squared timber. Each car used two trucks.

The greatest operational problem was the correlation of weight and friction on the track. Too much weight risked chewing up the rails and not enough weight produced slippage.

The first locomotive, Mouche a feu, was built at New France, by the same Acadian artisans who had built the complicated water powered mill. It had a twenty horse power stationary engine which transmitted motive power to the front wheels by means of two driving gears. When all the various wheels and pieces, most of them made in the blacksmith shop, were synchronized, the engine worked perfectly and gave many years of valiant service.

Enthused by this first success and no doubt dreaming of the big trains, these same men went about building a small passenger car. It was very carefully built, a work of art. It looked like a miniature of a real coach of the day. Its hardwood sheathing outside was painted maroon with white trim along the edge of the rounded black roof and around the windows and the door. There was a window on each side and at the back, the door was at one side under a covered platform and another small window. The inside was finished in natural pine and maroon trim. On the side, one read "Mouche a Feu" in white lettering. This conveyance was indeed a gem of ingenuity and artistry. The only trouble was that it accommodated only four or five passengers.

By the end of the summer of 1897, the track was finished to Riverdale, the railroad was in business, the Fire Fly hauling logs to the mill and lumber as far as Riverdale. The speed was only ten miles per hour, but this was a tremendous improvement over the two miles per hour by ox team.

On August 6th, 1897, two carloads of equipment for the railroad arrived at Weymouth by D.A.R. freight from Robb Engineering Ltd. and Rhodes Curry Ltd. The passenger car "Caribou" arrived on this consignment together with trucks to make more flat cars. The coach was twenty feet long. The siding was of narrow sheathing painted eggshell blue with maroon trim along the edge of the roof. There were four windows on each side and a door at each end. There was an observation platform at the back. The roof was rounded and covered with brown coloured canvas. Just above the windows in large yellow letters was painted "W. and N.F. Railway" (Weymouth and New France Railway). Below the windows also in large yellow letters was the name of the coach, Caribou. The inside was divided into two compartments, the forward one, equipped with fixed wooden seat, was smaller than the rear one and was for the use of the workmen. The rear compartment with observation platform was for the family and had no fixed seats. Easy chairs would be taken from the house when the ladies and the owner were to travel. The Caribou was hauled to Riverdale by several yokes of oxen, and tried out with the Fire Fly. Everything seemed to work well, although the extra load slowed down the train to about eight miles per hour. But people travelled in comfort and the journey took under one hour. One can imagine what this sort of luxury travel meant to these pioneers.

On September 3, 1897, also by D.A.R. freight, arrived at Weymouth, the locomotive built by Robb Engineering Ltd. Laden on an open flat car, it had passed through Digby the day before and as it had remained there for several hours, a large number of people from the town came to the station to see it. It took eight yokes of oxen and two days to haul it to Riverdale and set it on the track. It had a brass bell and a brass oil lantern in front of the smoke stack, as well as a whistle. In yellow letters, on the sides of the drivers compartment, was painted the name "Maria Theresa". There was a fuel tender behind the locomotive, all black metal, with the inscription, also in yellow letters, W. & N.F. Ry.

The engine, run by steam from a wood burning boiler, had four cylinders, each developing twenty horsepower. The locomotive was mounted on two trucks of four wheels each and the tender was on two trucks of two wheels each.

The arrival of the Maria Theresa at Weymouth was a cause of great excitement. It took time to unload it onto a special carriage to haul it, and there was ample time for people to come from some distance to see it. The newspapers, L'Evangeline and the Digby Courrier, covered the event well.

The contract for the locomotive was simple, contained in a letter to Emile Stehelin from Robb Engineering Co. Ltd. as follows:

Emile Stehelin
New France, May 1, 1897

1 Pole locomotive complete per plans and specifications
Engine
0431 Boiler
0432 Tender Tank
0430 Trucks tender, etc. and erecting
$3,300.00 F.O.B. Amherst
$75% on delivery
$25% 30 days

A later memo date August 18, 1897.

Emile Stehelin
New France, N.S.

Dear Sir:

In accordance with conversation, we will agree to make a discount on locomotive of 20% on contract price, on account of delay and will accept 50% of new price cash on delivery, and balance in four months after shipment. Please acknowledge and oblige.

>Yours truly,

>Robb Engineering Co. Ltd.
>President
>(Signed) D.W. Robb

The locomotive was put on the rails, and the trials carried out that fall were disappointing. There is no clear record of the trouble but it would appear that it was related to the mechanics of construction and the excessive weight for the track. Because the locomotive had been delivered later than the contract specified and there was, therefore, little time before winter to properly evaluate its performance, it was agreed that acceptance of it would stand until the following spring.

It had always been intended to use the snow packed road in the winter, rather than try to keep the track open. There was nothing lost by closing the railway down for the winter months. Living in the woods in the winter time was, in many ways, much easier and just as pleasant as in the summer. Hauling lumber out was easier and quicker also.

Because communication was easier, there were many visitors to New France during the winter months. They would arrive on moonlit, cold and still nights, in large sleighs. Sometimes several sleighs would come together, making a big party of the outing. On such occasions, a huge bonfire would be lit in the middle of the square and around it there was dancing and singing, followed by a picnic lunch. Sometimes they opened the large doors of the barn and danced the traditional reels to the accompaniment of the mouth organ, the jew's harp and the fiddle. These parties invariably brought plenty of whiskey and rum and the hay lofts always provided a soft and warm place for lots of spooning. Some groups used a hay rack filled half full of hay as a conveyance. On the way home late at night, the popular game was to reach around in the hay and grab a leg and see to whom it belonged.

At the big house, of course, life was pleasant and restful, always lively, sometimes even tumultuous with thirteen young people, eight of whom were healthy young men. The parents tried to maintain the old way of life of St. Charles. Sunday was the special family day. Dinner in the evening was later than usual and was followed by a family evening of games, singing, dancing and good conversation. Jean played the violin, my father the cello and my mother the piano. The others sang under the direction of Louis. One can readily perceive how these evenings ended in arguments about who had produced the sour note.

Life was very lively at Weymouth Bridge also, and the Stehelins often went in for evenings at the hotel or in homes, to play whist, dance or just talk. There was a Winter Club for young people. They gathered in the Sissiboo Hall to dance and enjoy a lunch provided by the girls. There was the Literary Club for married ladies only. They met to discuss contemporary literature and social problems of the day. At one of these meetings, the subject for discussion was "How Best to Manage Husbands". The Independent Order of Foresters was the men's club. They had dinners and held their ceremonious High Court regularly. Of course, the Temperance Society was active under the leadership of Father Sullivan.

There were, from time to time, the passing of notable citizens. One who deserves mention was John Hood, a very intelligent and cultured man who died in 1897, having spent the last seventeen years of his life at Weymouth, teaching school. He was born in 1811, in London, England. He had lived in Calais, France, and in Penzance, England, before coming to Weymouth. He left ten children, some of whom moved to Yarmouth. My grandfather enjoyed conversing with him in French.

After many days of experimenting, it finally had to be admitted that the locomotive did not perform satisfactorily. It is not clear what the trouble was, but it seemed the machine was too heavy. During the summer, my grandfather went to Amherst and Mr. Robb came to New France. Adjustments were made, but to no avail. Finally it was agreed that it should be returned to the factory and rebuilt. Apparently, a satisfactory compromise was reached, as to work to be done and cost to be adjusted. The contract or agreement was contained in a letter dated September 3, 1898 from my grandfather to Robb Engineering Co. Ltd., which reads as follows:

Robb Engineering Company Ltd.

After receipt of your favour of 19 August, I had with you at your office a conversation of which it has resulted:

1. That I spoke to you of the necessity to fix a certain time for the delivery of the new locomotive you are constructing for me, and we have agreed together that she shall be delivered at 1st November next.

2. That I have to pay you the due amount of your note of $1,288.49 with addition of $600.00 each in two terms, one

half payable the first, cash after testing the new locomotive on my pole railroad, according your letter 19 August and the second at 30th June, 1899. Also to guarantee for the new locomotive they are satisfactory as stipulated in your letter of 19 August.

I would say that, answering your said letter, you ask the large locomotive you supplied to me delivered on board cars at Weymouth and $600.00 in addition for the payment of the new locomotive. This seems to be in contradiction with this part of your letter 29 August received only yesterday: "and that the payment of the $600.00, only is conditional on the success of the new machine".

Do you think that the whole (total) value of the next locomotive shall be conditional on the success of this machine, or in other words, what conditional value would you assign to the big locomotive included in the price of the new one?

I expect to ship middle of next week the parts of locomotive you wish returned.

Yours truly,

Emile Stehelin

If you have convenience to redraw the note of $1,288.49 as you write me, it is no difficulty in it.

(The above letter was written, longhand, by my grandfather who only two years previously spoke only French and German. He had taught himself enough English to do business in the language).

The note from Robb Engineering, setting forth the new contract, reads as follows:

Emile Stehelin
New France, N.S. September 3, 1898

1   Pole locomotive consisting of:

    1 -special impd. monarch 44x
    1 -Right hand, 1-left hand, 9x10 reversing engine coupled together with flange or compression couplings.

-8" steel pinion, 16 teeth on centre, gears 30"x4½ face, 60 teeth
-driving wheels 36" diameter

Use from old locomotive the following:

Housings, shafts, gears, pinions, cab, tender, sand box, reversing lever, boiler fittings and all old parts that will come in.

$600.00 and old locomotive

Robb Engineering Co. Ltd.

What they were trying to produce was a lighter machine that would run better on the wooden track. There is no record to tell us when the new locomotive was delivered, but it would be safe to assume that it would have been late in the fall of 1898. The cost of the rebuilt machine would have been $3,300.00, less 20% and plus $600.00 or $3,240.00.

The cost of the track was in the vicinity of $3,000.00 per mile. The factory made passenger car cost around $1,000.00. The wheel trucks to build about ten or twelve flat cars might have cost another $1,000.00.

To these costs must be added the cost of building the Fire Fly with its tiny passenger coach, the station at New France and the shelter at Riverdale. All in all, it represented a very large investment for one man to make.

The station was not a pretentious building, being intended primarily as a shelter for the locomotive. It was built near the old woods road, where it entered into the village square. It was open at both ends so the train could go through and it had a narrow platform on one side.

The track crossed the road and went around close to the back of the barn so that it could unload directly through the large door, onto the barn floor. There was always animal feed, hay and flour as well as hardware to be unloaded at the barn. The track thence continued past the side of the big house to the mill where the finished lumber came out, and could be loaded directly onto the flat cars.

On the last day of February, 1898 another daughter, Jacqueline, was born to my parents, living in the little house on the hill above the mill. There were the same worries, the same pain for the mother giving birth in the deep woods, assisted only by a midwife. She came so near death that there was talk at the mill about making a coffin. But the brave little English lady pulled through and there was great rejoicing in the colony. At the big house, there were the customary toasts in champagne.

In the spring of 1899, the railroad was opened again and in May, there was an inaugural celebration. Many people came to New France on that beautiful Sunday for the christening of the Maria Theresa by its godmother and namesake. The locomotive, all brightly polished, stood on the track with the Caribou in tow, all ready for the official ceremony and inaugural run. Some bunting of various colours was flying from the train and on one side of the locomotive flew a Union Jack and on the other, the Tricolor. At the appointed hour, the godmother, in her smart Parisian dress, always in style, approached and smashed a bottle of champagne on the nose of the Maria Theresa. There were loud hurrahs and the breaking out of singing. Amid all the good wishes of the friends, the train, blowing its whistle and ringing its bell, started off for a short run. In the car sitting in the best chairs from the parlour of the big house, rode the founder, his wife, several members of the family and a few friends. While the train was away, merriment broke out all over the place. There was dancing, singing and lots of laughter around the usual bonfire in the middle of the square. By late afternoon, a picnic lunch was served and by the evening of that memorable day, the friends, well enlivened with wine, left for home. New France was quiet again for late family dinner.

The eventual decision of the Government, after the railroad had been built, not to build the road as agreed alongside the track was a blow. There is no record of the reasons for this apparent reversal of what was thought to be a firm engagement. It was a blow to the whole project and especially to the overall development of the entire area. My grandfather felt he had been "had", and the people were disappointed and the pulp mill was concerned. Traditionally, governments have never supported meaningful economic growth in this part of the Province. The result has been near stagnation. In time, most of the timberland passed into American hands and was held for capital appreciation, thereby contributing to unemployment and migration.

The Stehelins were on their own once more. They had to think of a way to expand the business, if there was to be a livelihood for eight sons and three daughters, the latter having no plans for earning their own living.

The sawmill at New France, a wonderful piece of machinery, was a permanent fixture and logs had to be brought to it. So far the logs had been cut along the water way, but the day would come when this supply would be drained and they would have to go out further into the woods, away from water courses for their raw material. Finally, the mill had to remain idle during the summer due to lack of water. It was very obvious that the old methods could not produce the desired expanison. New methods would have to be adopted.

My grandfather turned his attention to portable sawmills. These mills usually consisted of the bare essential machinery to produce rough lumber and deals. They were equipped with a rotary saw, a carriage, a trimmer and an edger. Some had a planner. A steam engine, powered by a boiler which burned scrap wood provided the motive power. These mills could be set up very quickly. The time consuming task of bringing the machinery on site without adequate roads, was the only limiting factor to their wider use. Shelters for these mills were build of scrap lumber, once the sawing began. Alongside the mills, cookhouses to house the workmen were built. My grandfather would complain that the men had bottomless stomachs and that they ate more when they were not working, Sundays and rainy days. Lumber was selling between $9.50 and $10.50 per thousand board feet F.O.B. (Free on Board) ships. One had to run a tight operation to make money.

The first portable saw mill was installed at Lake Doyle on a strip of the Seven Pence-ha-penny River which served as a log storing pond. The railroad was alongside, to bring logs and take away the lumber. Logs were also cut on the land around the mill. Thus the family now had one year round operation. The work of supervision of the operation required two sons. One, usually my father, was in charge of the mill and the other, usually Paul, in charge of the logging operation. The mill crew consisted of about eight men and the cookhouse was run by a cook and a helper.

Moving this sawmill into place had been a very difficult job. Several yokes of oxen were needed to haul the machinery, piece by piece. At Seven Pence-ha-penny, they had to leave the road and make a very rough road up the river to Lake Doyle about half a mile away. It was in the summertime and hot and the flies made life very miserable. It took seven days to move the equipment and machinery that short distance.

The mill at New France continued to operate in the spring and fall of the year. The railroad took the lumber out, brought in some logs, and, of course, handled all the provisions from Weymouth Bridge.

Attention had to be turned to the wharf at Weymouth Bridge. The barn on the wharf was repaired, as well as some parts of the wharf. Ships were coming in to take on lumber and Charles was put in charge of this aspect of the operation. This job kept him away from home for weeks at a time, when he lived at a boarding house at Weymouth.

Jean remained with his father, more or less in charge of the entire operation. Louis, now home permanently, took over the running of the office. Maurice, coming on to seventeen years, was given different jobs, but what he liked most was finding some reason to go to Weymouth for a day, or running out to the Corner at Southville to attend a dance. As a child, he had not been too robust, but now he could run the six miles to Southville and back the same night. He had not taken yet to the work in the woods, or around the office. Roger was occupied looking after the mill at New France. Bernard was about fourteen years old by now and he was given jobs at the office helping Louis.

In October of 1898, my grandfather went to France on business, taking Therese with him. She was now about twenty-eight years old and she had to face diminishing chances of marriage, which was what she thought she wanted above all else. Maybe this visit home would give her a chance to renew friendships and maybe an eligible young man would be fired by the prospect of living in Canada or perhaps another one would be taken by the charm of a woman who lived in the forest. No doubt her father hoped also.

They stayed at St. Charles nearly three months, returning to New France just before Christmas. Alas, Therese was returning as free as she was when she left, but a bit more reproachful of her parents having brought her into this hopeless situation. She had been very seasick on the boat and still took pills for it long after she was back. In fact, she began to rely on all sorts of pills and medicines. My grandmother said that in fact Therese was very happy at New France, but she didn't know it.

Problems and disappointments, of course there were many, but the parents, in spite of them all, were still very content and happy to have come to Canada.

SOCIAL AND BUSINESS WEYMOUTH

Around the middle of January 1899, unannounced, Maurice and Bernard arrived home from Church Point. Ste. Anne College had been destroyed by fire the night before. The students were asleep in the dormitory upstairs when the fire was discovered, well under way. It was impossible to save the building but the boys were evacuated safely. Maurice distinguished himself that night by ensuring that his younger brother, Bernard, who was fourteen, was led down the stairs, filled with smoke, to safety. He went back to bring out another boy, who was not accounted for at roll call. Fortunately, he was able to find him, lost in the smoke, and bring him out.

The fruit of so much hard work now lay in ashes. But Father Blanche was an unconquerable soldier and soon his spirit was leading the people in rebuilding the college, starting once again from nothing.

It was time for Momo to move on to new experiences, when the fire ended his student days at Ste. Anne. He was very intelligent, but an inveterate practical joker. His brain worked overtime thinking up stunts and tricks. He didn't like the food at the college, so he boarded with the Stuart family, living in a big house very near the college. One of his masterpieces was a cannon he built in the field behind the Stuart house. He was also a good promoter and it was not long before the villagers were talking about Maurice's invention. The men, good naturedly, teased him about it, but the women were alarmed, as Maurice had noised the possibility of the whole village being blown up. The cannon was simply a piece of four inch iron drain pipe, filled with gunpowder. The effect was so satisfying that he decided to build several cannons and fire them all in one salvo, at a time he kept secret. On Spooks Night in November, the population was awakened in the dead of night by many explosions in the cemetery and the women thought for sure Judgement Day had arrived. The good Fathers at the college laughed inwardly, but they enjoined Maurice to restrain his imagination.

Maurice moved on to other exploits. He knew his audience and played on their gullibility. He leaked the news that in his little bedroom at the top of Stuart's house, he was holding seances and making the spirits move his table. This was more serious indeed, disturbing the very religious beliefs of the people. The good Fathers had given him a sound reprimand and had threatened him with explusion.

It was spring when Father Blanche, absorbed in the new construction, received orders to report back to France. His term had expired, and besides the turn of events at home required his strong hand. Before leaving, he went to New France. He always brought conviviality to the table talk and intelligence to the more profound discussions with his old comrade. Both men were terribly concerned about the avowed determination of the government of France to banish all religious orders from the native soil. Father Blanche had not forgotten the first precept of military tactics, "we are condemned to die, therefore we attack".

It was during this visit that Katie made her historic and oft recounted gaffe. She had never had the chance to learn elegant manners or the art of fine conversation, but she was intelligent and she diligently worked at acquiring the Savoir Faire of her mother-in-law. She had observed an expression and a gesture which she liked very much. Her mother-in-law, offering a second helping of chicken to a guest, passing the plate, would say "laissez moi vous tenter avec une cuisse" (let me tempt you with a leg). At dinner on this occasion, watching her chance, at the right moment, Katie seized the platter and passing it to Father Blanche said, "Mon Père, laissez moi vous tenter avec ma cuisse" (Father, let me tempt you with my leg).

There was dead silence and Father Blanche treated the incident very calmly by smiling and saying "Non, Merci, Katie".

This was the last reunion for the old comrades of the battlefields of 1870. Father Blanche, upon his return to France, was posted to the famous Ecole St. Jean, the prestige college of the Eudists and from there, immersed his whole being into the fight to save the Eudist Order. He led his religious brothers back to Canada, to the missions and in 1903, he was consecrated Bishop of Northern Quebec/Labrador. He died suddenly in Paris in 1916. To students he had given the vision of honour, self discipline and excellence. Those entrusted to his pastoral care had felt the warmth of his love. All he had wanted was to be a brave soldier of France and a worthy soldier of Christ.

One interesting visitor following Father Blanche, was Baron Engel, a distant relative whose home was on Lake Geneva. He came to New France from India where he had spent the last two years hunting big game. Having landed in Vancouver, he had hunted in the Canadian Rockies. He had hired a box car to carry his trophies, skins and various specimens of wild animals. His physician and his taxidermist accompanied him, as well as several other hunters. He stayed at New France about three months during which time his party were busy collecting wild animals. They took back a moose, a bear, a wildcat and a number of birds. The hunts under his direction were enlivened by the new methods he taught Paul, Roger and Maurice. Small bears, wildcats and foxes were caught alive and the Baron's men experimented trying to tame them. A large male bear was caught by a hind leg in a steel trap. Full of life, it was decided not to shoot him and they organized a duel between it and one of the experts of the Baron's team. The man was armed with a bayonet and the bear parried blows with his front paws as he stood on his hind legs. The battle went on for some time and eventually the armed man killed the bear. This may seem cruel sport, but in those days, it was not considered so.

As much as my grandfather sought and enjoyed the social life that so many visitors brought into his home, in the quiet of his office, he philosophied on the fortunes of his life and if only momentarily, felt some disappointment with it. Two letters to Mathilde reveal some of his thoughts.

(Translation) 15th October 1898

My Dear Mathilde:

 I have not yet replied to your good letter of July last. I had completely forgotten my birthday (July 28) and it is you who reminded me that I am sixty-one years old, already a long life, as I go over it.

 I find it a failure and useless, and I tell myself that it is useless for one to take so much trouble and worry to arrive at the same ending that awaits all. That one arrives at the end just as well without worry and work.

 Except for your letter, I have no news from France. I see by my newspaper the mess and the filth in which the good French people wallows.

 Another disillusion for me, as I come to know the governments of America, I come to see, by comparison, the French Republique as a virgin, white, honest and pure. I can see now that the distance caused me to see things in a deceiving mirage. Unfortunately that is how I have seen things so often in my lifetime.

 We have had an excellent year and I can see that my sons, more and more, are taking to this life of freedom, half woodsmen, half farmers and coureurs des bois. They are very busy during the nice season, very busy in the woods as well as on the farm which is beginning to look like something, and from which we already almost live. It is growing every year and in the end, will become a source of profit. But what labour all this requires when one is far from everything and left to one's own resources.

 Therese looks after the cows and the milk with Germaine. We now make, for our own use, little Swiss cheeses, like the Gervais, which are as good as those in Paris. It was Germaine who tried it first and succeeded perfectly. As for my wife, she raises chickens which is really very simple because during the good season, they run freely and we don't have to feed them. They are as good to eat as any fattened fowl. Simone has gone back to the Sacred Heart.

A few days ago, I caused the family a deep shock by loosing myself in the forest. I am in the habit of taking my gun and four or five dogs after dinner and going out until five or six o'clock. I must have been distracted, because at a certain point I didn't know where I was. I continued walking, thinking I would find the road again. With the approaching darkness, I found myself in an open space, unable to reenter the woods because it was so dark under the trees. I lit my fire to camp there. By nightfall, at the house, they surmised I was lost. They formed several groups and with lanterns and guns, they started looking for me, firing shots and hollering. Around ten o'clock, my dogs gave voice and hearing their guns, I fired mine in reply. All this directed the search towards me and we finally got home around one o'clock in the morning. The moral of this is that one must never go alone in these woods in America, which is what I was doing up to this point. It is so dense that one does not see the sky and if one has not a compas, there is no way to get out.

The impression that this creates, left to your own resources, is pleasant enough. One is alone and peaceful, until hunger and thirst arrive, and lying by your fire, you let yourself go, putting your trust in the Good Lord, who appears so much greater here than in the houses of the cities.

If I had not had to worry about my wife, I would have been perfectly safe until morning. In the final analysis, life is not worth too much attachment to it. We are going downhill, may God come to our aid to finish it well. That is the essential.

Au revoir my dear sister. If nothing hinders me, I will come to France in December or January.

My Dear Mathilde: 11 December, 1898

I had planned to be in France for New Year, but I can't leave yet because I am detained by the loading of a ship that I am sending to the West Indies, where a recent cyclone has destroyed about everything, which makes wood in great demand.

Winter has started early this year and we already have snow permanently. This happens rarely before Christmas. We are warm and my sons go to the woods with the workmen to cut logs, which does them a lot of good and they enjoy it.

My wife and daughters are very well and probably I will take Therese with me to France next month and we will spend a month there.

I have sent M. de Clery an article from "The Canadian Lumberman", describing my business. There are a few pictures. It is in English, but you will find someone to translate it for you.

I wish you and your children a Happy New Year without forgetting Grandfather. I embrace you all with all my heart.

E.S.

The beginnings of the dispersal came around the turn of the century, when Jean Jacques announced that he was going to leave and seek his fortune in New York. Since the beginning of the enterprise, he had had more sharing of responsibility with his father than the other sons, because he had been longest in the country and had started the business. He had been the prime mover of the railroad and the road alongside it. In New York, he had his period of hard times. Without money, he had to take the only job he could find, that of a labourer in a factory making silk trimmings. In a short time, he had his own factory making tassels and cords and he ran it very profitably and prospered. Katie never rejoined him and Jean came back to New France only once. The marriage ended in divorce but not until 1906.

Two more buildings had been erected in 1898; the chapel and the bachelors' den. The chapel was a log structure, sited next to the office and connected to it by a narrow passageway. It was not a very pretentious building on the outside, but it was discernible as a church by the large cross above the front peak and the norman style crenellated bell tower at the front side, which also formed an open porch to the entrance door. A large window, of many small panes, took up most of the front wall. There were smaller windows on each side, with tinted glass panes. The altar, on a raised section of the floor at the back, was a very artistic decoration, made of many panels with raised crosses in each one. The same motif carried through in the wooden backdrop and the tabernacle, which was well proportioned and quite elaborate. The background woodwork was painted white, the trim azure blue and the crosses gold. This fine work had been executed by the men at the mill, mostly in their spare time. The altar cloth, draped to the floor, made by the women, was of maroon silk, embroidered around the edges, and with very small gold crosses embroidered all over its field. On either side of the altar was a statue, one of the Infant of Prague, and the other of St. Theresa, the patron saint of my grandmother and of course her eldest daughter. The famous statue of St. Roch was on the dressing table in my grandmother's room. There was a large fireplace on one side wall and there were several pews in the nave. At the front were two chairs with "pries Dieu" for the parents.

The chapel, dedicated to Our Lady of the Forest was a place to meet on Sundays for prayers and singing of hymns. It was also a very necessary little place for private meditation and reflection at any time. It was quiet there, with the warm sunlight casting shadows of different colours on the dried out logs and the black bear skins on the brightly varnished hardwood floor of the modest sanctuary. It was conducive to prayer.

One can find God anywhere, but it seems He feels closest to man in the forest, among the tall pines and hardwoods, when the sun shines through the branches and at night the beams of the moon light its green carpet of leaves and shrubs. Not only the Indians thought they heard Him in the rushing, foaming waters of the swollen rivers and the overflowing lakes. But surely He penetrated also the silent thoughts and heard the prayers from the little chapel.

The first ceremony, intimately family in nature, and the most memorable in the life of a Christian, was carried out in the chapel when it was shining new. Bernard, who was then about twelve years old, made his first communion. It was a beautiful warm day toward the end of June, when the entire family, the maids and the workmen gathered in the chapel, which was decked out in greenery with multi-coloured flowers from the woods and the garden.

Bernard was dressed in his first long trousers with white shirt, flowing silk bow tie and an armband pinned above his right elbow with wide ribbons flowing to his wrist. It was an occasion for his father to wear his morning suit with top hat and for his mother to wear her best Parisian dress and hat and carry a bouquet of wild violets.

A Father from Ste. Anne had come to spend a holiday at New France and he said mass assisted by Louis, who also acted as choir leader and by Paul and Roger who acted as acolytes. Dinner that day was the occasion for special toasts to the happines of Bernard, and Simone who had received her first communion at the Sacred Heart a short time before.

Religious ceremonies were few, depending on the visits of friends from the college or the parish priest at St. Bernard, Father LeBlanc, who became a very good friend of the family. He was a native son, born at Ohio, a village above Weymouth on the way to the back country. In 1912, he was consecrated Bishop of St. John, New Brunswick, but throughout the years hs maintained his contact with New France. Hence the "Bishop's Room" in Louis' camp at the foot of Langford Lake.

The bachelor's den, the sole and exclusive property of Paul and Roger, was built next to the cookhouse, between it and the blacksmith shop. It faced onto the square and consisted of one large room with a very large window at the front, facing south and therefore full of sun. On one side a little ell provided a little bunkhouse with two beds. The roof was high pitched and the inside finish, in varnished hardwood sheathing, went up to the top of the roof, cathedral style. The door was at the side near the front and the fireplace was at the back. On the walls were mounted moose heads, and on the floor were the ubiquitous bear rugs and moose skins. The windows had bright red drapes. The guns, traps and rods were kept on racks near the door. With a few good chairs and good books, the boys spent happy hours here reading, talking and smoking by their own fireplace.

It was always enjoyable to visit friends at Weymouth and join in the village activities and special celebrations. The men of the family, except my grandfather who was always quite content to remain at home and receive visitors, joined the

Foresters (I.O.O.F.), and attended meetings and dinners nearly every month. There were dances, and of course, card parties.

With the arrival of spring, people everywhere feel the need to rejoice outwardly and together, in some special celebration. This is an instinctive desire going back to the first days of any society. In Weymouth, the occasion was the Queen's Birthday on the 24th of May. It was called Victoria Day and even in this little far away village, the people wanted to show their affection for the beloved Mother, in their own special way. It was a national holiday of course, and at Weymouth Bridge, the festive mood was excited and uninhibited. Flags were flying everywhere and strings of bunting crossed the road. All the people in their Sunday best were out in the sunshine of a beautiful day always referred to as the Queen's Weather. There was the parade in the morning. The floats were built on dray carts, by the different patriotic and fraternal societies. The horses, usually in spans, were dolled up too, with red pom poms, bells and shiny harness with polished brass decorations. The last float was always the most beautiful one. It carried the Old Queen herself, on her throne, with crown and staff, waving to the people who applauded wildly. A lady of the village most resembling the Queen in size and countenance, was chosen year after year for this honour. It was said that she even had the flushed complexion of the Queen through her Irish habit of imbibing her daily ration of the best spirits. With an extra tot before the parade, she was grace, manners and charm befitting the finest lady, playing her role with warmth and dignity. There were some extra hurrahs and some snickering as she went by, however, because the lady was also known as Potiphar, the husband beater. It was no secret that she beat up her husband regularly. On those occasions, he could be heard hollering right across the bridge.

Being a day of rejoicing, there was a little extra drinking in public. Most men carried flat bottles in their hip pockets. They treated friends, as they went their way along the street or in the shops. They were drinking to the good health of The Queen, very seriously raising the bottle and saying God Bless Her.

At noon, there was a picnic at the park. In the afternoon, there were sports. At Muise's Trotting Park, there were horse races. This park had been set up by Joe Muise, the village tailor, just above the railway crossing on the main road going towards St. Bernard. The popular events were trotting races. There were good horses around the countryside at that time and these races were interesting. The main attraction one year was the entry of a moose harnessed to a sulky. It was equipped with blinkers. For the moose, it was free racing, heeding to the reins only enough to keep direction. The moose easily won, it took so enormously long strides that nothing could pass him and it never had to be checked for breaking into a gallop. But a bull moose always remains a wild animal, and the horses, expecially the mares, were afraid of him. Eventually the moose was returned to its natural habitat, where, no doubt, it led a happier life.

The Stehelins tried to introduce jockey racing. They entered their particularly fine little white mare, Lady. There were very few good riders in the country at that time, and the only opponent was a little bronco. Unfortunately, it was as untrained as its rider and after one circle around the track, it galloped off the field and into the crowd.

At the other end of the village at the Cricket Field, a cricket match was going on. This was the game of middle aged patriotic British types, the doctors, the dentist, the lawyer, and the elite of the Weymouth society. They were, properly dressed, white flannel trousers with black pin stripes, white shirts and green visors, and, of course, white shoes. It was a gentlemen's game. Soft drinks were available, but eventually the sportsmen and the spectators gravitated to the bars, Brown's and Beaton's, where some proceeded to get royally drunk, to the patriotic toasts.

Weymouth was a very busy place, a very prosperous place indeed. Besides the lumber business, ships were being built in yards along the muddy river banks. The Merchants Bank had established a branch at Weymouth Bridge in 1871. Mr. Kemp was the manager at the turn of the century and he was the most respected man in the village, even if he bore a stern contenance, as every one expected a banker should, seeing that he was guardian of so much money. In 1900, the bank was sold to The Royal Bank of Canada. Very few individuals would presume to approach the almighty Mr. Kemp for a loan, even with cap in hand in due reverence. Such a request would have been tantamount to a confession of leading a wasteful life, if not a sinful one. The Bank was the most revered place in town and little people were expected to dare enter its portals only to deposit their savings, like an offering to the gods of mysterious finance.

Of course, there were characters around the village who enlivened the place and were loved by all. For example, we could look at Sam McCormick, an Irish immigrant who started out as bookkeeper at Burrill's and after it was destroyed by fire, was appointed Magistrate. He was a joker as well as a good drinker, a combination which made his court sessions very amusing. In fact, next to the blacksmith shop, Sam's court was the best place to spend a riotous afternoon. The subject matter of the trials nearly always touched on drinking and the fine points of sex and morality. Sam felt he had some responsibility to his large audience as well as a sense of justice. He, therefore, loved to go to the bottom of things, putting the questions and making appropriate remarks at the answers. He would get in a rage, much of which was put on, if a witness or a complainant showed the slightest modesty or reticence in divulging the grossest facts of the case. The Blacks made the best litigants and the best actors. They had no inhibitions about relating the facts, and even embellishing them if it would enhance their own prowess. Bastardy cases were sure to be interesting and having a thought for his audience, Sam never allowed many to be settled out of court. All the facts had to come out in open court and strangely enough, the parties involved did not mind this a bit.

The two bars operating at the time, were located near the top of the hill where four roads converge, called Weymouth Corner. Alex Beaton's bar was painted red and Brown's bar was painted yellow. Both were pretty grim looking outside and dark and dingy inside, but for many men, they were the paradise of the village. Behind high bar counters, the owners served, selling by the glass or bottle, gin, whiskey or rum. Men bought the flat bottles, which they carried in their hip pockets. Walking along the road, if they met a friend, they stopped and passed him the bottle for a swig.

Old friends exchanged the niceties of convivial drinking as they knew it. Raising the neat stuff, serving in a tiny glass, they said, "here's luck" or "down the hatch" or again if they were Acadians, "en levant le cul". To Frenchmen from Paris, where one went to a bar to quietly sip a cognac with a cup of black coffee, this method of drinking appeared uncivilized in the extreme.

The barter system was in effect, as most merchants were in the lumber business and the people sold their lumber to them or worked for them. Until the bank got better known and trusted, people who needed money went to the money lender. He charged usurious interest rates, but he was a respected citizen, sending his children to fancy schools, himself not having to work at all.

The butcher shop, with sawdust on the floor, was a place where few customers came out with a square deal. The upper crust of society got fresh meat as they knew what they were offered, but the Blacks and the common people, who didn't know, got taken in every time. The butcher flicked the maggots into the sawdust, put a finger on the scale with the meat and assured them it was "just ripe, Amos". When the unsold meat got too high, even for the Blacks, it went into the pickling barrel, to make "just right" corned beef.

At New France there was no telephone and the only communication with the outside was through correspondence and newspapers. But there were all kinds of papers and magazines and what difference if they read about events weeks or even months after they had occurred?

And so there were no great anxieties, no great problems, safely away and oblivious to the worries of the world that caused so much suffering and pain, even to the remotest onlooker. When one learns of dramatic events some time after they have occurred, their impact is greatly reduced.

From the beginning of the development of the property, my grandfather experienced some opposition from the Weymouth merchants to the way he paid his men. He paid according to the wage scale then prevailing but always in cash, or deposit in bank accounts. This method of cash payment was upsetting the established barter system the merchants, cum lumbermen and ship builders strictly maintained. Instead of paying cash, they gave credit notes for future purchases at their stores. There was no competition and the people were bound captives of the system. In self defense, the merchants maintained that they extended credit to people when they were in need of goods, and had no credit balance. However, very little credit was granted to ordinary labourers. Some small operators undoubtedly got credit. My grandfather never intended to run a store for this sort of trading which he sometimes called "white slavery". Besides he reasoned that he would get more work and loyalty from workers who were free and enjoyed some independence. After several years of operation under this policy of weekly payment of wages, he was naturally upset when a representativce of some merchants approached him with the suggestion that he pay in credit notes to their stores for which he would receive a 10% commission on resulting sales. He politely refused but he was indignant. However, he had the inward satisfaction of knowing that he was helping bring an end to the system.

Paying wages in cash brought him unexpected problems however. A few workmen didn't want cash, rather, they wanted a credit on which they could draw as they needed money. Naturally, my grandfather didn't want to become a banker, so with some reluctance, his workers agreed to their wages being deposited monthly to their accounts at the bank. The amounts in these accounts accumulated and people were able to get a little money ahead against the bad days that were sure to visit them.

The founder of New France became affectionately known as the Old Gentleman. He derived great personal satisfaction from the gratitude and loyalty all his workers showed towards him. Once before in his business life, he had shown a similar concern and respect for those who gave him their best effort by taking his factory workers out of Alsace so they could remain free French citizens.

New France was already building its legend which was

to grow as it travelled among the people far and near. So many people had visited the colony, so many others had worked there, side by side with people they would never have known or understood otherwise. The Acadians, the English and the Blacks worked together and came to know and respect one another, living harmoniously, each making his contribution happily, according to his or her capabilities. There was contentment and happiness living in such a small community. In after years, the memories that lingered in the minds of old men who had worked there, were of pleasant happenings and experiences, those that had brought them joy, laughter and even sadness. To one old man, it was the recollection of being down and out of work, arriving at New France late on a fall night after a long walk from the Corner, bursting out onto a lighted and cheerful looking village and being given dry clothing, food and a job. To others, it was the memory of hunting trips and the tall stories about bears and moose. Yet to others it was the recollection of the hospitality at the Big House. Be he tramp or Governor, he found the hospitality that warmed his spirit.

From time immemorial, it seems, a small cabin has stood at the end of the road at Fourth Lake. It didn't seem to belong to anyone, and was used by anybody and everybody. It was a small cabin, perhaps twelve feet square with a lean-to at the back where firewood was stacked, venison was hung and oxen could be sheltered. Beside the door at the front was a small window, about two feet square. Inside there was a large bunk filled with fir boughs, dried to a deep brown, which gave off a pleasing aroma. To one side was an old stove resting in a box filled with gravel and under the window were a rough table and two stools. The walls had been insulated with many thicknesses of corrugated cardboard, nailed between the studs. The outside was well shingled, which gave the little haven some air or permanency and snug comfort.

My grandfather was immensely interested in seeing and talking with the various people who went by his house on their way to this little cabin, five miles beyond. In the fall of the year, there were the hunters. At any time of the year, there were all sorts of people passing through, many for no other reason than to go there to live the freedom and leisure of the woods as long as their meagre supply of grub lasted. There was old Tom Whitfield and his young son who went through every fall with their team of oxen, on their way to the cabin for most of the winter. They lived frugally, eating mostly rabbits, squirrels and porcupines.

One summer day, appeared a middle aged man accompanied by a beautiful young blond girl, on their way to the cabin, laden with what provisions they could carry. They were given a cup of tea, no questions were asked, and they went on their way. The next day a clergyman arrived in hot pursuit, inquiring if a couple had passed through. It appeared that the man had a wife and several children and had simply eloped with this really beautiful young girl. The excited good man was out to catch up with the errant husband and bring him back to his senses and his family obligations, but he was exhausted already after walking the six miles to New France. Yes, such a couple had gone through he was informed, but it was now late in the day and it was suggested that he stop for dinner and a rest, during which the thorny problem could be discussed. Fourth Lake was far away, he would probably never be able to find the cabin and in any event the erring couple would have to come out soon, as they had very little food. Besides, the misdemeanour had been committed and a little extension of the illicit concubinage would not increase the magnitude of the offence materially. So my grandfather argued, and the Reverend was won over, perhaps more by fatigue than by the arguments put forth. He rested and turned back for home the next day.

The sequel to the episode is not what one might expect. Indeed the couple did come out in about a week's time, having exhausted their supplies. They were given food at the cook house before continuing on their way, to meet the judgement of their society. But they braved all condemnation and conventions and set up housekeeping in a shack opposite the man's home where his wife and family continued to live. The couple started a family, which came to number many very beautiful girls and sturdy boys, all blond. My grandfather called this "Divorce, missionary country style".

Every Stehelin man wore a fine waxed mustache and shaved every day. They wore riding clothes nearly every day. The Old Gentleman wore funny corduroy suits and a long coat and funniest of all, a high stiff collar and necktie every day. The girls wore skirts to the ankles, blouses to the wrists and practically up to their chins. They looked funny too when they got on a horse and rode away riding sideways. But the men admired the daughters for taking a gun and going shooting with their brothers. The Old lady, a term which no one dared use in her presence, always wore earrings, and Parisian styles. The sons were awkward with a cross cut saw or an axe and that was funny too. Paul was the exception though. He loved to live like the men, not shave, wear old clothes, team the oxen, take his end of the cross cut saw and wield his axe. But when it came to hunting, fishing and trapping, the Stehelin boys had learned well and were a match for the Sullivans, the Cerenos, the Sabines and any of the best.

The servant girls working in the house were certainly not lazy, but they had had no training and of course had to be taught the European way of keeping the house and cooking. Most of them never despaired getting one of the sons for a husband. They were eligible, young and full of good healthy life. Madame ran her house from her "fauteuil" (arm chair) in the living room. Every morning, there were orders and instructions to be given and the ritual was well established. The girls lined up in front of the mistress of the house. This stage setting was very important. The day's work was laid out and this was the time and place to bring up any matters of questionable conduct. When good morals had been forgotten, a delicate but stern reprimand was administered as diplomatically as possible. There is always a leader in any group and among the servants, it was the buxome wench, mentioned before, well built with warm eyes and a ready tongue. She was a good worker, was well liked and could more than hold her own in repartee or in fun and games with any man. At a morning meeting, she felt that a reprimand had been intended for her. She could contain herself no longer and with fists on her hips, she said, "Alright, Madame, but when I am your daughter-in-law, I too will throw my "derrière" in a big chair, give orders around here and make big sermons". My grandmother once again went into shock and fainted. The saucy servant girl never became a daughter-in-law, but she was not fired either.

Of course, in some cases, my grandmother was deceived badly as some of the girls pulled the wool over her eyes. One girl made the best tea biscuits and cookies, and she just loved to make them every day. The secret of her success was having the oven just right and to ensure this, she would go to the mill and bring back very special wood chips. Such dedication won the heart of my grandmother, until one day she discovered what my grandfather and everybody else had known for a long time; that her docile little cook met her man at the mill. Indeed, as she said when being mildly laughed at for having been duped, "one would need eyes at the back of one's head to keep up with these "gaillardes" (hussies) or "sauvagesses" (savages).

The Sissiboo Pulp and Paper Company Ltd. came into being in 1899, incorporated under the laws of Nova Scotia. Charles Burrill had promoted the venture. He had gone to London, England to interest the big newspapers in a pulp and paper mill. The new company acquired the capital stock of the Sissiboo Falls Pulp Company Ltd. Its' old mill at the Falls was enlarged and retooled to produce five thousand tons of dry pulp per year. The new mill with a capacity of seven thousand tons per year was erected down river at a site called Weymouth Mills.

Charles Burrill, in his promotion, had made much of the timber available for the mills. In addition to lands of the old Sissiboo Falls Pulp Co., the new company had an option on twelve thousand acres of spruce lands and full control of the waters of the Sissiboo River. He had estimated that between one hundred and twenty-five million and one hundred and fifty million feet of timber would be available, with a replenishment growth of 6% per year.

The significance of this new enterprise for the Stehelin business could be very favourable. Much of the family lands were adjoining those of the company. Roads would be built that would facilitate exploitation of lands hitherto impossible to reach, and finally small spruce might be sold to the new company. A government wharf at Weymouth would benefit all shippers, making it possible to ship by steamer.

This exciting development gave Paul his chance to push out into the business world on his own. We shall let him tell his story, which he wrote when he was, past eighty years of age.

(Translation)

"I made my first venture into the business of a lumberman around 1903. At this time, I was between twenty-four and twenty five years of age. Roger and Germaine were at sea and I found myself very much alone and somewhat lost, because we were always together, running the woods, trapping and hunting. I knew the lands around New France like the inside of my pockets and furthermore, I knew all the good stands of timber from Barrio Lake to Sporting Lake, Rocky Lake, Uniake Lake, Fourth and Fifth Lakes on the Sissiboo and, of course Lake Doyle. I didn't know why, but suddenly I thought I would like to make some money. I had heard the pulp mill wanted to let out some contracts to cut two million feet of timber on their lands up Long Tusket Lake to the east of our lands along Sime's Brook and beyond the meadow. The pulp mill company was selling this wood to Dickey & McGrath, a lumber firm way down the river system ending at Tusket in Yarmouth County. The logs were to be driven on the rivers down to their place of business at Tusket. I thought about it for a long time, figuring all angles and I finally decided I could make money at the price the company offered.

I told no one of my plans and I went to see the manager of the pulp mill and offered to take his contract. The lots to be cut were one of one hundred acres along Sime's Brook and two smaller ones around the meadow. Another lot of one hundred acres was situated between Long Tusket and Collibri Lakes. (See map)

After long discussions with the manager of the pulp mill, I signed a contract to cut and deliver on the ice on Long Tusket Lake, two million board feet of logs. This was in November and I started at once by building my logging camp between Collibri and Long Tusket. I hired my crew and started cutting. Every week, Emile, representing me, and a Mr.

Burgess representing Dickey & McGrath, came to survey the week's cut.

I was terribly scared of going into debt. I had six pairs of oxen and thirty men, and many nights I did not sleep peacefully. Finally, I stopped worrying, saying to myself that if I went into the hole, I would not die of it.

With Easter, came the breakup on the lake and I had to stop my operation. I paid all my debts and made a profit of more than two thousand dollars. You can imagine how excited I was. I had never had so much money, but I had worked hard for it.

Most of my men were Blacks from Weymouth Falls, and they were good workers. We lived in one big camp and the nights were entertaining. They sang old songs and were very fond of ghost stories. I stayed at the camp, going home for weekends".

The winter of 1903-1904 was a particularly hard one. The snow came early and piled up all winter long to heights never known before. The old road once flattened with loaded drags and frosted over hard was excellent for sleighing. The trips out to Weymouth dressed in fur coats and covered with fur rugs were beautifully pleasant and short in comparison with the four hour buggy drives in the summer. But the mail was often very late arriving. Bad storms paralyzed everything and sometimes the trains did not run for days.

A notable visitor was a banker friend from Europe, Mr. E.J. Poisson, Governor of the Russo Chinese Bank of Yokohama. From the Orient, he was on his way to St. Peterburg, Russia, via New France. He came across the Pacific, thence by train across Canada and was to cross the Atlantic and finally reach Russia. A long way around, which makes one realize that people in those days were just as adventuresome as we are, today.

In summer especially, the forests were very dry and forest fires were a constant worry. It seemed impossible to determine how they started. They could have been set by careless travellers, fishermen, workmen, but also spontaneous combustion and lightning were sometimes blamed. Forest fires are hard to put out. They can smoulder under ground for a long time, spreading in the tinder and suddenly burst out over a large area. The wind then takes over and a conflagration ensues. Anyone who has seen a forest fire knows how terrible it can be, galloping at a tremendous speed and making dense smoke.

One summer, the colony itself was threatened and everybody was terrified. The fire started on the other side of Langford Lake. There was no cutting going on there, or any where else and in the middle of the summer, there were no fishermen in the woods. The fire was coming towards New France and there was little they could do to put it out or control it. There was no point trying to get out on the road. The fire might have overtaken them and they would have been trapped. Instead, they decided to pack boats and canoes with their most precious belongings and some food and be ready to get out in the middle of the lake. For five days, they kept watch on the shore of the lake. They could see acres and acres of prime timber lands going up in smoke. By dusk on the fifth day, the wind suddenly changed course and the flames turned about towards the lands already burnt and by the next morning, the fire extinguished itself. Saved by an act of God brought about, my grandmother was certain, by the intercession of St. Roch.

When fire goes through a forest, it does not burn the trunks of green trees. The flames devour the green branches and leave the tree dying. These trees, however, can be salvaged, if cut before the worms get into them. The lumber they produce is just as good as that sawn from green logs.

In the fall, therefore, three logging camps were set up in the burnt area to salvage the logs touched by fire. The crews were busy all winter and in the final accounting, the loss was negligible. That winter, they produced more lumber than in any previous year. The market was good and took it all.

THE CALL OF ADVENTURE

In 1899, another crack appeared in the solidarity of the family. It came from a yearning of young people for adventure beyond the confines of the family domain at New France.

Roger and Paul were of the original group of four sons who had spent the first winter in the little cabin on the banks of the Silver River. They were very young then, and they had stuck together very closely ever since. They were the inveterate hunters, the coureurs des bois, the boys with their own private den. They had always been the most enthusiastic of the sons for this new life and they seemed to understand its value more than any other. They had no intention of ever leaving. However, at this point, Paul, as he examined the sailing vessels that lay at the Weymouth wharves, got the itch to see just a little bit of the world. He had heard so many tales of the wonders of South America, United States and the West Indies from the captains who visited New France and the sailors he met in Weymouth.

One ship fascinated him especially. She was the Florence B. Edgett, a beautiful all white braquentine. With Roger, he visited the ship several times after the Captain, Nevius Kay, had befriended them, noticing that they kept coming back to sit on the wharf and look at his ship. Paul was simply fascinated by the beautiful quarters, the tall masts and all the ropes and sails. He was even more wide eyed when the good captain told them of far away places, tropical islands, strange people and strange happenings at sea.

The Florence B. Edgett was launched at Bear River on July 31st, 1891. She was one hundred and forty-eight feet long, thirty-two feet wide, a thirteen foot draft, with a gross tonnage of five hundred and nine tons.

Paul was very much taken with the living quarters. The aft house had a suite for the Captain, a mess room, a wash room and a room for two mates, the bosum and the steward (cook). The walls were varnished panels of fine hardwood and the ceiling with skylights was panelled and painted white. The forward house had the galley and a bunkhouse with space for six sailors.

The friendship between the two young men and Captain Kay developed and eventually they invited him to New France for a visit. Paul was twenty-one at the time, and upon learning that the Florence was going to South Africa and would be returning to Weymouth, a trip that would take about six months, there was no way of holding him back. The captain argeed to ship him as the bosum, although he had no experience at sea, and his father agreed to let him go. Roger would have none of it and resigned himself to the separation. There was frantic activity at the big house, collecting clothing and gear for the trip. Meanwhile, the captain made several further trips to New France, paying special attention to the daughter of nineteen, Germaine.

Eventually the day arrived for Paul to join the Florence. Roger and Paul had been so inseparable that it was a sad day for both, but especially for Roger.

As they stood by the ship, they were silent and when it came time to say farewell, Paul's courage faltered. Leaving home proved too much. He hesitated. But the vessel was ready to let go her lines and a quick decision was needed. They couldn't let the Captain down, leaving him short handed. So Roger grabbed Paul's kit bag and jumped the railing. He would go in his brother's place, although he had no desire to do so. Once away and sailing, however, Roger became quite happy and seeing Cape Town and other places excited him and he became eager to see more of the world. Thus he became a sea captain and New France dimmed behind him. Paul returned to New France alone, much happier in his old clothes, his guns, his dogs and his oxen. He would carry on during Roger's absence but when he returned, everything would be the same again.

At New France, the year went round its usual cycle and it was hunting time again. There were the pigs to be butchered, most of the meat also being salted down. However, hams were smoked and hung in the pantry. From the Acadians, they learned to make blood pudding and blood sausages. The women prepared the intestines for casings. They scrapped and scrapped them until they were clean, after which they salted them and filled them with the blood collected when the pig was bled. The same casings were used to make ordinary pork sausages which were spiced like the ones in France. Being Alsatian, of course, my grandfather supervised the stomping of the sauerkraut. He found lots of berries in the woods, such as juniper which went into the process. Nothing was wasted. They had headcheese, pickled pigs feet, liver paté, bacon and all the other pork products.

In October, sometimes early in November, after the first frost, the women went on cranberry picking expeditions on the shores of Cranberry Lake. It was a day's trip to get there by ox team loaded with provisions for a week's stay in tents or lean-tos. Cranberry Lake is above Sime's Brook and was reached from the old road to Fourth Lake. It is a very beautiful little lake, hidden in the forest, which few people have ever discovered. They brought back great quantities of cranberries, some of which were made into preserves and others kept in oats feed bags in the cellars by Langford Lake. In this way, they kept perfectly until well after Christmas.

There were dams to be repaired before the fall rains. To patch holes between the logs, they placed birch bark strips against the logs and they banked the front with gravel, which was very plentiful everywhere. Leaks in the dams were caused mostly by eels, that dug under the sand below water level, in their effort to get down river on their migration to the sea late in summer and early fall.

Eels were caught in the fall of the year, in improvised traps, using large casks that had brought wine from France. These held around two hundred liters and as soon as they arrived, the wine was decanted into bottles which were stored in the cellars to rest and age further. It was said that wine shaken in transit and exposed to varying temperatures tired and had to rest for at least three months.

In building the eel trap, the first task was to drill one inch holes, about two inches apart all over the bottom of one end of a cask. In the center of the other end, an opening about six inches square was sawn out. On the side of the cask, an opening about a foot square was sawn out and a cover was hinged over the opening. A six inch square opening was made in the dam gate. The cask was then positioned on its side behind the gate and the two six inch square openings were matched up and connected by a piece of the leg of an old overall or some piece of canvas. The trap was finally weighted down with big stones and was ready.

The eels travelling downstream to the sea, held up at the dam, would search for an opening and drawn by the current, they would fall into the trap, held captive while the water continued on through the small holes. These one inch holes were also designed to let the very small eels through. Every morning the men opened the trap door and pulled the eels out, putting them in hessian feed bags, no mean feat.

Bear hunting was also very popular in the fall of the year. It was difficult to track down a bear and shoot it. One could pass ten feet from one and never see it. Dogs were no good either because bears never circle back to the hunter to be shot at like a rabbit. They had to rely on traps and deadfalls which they contrived themselves. Usually the deadfall was built over the offal and other remains of a moose on the spot where its carcass was dressed.

Charles (Lolo as he was called in the family) never took to the woods very much, nor to working in the logging camps or the mills. He liked fishing, but was not enthusiastic about hunting. He did some scaling of logs in the winter, never straying too far from the comfort of the home. He spent a good deal of his time at Weymouth Bridge, looking after the loading of ships and the stacking of lumber on the wharf. Having served with the French Cuirassiers Regiment, he was a superb horseman, and rode between New France and Weymouth Bridge with great ease and much enjoyment. On Sundays, he always enlivened the dinner table with stories about his experiences in the army and he kept the family abreast of happenings in town, especially gilding some of the juicier bits of gossip.

The famous blacksmith shop at Weymouth, occupying a building owned by the family, was situated just a few yards from the wharf. Charlie (as he was called in Weymouth) soon became one of its many habitués and in time the leader of the gang. He was very popular, because he was very good at ribald repartee with passers-by, inventing clever jokes, finding apt nicknames for characters in the village, and drinking his share with the best of them.

By this time, "la source de la tentation" (the spring of temptation) had become very popular. This beautifully limpid little spring was situated below the little house, across and off the road and slightly up along the hill. The servant girls always preferred the water from this spring and every time one went to it to draw water, it so happened that a stalwart from the mill was thirsty, stealing his way to the little grove. None other than Lolo could have given the spot such a charming name.

Letters from Roger had been enthusiastic about the sea voyage, and the places he visited in South Africa. He had had his first photograph taken at Cape Town and he looked very well indeed. At the Big House, there was an air of new expectancy and some impatience; he was due home soon.

Early in May of 1900, the *Florence B. Edgett* sailed up the Sissiboo river and tied up at the Stehelin wharf, safe and sound. Roger's return to new France was an occasion for a great family celebration. Paul was especially glad to see his favorite brother home again. Together they would pick up the thread of their former way of life and all would be well again. As the account of the adventure unfolded, those far away places, those mushrooming cities in the Pacific, balmy climates, the Boer war, it soon became clear that Roger was taken with a new perspective of the world. Life for him could not be the same again and Paul was saddened when he learned that Roger was shipping again on the *Florence*, for at least another voyage, this time to the West Indies. My grandfather could read the ominous signs of the beginning of the dispersal. He had worked hard for his children and he had taken it for granted that the family would always remain together. The sons would build their own homes in the shadow of the big house, and the grandchildren would be the joy of the whole clan. Would he now have to realize that life is different than he had envisaged it, and that his grand design must crumble?

Captain Kay was not far behind Roger in reaching New France, where he was warmly welcomed as a friend. It soon became apparent to the parents, and to all the family, that the gallant captain was very much interested in the beautiful and very charming Germaine, in all the freshness of her twenty years. There was no whirlwind courtship, as all the proprieties of good manners were observed in the well regulated society and family of those days. The Captain's visit came to an end, but there was a feeling of certainty that he would be back. On this trip, Roger signed on as mate, in preparation for taking the examination for his first sea ticket.

There was little doubt in the parents' minds that the Captain entertained serious intentions towards their daughter Germaine, suddenly a woman, sensing herself attractive to men, somehow knowing how to fan their ardour. She was the type of woman who could have found a husband anywhere and at any time of her life. She was full of life, pretty and knowledgeable in the womanly art of using her charm. In her old age, she would say that after a long life she was certain that a woman's best friends were her eyes and legs. When the captain came on the scene, already two young men in Weymouth were pressing their suits assiduously. One was the young dentist, and the other was the son of a well to do merchant. Either would have given her a comfortable and secure life. Nevius Kay was of Irish and Scottish descent, born in Canada and at the age of thirty-eight, he presented the picture of a mature, dashing and, of course, adventurous man of the world. Germains had a yearning for adventure and excitement even at the cost of security and ease. She would dream such a husband would take her to far away places, deliriously exciting, even if some risks would have to be incurred. These dreams were not, however, in full prospect, yet.

Nevius and Roger were back from the voyage and at

New France, early that summer. It was not long after arriving that the captain asked to talk with Germaine's father privately. Of course, it was obvious to all what he wanted to talk about, but the course of etiquette had to be run in due form, and the play had to be acted out. The two men met in the privacy of the office. The proposal of marriage was made and received in all proper form and the father agreed to consult with his wife and Germaine. Events moved along the course of the best romance, and the next day the two men met again, at which time the father announced that his daughter had chosen him. Germaine was terribly excited and never gave another thought to the other two suitors. She dismissed them from her life, for the good reason that either would be "monotonous". Her big adventure was about to begin.

There was general satisfaction in the family, but in the privacy of it, Therese was disappointed. She felt her father should have suggested her to the Captain. After all, she was the eldest and, therefore, should be married first. She confided to her parents that at first Nevius had shown her some attention but that Germaine had stolen him from her. Therese had not yet realized that in America, marriages are not "arranged" by parents with a dot to bargain with. Unlike in Europe, couples married for love. "Mariages de raison" (marriages of reason) would not be understood here.

That night, the dinner "de fiançailles", the formal occasion to announce the engagement, was held with all the family present. The champagne flowed to celebrate the momentous event. The wedding date was set for October 30th next. In the meantime, Captain Kay and Roger went on another short voyage to South America. Nevius was a happy man, having triumphed over his two opponents.

The remainder of the summer was committed fully to making the preparations for the wedding. By this time, New France was part of the family and loved as "home". It would have been so romantic and warming to the heart to have the wedding in the little chapel, followed by the reception in the home. However, it soon had to be accepted that this could not be. The guest list was long and it would be impossible to lodge and feed them for two days. In late October, there was the added difficulty of transportation — snow might even hold up the *Marie Theresa* and the roads would not be fit for comfortable travel. In the end, it was decided that the marriage would take place at St. Bernard, the nearest church, and the reception would be held at the Goodwin Hotel.

The Goodwin family began preparations early. Annie, one of the daughters, came home from Boston to help. Besides she wanted to participate in the merry making. She said in later years that she never had regretted interrupting her career and coming home for "The Wedding", she had had such a good time. At New France, two seamstresses and two embroiderers and a milliner moved in to make the dresses for the mother, the bride, and the bridesmaids.

On October 29th, the entire family, with the exception of the two grandchildren who remained at New France in the care of the maids, moved to the Goodwin Hotel. October 30, 1900 was a beautiful crisp sunny morning and by noon the air was warm. The religious ceremony was performed by Father Sullivan, a good friend of the family.

The bride wore a white satin dress with train and a veil of orange blossoms. She carried white roses. Her attendants were her sisters, Therese and Simone. Therese was in a long blue gown and Simone in a pink one. They carried pink roses. The best man was Dr. Sanborne of New York, a friend of the groom.

The wedding party, in stylish horse drawn carriages, rode through a brightly decorated Weymouth Bridge on their way to the Goodwin. Many streamers of different colours and pennants were strung across the street. There were a number of ships of several nations at the different wharves and all flew their signal pennants, flags and bunting.

There were about one hundred guests for the luncheon, and many more for the reception. The meal was excellent, the best the Goodwin family had ever prepared, enriched for the occasion by the bounty of the forest and the streams of the family domain and the wines and champagne of the old homeland. The speeches were joyous and the wishes for the happiness of the newly married couple were many and warm. The bride made the usual little speech, thanking her parents, adding the heartfelt regret and apology at having shot a moose out of season, which had cost her father a $200 fine, the only one he had ever had to pay. At the time, he had been furious, but now all was forgiven and he gave his daughter a present of a five hundred dollar gold piece.

The irony of the moose story was that Germaine had not in fact shot that moose at all. Either Paul or Roger, had shot the moose, and fearing the wrath of their father, propped the animal against a tree, went home and coaxed Germaine to go out to shoot a moose they had just seen not far from home. Faced with such a lucky target, she fired, and her brothers going forward, congratulated her on her lucky shot. She had brought down a fine bull moose, so they told her and so she believed.

After the dinner, the hotel was open to all who might wish to come in to congratulate the bride and groom, and partake of a coupe of champagne, with which to propose their toasts. The ladies admired the beautiful wedding dress with its embroidery as delicate and fine as one would find in Paris. The men admired the beauty of the bride in the lovely dress. She was a beautiful bride and she knew it, acting perfectly every moment, as she gracefully accepted the many compliments profused upon her. The local papers covered the event, with enthusiasm, describing the colourful decorations and the reception. The English paper stated "she was the prettiest bride that ever crossed the Weymouth bridge". The French paper ended its report on a somewhat jesting note, that the beautiful bride was "hardly out of her infancy".

The celebration was still in full swing, the bride still in her wedding dress, in mid-afternoon, when the station agent, in a joyous mood also, announced that the train that was to take the couple to Yarmouth on their way to New York on their honeymoon was standing at the station, only a few steps from the hotel, waiting for them.

The father asked the station master to invite the conductor and his crew to come to the hotel to drink a friendly glass of champagne to the health and happiness of the newlyweds. The conductor and his men were at the reception in two minutes, and from then on no one seemed to give a thought to the train standing at the station.

Eventually, the bride, in her beautiful travelling "toilette", feathered hat, veil, parasole and her new fur coat, the gift of her husband, stood with the guests outside the Goodwin for the photographs.

Finally the whole party moved to the station grounds and the noise of firecrackers, the clouds of confetti and rice and the waving of hats and kerchiefs and Bon Voyage wishes, the train pulled away. For Germaine, the big adventure had begun.

While the honeymooners were doing New York in grand style, the *Florence B. Edgett*, under the temporary command of the mate, Roger, was at Bear River, loading lumber for Cape Town. When the captain and his bride joined her two weeks later, she was ready for sea.

The *Florence B. Edgett*, a beautiful barquantine, was well appointed, well maintained and fit for a bride. The Captain's quarters were commodious, consisting of a small bedroom, a living room, with its own companionway leading to the aft deck and the wheel block and a tiny bathroom.

It was mid November when the *Florence* cleared for the high seas. For a young bride of twenty, whose only sea experience had been the crossing from France, on a huge steamer, five years earlier, heading for Cape Town with her husband in a sailing ship, promised to be a deliriously happy adventure. The presence of her older brother would help keep away any loneliness at leaving the happy family life behind. Besides several cases of champagne had been stored aboard, the gift of her thoughtful father, just in case of seasickness. Indeed she was deathly seasick during her first week at sea. Fortunately, however, the malady passed away, never to return at any time during the next seventeen years she sailed to many parts of the world. During those years, the cabin of a ship was the only home she knew. She never felt too far from New France to return as often as possible. She made the trip from San Francisco by train one year to be with her parents at New Year. Indeed there was a deep feeling of solidarity in the family. The children left the home, but their hearts in great part remained behind, and they returned often to be with their parents.

In the family home, the leaving of Germaine left a void that was felt by the parents of course, but also and particularly by her younger brothers, Maurice and Bernard. She had enjoyed life at New France, much more than her sisters. She went out fishing and hunting with her brothers. Perhaps not an enthusiastic homemaker, she nevertheless enlivened family life. There were still seven children left at home, and there were two granddaughters in the little home on the hill who brought the greatest joy to the grandparents and the uncles and aunts.

There was anxiety too for the safety of Germaine, so young to be on a wooden ship on the way to Cape Town, so far away. It would be weeks before a cablegram announcing a safe arrival would reach the home, and more weeks before letters, postcards and photographs would be avidly read, looked at and discussed. In the meantime, to the philospher and hopeful father, the day to day solution was to drive on, and keep everybody very busy and cheerful, ready to fall into sleep every night dead tired.

Visitors always brought gaiety and change into the home. Judge Longley and his daughter always brought lively conversation. To my grandmother, he was the epitome of the fine gentleman, appreciative of good food, and to my grandfather, he was the lively story teller and fine speech maker at the table. Mr. Robb, the builder of the Marie Therese, was a charming gentleman, always gallant with the ladies and knowledgeable of fine things and events. There were also the more frequent visitors from Weymouth, the Hogans, the Campbells, the Burrills, and others.

From Europe came the young Baron Maurice Hottinger, the son of the Regent of the Banque de France, a friend of my grandfather from his business days. This son, privileged and very rich, with nothing to do but amuse himself, spent the whole winter at New France. He enjoyed the hunting, the activities in the snow, and the healthy life in the wild of Canada, a welcome contrast to the gay life of the rich circles of his age group in Paris. Therese tried very hard to make herself attractive and pleasing to Barron. However, obviously the too rich Baron had other ideas in mind. In the spring, well rested, the Baron left for the Pacific coast and a tour around the world, via Japan, through Russia and on the then new Trans Siberian Railway back to Paris.

My grandfather always leaned towards those people who had not been too fortunate in life, usually because they were not too well endowed mentally. New France at times seemed to be the heaven for many men who were "not too bright". These men always rewarded their master by their honesty and conscientious hard work, which, in his view, more than made up for their lack of intelligence. As he would sometimes say "one does not need to be the ace of spades to wield an axe, or carry lumber on one's back". They earned their wages, and were happy.

One such character was Zozime. He arrived at New France late one autumn night. He had walked the six miles in the dark, and when he suddenly burst into the village square, lit up with many lighted windows in buildings all around, he said he stood in amazement, and removed his old cap because he thought he was entering Heaven. He got a job and he begged my grandfather to let him work for nothing, because he wanted to stay there the rest of his life. He worked in the woods, and became Paul's shadow, he loved him so. In time, he became the teamster entrusted with a routine job of going to Weymouth once a week for provisions.

Zozime was completely honest and reliable, but he had one weakness that was easily forgivable. The four wheel cart had a high body and Zozime always put a good bunch of hay on the bottom. When he had done his errands in town he liked to have a few drinks on the way home. If he drank too much he simply went to sleep in the hay and the oxen took him home.

On cold, moonlit nights, it was a glorious adventure for parties to visit Electric City. As they turned the last bend in the road, they would suddenly find themselves in a fairyland village, houses covered with snow, with shining lights from so many windows. Sleighbells and laughter and singing added to the charm of the scene. To the accompaniment of their fiddler's music, clapping of hands and singing, they danced the old reels and square dances. Around one o'clock in the morning, the party would leave, and when the last echo of the sounds of the merry makers had died away, the night seemed to settle deeper in its stillness and cold. The stars and the moon shone ever so brightly, as if they had hung from the sky forever, making a picture of light of so many hues, mixing with the electric lights, in this hamlet, lying sparkling and so quiet under its blanket of thick pure white snow.

My grandfather once again asked the government to provide funds to upgrade the road. After all he employed some forty men, plus hauling contractors and business for merchants in Weymouth. Other tracks of land along the road would be exploited. The government did respond favourably this time and in 1901, spent two hundred dollars on the road. In subsequent years, smaller amounts were allocated for further improvement. My grandfather was greatly encouraged and he made long range plans for exploitation along the road and possibly towards Fourth Lake.

Charles was not fully occupied running the lumber yard on the wharf. It was decided to open a store in a vacant building on the property in Weymouth. Charles would run it in conjunction with his present duties. The outside of the building was freshly painted a deep maroon, the inside was repainted white with brown trim, and the existing counters were cleaned up and varnished. Louis would keep the books and so Charles was in business. Every Sunday, he reported on the state of affairs. My grandfather was anxious to keep informed, as he was dubious of Charles' business ability. The Army had not prepared him for this type of work, nor indeed for any occupation or profession. He had been taught to be a good comrade and enjoy life, such as one found it, which explains why he was such a success with the "gang".

The store somehow didn't seem to prosper and expand. Unfortunately, the forge was too near, and Charles sometimes had trouble explaining to his customers why the beans tasted kerosene. Indeed he had more trouble explaining to his father why there was always a loss on accounts day at the end of every month.

Marie Brown was the widow of the former proprietor of Brown's Bar. She had a home, money and a good horse. Charlie was a handsome, charming young man, and in due time, Marie fell for him and they were married. Charlie now had a home and he continued the business for some years. Marie was a fine woman, quiet, spending most of her time looking after the home. She visited New France on many Sundays, but never stayed for longer visits. Her good influence, however, was never enough to keep her husband from the gang at the forge.

It was a happy day when in the summer of 1902, the Florence B. Edgett brought the honeymooners back home, from their near two years absence. After discharging cargo at Cape Town, they had freighted coal for the Americans from San Francisco to the Phillipines. They had also made one voyage from British Columbia with a cargo of lumber destined to Callao in Peru. From there, around the Horn they went back into the Atlantic, bound for Nova Scotia and home.

There was great rejoicing at the big house, thankful that the three were safe and sound after such a long absence. There were great stories to tell about the war in South Africa and the many countries visited. After three weeks at home, Germaine, her husband Nevius and Roger rejoined their vessel at Bear River. Late in August, the Florence sailed out of the Annapolis Basin for Buenos Aires.

The weather was beautiful as they sailed afore a mild westerly breeze. Early in September, they reached the Carribean where very suddenly on September 18th, they encountered a strong wind and very heavy rain squalls. After a day, the rain stopped and the wind increased to tornado force. There was not even sufficient warning to take in canvas and the sails were torn to shreds. The lashings that secured the deck cargo let go and boards were flying everywhere. The fo'c'sle and the aft house were flooded, the riggings let go and all three masts snapped. Nevius lashed himself and Germaine to the stump of the main mast and crew members did likewise around the fore mast. Roger and one seaman lashed themselves to the wheel. The tornado raged all night, the seas washing what was left of the *Florence* as she tried to ride the smashing seas.

As daylight came on a scene of disaster, the wind abated and during the day, a calm sea returned. No crew member had been lost or hurt, but the Captain decided to abandon ship, get into the longboat and make shore somewhere or better still be picked up by a passing ship. However, when they examined the lifeboat, they discovered it had been damaged. They set to work repairing it, but it was a long job. The vessel was doomed, awash but afloat, drifting aimlessly. The cabins were flooded and the crew had to live on the wet deck cargo, under an improvised shelter. The sun was hot, a blessing really as they would have perished in cold weather. For food, they had salt meat, two hogsheads of fresh water and very little bread. While on the wreck, they sighted two freighters, and sent flares to attract their attention. Unfortunately, the distance between the ships was too great and they were not noticed.

On October 15, after one month of hardship, the life boat was ready with two small sails, and the oars. They had built a small cuddy aft for Germaine. They took the little food left and set a westerly course. Fortunately, the ship's compass had been salvaged. The Captain, Nevius, and the mate, Roger, sat together at the tiller, each with a revolver in case anyone went beserk.

The days were long and hot, with little wind to sail the boat. On the tenth day, as the food and water had practically run out, they landed on the Island of Grenada, where the British Consul assisted them to get clothing and passage to New York.

The end of this fine ship, in her twelfth year of service was a great loss as well as the passing of a piece of the romance of sailing ships. Years after, sea stories related that the *Florence* had roamed the seas for many years, just a ghost ship drifting at the whim of wind and currents. It was even said that she returned to the Pacific to roam there for years. Finally she returned to the North Atlantic where she disappeared.

Nevius and Germaine, after a month's rest, went off again to New York to take over another sailing vessel bound for New Zealand. In due course, they went into steam and sailed together until 1917, when steam ship owners put a ban on the captain's wife living on board ship. Germaine had to set up a home in Brooklyn, New York.

Roger spent a very happy winter home, but in the spring of 1903, he got the fever to return to the sea. He sensed that the days of sailing ships were drawing to a close. His first command was a freighter of the American Hawaiian Line. He spent his entire career with this company, trading mostly in the Pacific to the Far East from the west coast of U.S.A.

The passing of the wooden sailing ships was a gradual, but relentless process. These vessels had a life span of about ten years. One by one they began to disappear, wrecked or rotting. They were not replaced, because iron steamships had the advantages of greater speed, greater carrying capacity and longer life. This change, or progress, however, brought near economic disaster to thousands of lumbering coastal villages like Weymouth and Bear River. The bigger ships could not reach these too shallow ports and so the lucrative far off markets of the world were lost. There were no highway trucks to haul lumber to deeper ports, and shipping by rail was expensive and inconvenient. However, for New France, the business continued somehow throuth to 1907, when there was a slump which lasted until the war of 1914.

Families then as today, had their own joys, worries and sorrows. It was in 1902 that the first set of twins, a boy and girl, were born in the little house on the hill at New France. It was an anxious time for the whole colony as it was a long and difficult birth. The midwife was there but a doctor was needed. Dr. Elderkin hurried to New France, hanging on in the saddle on faithful old General. The doctor stayed for a few days and undoubtedly saved the mother. Roger the boy died at birth. Simone Louise lived about one year. Dr. Elderkin was most compassionate and consoling. "I have seen a child die in similar circumstances before and it was my own", he said.

The two granddaughters brought joy and sunshine to both homes, through happy and sad times. They were growing up however and the family began to concern themselves about their education. A bedroom, in the big house, now unoccupied was set up as a school, with two little desks made at the mill. Mother would teach English, Simone French, and Louis religion. Therese soon gave up trying to teach writing. Louis was a kind and gentle person. The children loved to visit him at the office and he had time to take them on little walks, talk with them, and even become an amateur photographer to take their pictures. The other uncles loved them also but in a playful way teaching them little tricks such as staying behind in the dining room after dinner and finishing off the wine glasses. Jacqueline got caught by an aunt and was promptly sent to bed.

A letter to Mathilde conveys the thoughts of my grandfather at the close of this period.

Translation   December 15, 1902

My Dear Mathilde:

Snce my last letter, we have had great worries about Memene (Germaine), who, with her husband and Roger, suffered a most terrible shipwreck. They were in the Caribbean Sea on the way to Buenos Aires, when a tornado, or storm like a whirlwind, suddenly caught them and in half an hour dismasted their vessel, now taking water everywhere and simply a wreck. The cargo of lumber fortunately kept them afloat and they were able to stay on the wreck for a month, hoping to be picked up by a passing ship. At the end of a month, they set out in their small boat with the crew and the cat and after fifteen days of navigation, they landed on the Island of Grenada, exhausted, without food, without water, with nothing.

The inhabitants of Grenada maintain that this storm was caused by a volcanic irruption and explosion in the Martinique and other islands in the area, because the sea is usually calm at this season. They came to New York where Germaine and her husband still are on business and Roger is home to rest and regain his strength. You can imagine our anxiety when we read about this in an English newspaper before we received a cable from Grenada.

We are in good health, my sons in the woods for the winter, Maurice and Bernard at the university, Simone at the Sacred heart and Therese and Louis at home. Louis acts as secretary and bookkeeper and Therese helps my wife. The snow makes it possible for us to travel fast by sleigh and we have excellent trotters (horses) so that we are not lonely and this season really is the most agreeable in Canada. Sometimes we are surprised around ten or eleven o'clock at night by sleighing parties filled with natives, men and women, who come to see "France" as they call my colony. We give them tea and after a few good words, they go back happy.

I wish you and yours a good New Year, and I kiss you with all my heart.

E.S.

A GRANDSON IS BORN

November 13, 1905 was a momentous day for the family when Emile III (Mitt) was born, healthy and strong. The loss of the first boy, Roger, had been a bitter disappointment, not only to the parents, but also to the grandparents and the uncles. The birth of daughters brings great joy, but of a different nature than the birth of a son. He assures the continuity of family tradition through the male line. He provides the essential link in the chain towards hopeful perpetuity of the family name. There was, therefore, reason for the greater joy at the arrival of this doubly wanted and anxiously awaited son and heir. The proud father recorded the event as follows:

"On November 13, 1905, New France was awakened at daybreak by a cannon shot, while the French flag rose triumphantly in the morning breeze. The first live boy was born. Our Mitt opened his eyes to the light of the rising sun, a beautiful sunrise that day, for we were in Indian summer. The woods, still covered with brillantly coloured autumn leaves, rustled gently, while the tall trees that sheltered the house seemed to bend towards it in the morning breeze, as if to welcome the newly born and embrace him in their foliage.

We had with us at the time a band of French sailors, birds of passage, who came every year to take shelter with us. Under the orders of René, who had been a qualified gunner aboard the *Formidable,* they had stood watch all night awaiting the happy event. They had built a cannon with a piece of four inch iron pipe and when the old midwife Jeanne-à-Henri called from the doorway "It's a boy", René, as if he were still aboard his battleship on inspection day, called his men to "Attention" around their gun. The Petit Carotier (The Trickster) held the lighted fuse, the Chat Botté (Puss-in-Boots) and Auguste stood one on each side of the gun. René, with the flag rope in his hand, commanded in a stentorian voice, "fire", and while he hoisted the colours, echoes awoke in the great forest as the voice of the gun circled New France from Long Tusket and Langford, reverberating in a long rolling rumble.

My father and mother, awakened by the noise, hastened to our home, full of joy. They tenderly pressed in their arms their first grandson they had hoped for for so long.

There were some thirty men in the cookhouse at the time, as the sawmill was in operation. It was a day of merriment. My father distributed a bottle of wine to each man and by midday, the rejoicing was general. René and his French comrades, of course, were royally full. Together they came to the house to see the new baby. We had to let René hold Mitt, and, following an old custom from Britanny, he moistened the baby's lips with wine. Poor René, if the wishes he made for Mitt that were to be fulfilled, his life will certainly be a happy one. As for the poor gunner, the war has claimed his life, for he was not one to desert the flag.

That night, there was a big dinner at Grandfather's. All my brothers and sisters were there and it was a general celebration. When it came time for dessert, my father toasted the health and future prosperity of his first grandson. The old woman, Jeanne-à-Henri, had left her patient and the baby to clink glasses with the family. With her black Acadian kerchief, her good old face covered with wrinkles, she seemed to symbolize "the past", a living relic of the first French who had come to Acadie. It was in a voice both joyous and firm that she toasted in champagne the "Health of Emile III".

As for your mother and myself, our happiness was immense, all our hopes realized, and on reentering the house after dinner, it was with a prayer of thanksgiving that I bent over the cradle, that cradle which thirty-five years earlier had been mine in the land of Alsace, and pushing back the lace ruffles, I looked with infinite joy at my first born son sleeping peacefully. Then I kissed also our two little girls, Bernadette and Jacqueline, for whom the arrival of a little brother was a gift from Heaven."

As was the custom in those days, Mitt was baptized by the midwife. A more formal christening would take place later. As it turned out, it was about three years later that the ceremony took place in the chapel. By that time, Mitt had grown into quite a sturdy little fellow who had already learned too many tricks from his indulgent uncles. Father Le Blanc, of St. Bernard's, came for a visit, and preparations were made for the event. The family and the workmen gathered in the chapel. The family silver punch bowl was brought forth to be used as the christening fount. Everything was ready but when Mitt saw all this and sensed that he was the center of attraction, he would have no part of it. To his little mind, it smelt like just another trick, thought up by one of his uncles, probably Uncle Momo. He ran away and got as far as the barn when his father caught him and forcibly brought him back. He had made his point, and from then on he must have felt he could bellow and kick as much as he wanted to. By the smile on their faces, he must have gathered that the uncles were enjoying the "show" very much, which gave him added courage and strength.

He made it clear that he objected to the water poured over his face and the salt they tried to stuff into his mouth, but when they tried to place a lighted candle in his little hand, he was terrified. The uncles had taught him to light matches, but his father had told him this was forbidden and it seemed he thought he was about to be punished by fire for having disobeyed a strict order. This was a traumatic experience for a child and he never forgot it.

The afternoon was concluded merrily at the big house with family supper with champagne. Wine and champagne are mentioned often in the story of the lifestyle at New France, but it must be remembered that very little spirits were drunk. The only exception was the ever present barrel of West Indies rum in the cellar, which was used very sparingly and only with black coffee after dinner. No one would have dared depart from the strict routine set by the master of the house and especially no one would have dared take a drink of any kind before the noon meal. This rule made for the proper use of alcoholic beverages and there were very few heavy drinkers in the family.

An event that had a very depressing effect on the family was the end of the railroad in 1907. It had been evident for some time that sooner or later its passing would come, but no one wanted to think about it, and no one dared talk about it.

The ending was brutal. It all happened in a few hours during the dry summer, when the drunken machinist, driving the train at full speed, set fire to the woods near the line. In no time, miles of track had gone up in flames. All hands available at New France were rushed to try to put the fire out. A gang of volunteers came out from Riverdale. When the two crews met, several miles of track had disappeared and the dammage was irreparable. That was the last run of the Maria Theresa.

The Maria Theresa, the Firefly, the Caribou and most of the flat cars were on the New France end of the track. Very upset by this shattering of his dream, my grandfather ordered all the remaining equipment out of his sight forever. It was indeed a sad day when the rolling stock, was shunted away and scattered along the remaining track between New France and Lake Doyle. The railroad had become the living symbol of the entire exploitation. There was enthusiasm and some excitement each time the Maria Theresa, towing the Caribou, chugged into the square. It gave the feeling of having a tie with the outside, only one hour away. It was exciting to work on it, to run it and, of course, to ride on it. It was close to being another person in the life of the colony.

The Caribou ended up on the high ground near the river between Little Tusket and New France. It was used for about twenty-five years as a hunters' cabin. One room was used as a kitchen and the other as a bunkhouse. Howard Steele from Southville had fixed it up into a snug little cabin and it became known as his camp. The Maria Theresa was abandoned near the old Langford road, not far from New France. It was eventually vandalized and no doubt today someone cherishes its bell, its kerosene lamp and its wheels as souvenirs. The wooden parts of the flat cars rotted away with the remains of the track, and disappeared. Only a few wheels were hauled away as souvenirs. Most of them must still be there covered over by new earth and will likely never be seen again. The new forest has covered all the wounds.

With the family smaller, the railroad gone, and the mother and father getting older, the pace of living was reduced. The portable mills had to be moved from time to time and if possible always nearer Southville, trying to reduce the cost and time of hauling the lumber out. The three grandchildren at the house on the hill were the joy of the whole family. There was as always before, happiness and contentment. They appreciated the free and peaceful life, and good open air, the shooting, the hiking and the lively family lifestyle.

My grandfather especially loved the winters. He liked to walk to the logging camps and to the mills in the crisp snow and the cold air. His life was very highly programmed. A man of habits: every day he did the same things at the same time and in the same way. During the day, so many hours were spent at the office, so much time for quiet meditation and thinking in the chapel, and so much time for exercise and relaxation, which usually took the form of walking in the woods with gun and dogs. The evenings were spent reading and playing exactly three rounds of double solitaire with his wife. He was interested in everything and kept abreast of events in the world. He became an amateur herbalist and concocted tonics and medicines. Goldenrod was a good spring tonic. Wild strawberries with some herbs made a good blood purifier, polly-poddy was a good digestive aid and an appetizer. Cobwebs stuffed in a bad wound would stop the loss of blood. A raw potato carried in the hip pocket during the winter prevented rheumatism.

The time came to face the dog problem. The dog population had increased steadily over the years and finally there were over thirty of them. Some were pets, some were hunting dogs, and the rest were just dogs belonging to no one. The big ones ran practically wild and were suspected of committing many crimes, such as killing sheep, even killing a pig, maiming some smaller dogs and fighting among themselves. The smaller dogs raided the henhouse, killed chickens, ate some eggs and stole food in the pantry. One such little dog was Major, a white and black terrier. His behaviour was amusing, but when he stole the Sunday dessert, the family council decided he had to go. They gave him to a sailor on a vessel that was leaving for Barbadoes, and would likely never return to Weymouth. Six weeks later, Major, happy as anything, appeared at the front door. In Barbadoes, he had jumped onto another ship that by chance was heading for Weymouth. How did Major figure out that the second ship was returning to Weymouth? Very simple. On the wharf, he had recognized a sailor from Weymouth who befriended him and he had simply followed him aboard his ship. The family had missed Major and had some qualms of conscience about the way they had stowed him away on that ship. He was a member of the family again, until, many years later, in Weymouth he was struck and killed by one of the two cars in the village.

Therese, passed thirty years of age and as the prospects of finding a husband slowly but surely receded, her frustrations agumented. At times, the flinging of the pots and pans in the kitchen rang through the house. She was always of the group that went blueberry picking and jam making at Cariboo every year. She was the self-appointed boss. One year something went wrong and she went into a fit and fainted. No one worried unduly because she often fainted. This time, however, she did not come to again after a few minutes. There were men working there at the time and they made a litter and had to carry her the five miles to New France. A Eudist, Father Conan, was visiting at the time and he was asked to administer the last rites, which he did, whereupon Therese regained her full consciousness and got up as if nothing had happened.

In the hope of getting her mind on something new and steer her towards the acquisition of the genteel graces of dignified spinsterhood, her father built her a small but very nice house on the brow of the hill overlooking the water on the road down Langford Lake. It was a very short distance from the house, but it was secluded. It was built of small logs with a verandah on the front facing the lake, and another one at the back facing a small clearing and the forest beyond it. The one room was tastefully decorated and furnished. Apparently, Therese found much contentment there, entertaining or just being herself in her own place.

Coming to a new world to live in the woods had been particularly and understandably hard on her. She found it very difficult to make new friends, mostly because she was never comfortable in the English language. But in spite of all, she, like the family, was captivated by the woods, the climate and the way of life. In her old age, far from New France, the vision of her life there never dimmed. In retrospect, it had been the best part of her life.

Ned Sullivan arrived one March day and coaxed Paul to go with him on a moose hunting trip to Barrio Lake. Let Paul tell his story:

"It was in March and a herd of moose that traditionally spent the winter on a peninsula jutting into the lake would still be there. This peninsula is about one mile long and at the base it narrows to about two hundred paces. At this narrow point, from a rise in the ground, one could usually see the herd very clearly as the moose travelled round and round their winter trail.

There was still ice on the lake, strong enough to carry us. We walked across the lake to the camp of the American doctors on the island. This camp had no stove in it but it had a very large fireplace with a cooking arrangement built inside it. Even with a big fire burning, we felt cold and so we set up a tent, that was there, in front of the fireplace. By keeping the fire going all night, we were warm.

Early the next day, we crossed on the ice to the peninsula and started hunting. There was snow on the ground and it was therefore easy to find the moose yard. I posted myself at the narrow part of the tongue of land, where I could see everything going by. Ned went towards the point and turning around started beating the woods, to drive the moose toward me. It was not long before a big bull moose appeared. I took a shot at him and missed. A second bull came running and I missed him also. A third one came past and this shot was luckier but not good enough to hold the animal down in his tracks. It faltered, fell to its knees, but after a few minutes, got up again and walked away. He was badly wounded. We decided to follow the blood stains in the snow and we walked until four o'clock in the afternoon, never catching up with our moose. We could see that he had gone down to ground to rest along the way, but he was too far ahead of us to catch up with him that night. We decided to give up the pursuit until morning. We had better get back to camp, cut firewood and get ready for the night.

We were comfortable enough with plenty of firewood, but from then onward, misfortune upon misfortune bedevilled us. During the night, it rained and rained and by morning, the ice was too thin to bear our weight. We were running out of food, having brought provisions for only two days. We decided to borrow the canoe that was there. We put it in the water and the one in the bow would break the ice as the other in the stern paddled. In that way, we would reach the other shore. We only paddled a few yards from shore when the canvas on the canoe was cut by the ice and we were sinking. There was no other choice than to come back to shore as quickly as possible. We looked around for something to patch the canoe with. If we could find a little fat, we could cut resin from the spruce trees, melt it and mix the two into a paste. We found no fat, but we tried resin and balsam mixed together.

We decided to wait until all the ice was gone before trying to get across. We planned that one would paddle and the other would bail the water out of the canoe as fast as he could. Fortunately, it started to rain again, which melted the ice faster. The thing to do was not to panic and look for something to eat.

Ned searched every nook and corner of the camp and came up with a little corn meal, half rotten and infested with weevils. We had a little tea and a little butter left. We made pancakes with the corn meal which we cooked in the fireplace. Thus we survived the next two days. On the fourth day, the ice was gone and we got into the canoe and paddling and bailing like mad, we made the other shore. Needless to say, we went home instead of going after our wounded moose."

Smitty, the general duties' choreboy, was still there, still the happiest man in the world. One year a male cook was hired for the kitchen at the big house. Oliver Cromwell was an excellent cook and he learned very quickly to do things the way Madame taught him. But he had one great fault; he was temperamental and he would disappear, always at a crucial time, when he was urgently needed, such as when visitors were staying at the house. He would go on strike and go home, always coming back in a few days, very repentant. He was the cook who used an old set of false teeth he had found on the road to decorate his pastries and crimp the edges of his pies.

Life was always full and satisfying, as one gathers from a letter written in 1905 by my grandfather.

My Dear Mathilde:

I wish the New Year which is approaching will be a good one for you, and I hope it will bring you at least some relief from all your tribulations. We each have our own to bear, and for those, like most in our family, who seemed to be doomed to perpetual misfortune, there is only the consolation that it will end some day and that we will have our compensation in the other world.

As for myself, I went back to work for my children. If I maintain my health, which happily is solid, I can hope to re-establish my affairs. The prospects are good, as wood sells well, at a very high price. But what work and worry to suceed.

We are alone at the house, my wife with my daughters and the children of Emile for a little while, during the confinement of his wife. She has just given birth to a fine boy and is very well. It comes when there is snow and it will be a month before the child can be taken outside.

The father, Emile Jr., and Paul are in the woods for the winter and come home only on Sundays. This year my operation is interesting. I have set up a portable mill that saws the logs as fast as the ox teams can bring them in. There are fifty men in two camps with oxen. All to be fed and what stomachs.

Roger just returned from London where he goes every month on a big steamer on which he is an officer. Momo

(Maurice) is in New York with Jean. Memene (Germaine) left yesterday after spending three months with us and will probably sail for Manilla which pleases her very much. Her husband commands a large steamer on which they have very good accomodation and a good cook, so the voyage is not uncomfortable. As for Bernard, he is at college and will be home for Christmas.

A good New Year, my dear sister. Take courage. I wish you an end to all your troubles. God will perhaps send you some consolation, if it is His Will.

I kiss you with all my heart.

E.S.

Mathilde was then the only surviving member of my grandfather's family. She was two years younger than he was, and had always been his favourite. She was living in Paris and her troubles had stemmed from the forced retirement of her husband, who was now in very poor health. In 1862, she had married Baron Max Gilm de Rosenegg. He was an Austrian, a Captain in the Cavalry and aide de camp to the Grand Duke of Baden. Through her marriage, Mathilde became Lady of Honour to the Grand Duchess of Baden. All this tinsel life eventually ended abruptly through a comedy of errors.

One night during a grand reception at the court of Baden, Mathilde, who was petite but of some hot temper, thought she saw her husband flirting furiously with a lady behind some bushes in the garden. She hesitated not one instant, rushed the couple and slapped the face of the man whom she thought was her husband. Horror of horrors, the man whose face she slapped was none other than the Grand Duke himself. Naturally her husband had to retire. They left the court and settled in Paris. Max died in 1908 and she returned to Alsace for a time. At the outbreak of the first war, she returned to Paris and ended her days there in 1926.

The three children at the little house were growing up too quickly it seemed and serious thought had to be given to their future education. In 1908, Bernardette and Jacqueline were sent to boarding school to the Sisters of Charity at Church Point. To the surprise of everyone, they were way ahead of the girls of their ages, which attested to the high standard of training at the home school at New France.

After considering all factors, my father, decided that it would be best to move his family outside. At first, quite naturally he thought of Weymouth and negotiated for a house. In the end, however, he opted for Church Point, chiefly because Mitt, after passing through the public school system, could enter St. Anne College. Besides, there was another child on the way, and he may be another boy.

It was time for a move. It was a sad break in the family, felt especially by the grandparents. At the last moment, my grandfather asked that Mitt stay a while longer. He did stay until the next spring.

The last few months that Mitt spent at the big house left a lasting stamp on his character. He always remembered life at New France as a fairy tale dream, always unfolding new wonders, new excitement with each day. It gave him a poetic view of his past, living nature, lakes, babbling brooks, snow, ice, birds and animals. With the uncles to himself, he listened to their tales and bravely did their bidding. It was not long before he could invent his own fantastic tales about wild animals and concoct his own schemes. Through this upbringing, he developed the well known characteristic of the family to love the romantic. Nothing is too fantastic to believe if it is pleasing to the imagination. But Mitt inherited wonderful qualities out of it, generosity, truthfulness and frankness.

Life at Church Point had a depressing effect on him, no flowers, no trees, always the cold wind. The ocean could not replace the lakes and the forest, and worst of all, the uncles were not there.

DEATH COMES TO NEW FRANCE

With the going of the family on the hill, New France became a home without the same gaiety, laughter and the running about of children. The house seemed to get bigger and the evenings and Sundays seemed to be long and quiet. Of course, there was the business to keep the men busy and the visitors to exchange thoughts with, but there was less activity around the mill, the forge and the barn.

Long afternoons were enjoyed on the lakes, along the rivers and in the woods, along the old roads, admiring the colourful foliage as it changed from day to day, according to a timed program, from green to yellow, thence to a soft pink, ending in a riot of all these colours and shades. The whole forest reddened in the sinking sunlight in the midst of the dark green of the spruce and pines, entwined in the soft green lace of the hemlock trees that rose high in the sky. As coolness returned, the lakes became the mirror of a cloudless sky of sapphire blue.

Nowhere in the world could there be such a beautiful place. A place to be healthy, to be free, to enjoy and often to meditate on the hidden questions that have tormented the mind and the soul of man since the beginning of thinking life. Who and what is Man in this universe? Not to ever find out can lead to doubt, which happily is resolved by the awakening of a tranquil and simple faith.

At this time, the founder of New France seemed preoccupied by thoughts of an uncertain future. He was seventy-two years old and maybe his dream was fading. He wrote of his feelings to Mathilde.

24 September 1909

My dear Mathilde:

I thank you with all my heart for your good wishes in your letter of July 18. At my age, a birthday is not a feast any more, especially considering the course of a lifetime as agitated as mine has been, which evokes rather sad thoughts. In spite of everything, I am very well and I note that if life in the forest sometimes lacks diversion and amusement, I have to admit it is good for one's health and that I would not have stayed alive in a more civilized environment. My daughter Germaine has just left for San Francisco on the steamer commanded by her husband, where she will see Roger whose ship is also there. Their ships carry coal for the American Fleet (Navy), which proves that in spite of all the friendly gestures between the Yankees and the Japanese, one does not want to be caught by surprise. My wife is in good health as well as those who are still with us, fewer now as they begin to disperse. My kisses my dear sister. May God help you in your troubles — everyone has his.

E.S.

Winter came early in November of 1909, when the snow first fell to stay all winter. New France under the snow was quiet. The laughter of children playing in the snow with the playfully barking dogs was stilled. At the cookhouse, only a few men were left with the faithful cook and her husband. Zozime, the man of confidence, although he still sometimes returned from his weekly trip to Weymouth dead drunk, was indispensible. The weekends were looked forward to, as the sons and the men returned from the camps for a night and a day. There was the gathering of what was left of the family for the Sunday dinner with the mother and father happily presiding.

Late in November, the revered mother came down, afflicted with some strange illness. Not responding to the usual remedies for "grippe", Dr. Elderkin was summoned. Trusted General got him safely over the rocky road to the bedside of a very sick patient. He stayed overnight and all the next day, studying the case very carefully. Finally, he alerted the family to the fact that his diagnosis was not reassuring. Diabetes had already made serious inroads and there was no known cure for it.

A few weeks later, the doctor came again. The diet and the medication he had prescribed had not brought any improvement. In fact, he could see that his patient was slowly weakening, while suffering great pain. He recommended a full time nurse to care for her in a more professional way. The nurse came and the family gradually had to face the inevitable.

Christmas that year was a very quiet one. The family was nearly complete and everyone tried to soothe the suffering of the mother and soften the grief of the father. Germaine left San Francisco on Christmas Day, arriving in New York on New Year's Day, and by her mother's bedside a few days later.

The next month dragged on, as the gloom of the impending end settled on this once joyful home, now a very sad house. Towards the middle of February, Dr. Elderkin came again. He knew the end was near and, sensitive to the religious beliefs of the family, suggested that perhaps they would like to ask the parish Priest at Weymouth to come. Bernard, with horse and sleigh, left immediately, and the next morning, he returned with Father Dion during the course of one of the worst snow storms of the season. The touching ceremony of the administration of the Last Rites was carried out in the bedroom, the family praying with their mother who retained full consciousness and a strong voice. Shortly afterwards, sensing that her end was near, she kissed her husband and her children for the last time, after which she fell into a coma and passed away on February 24th, two days following her sixty-first birthday, in the afternoon while a blinding snow storm was raging in the forest.

The storm abated the next day and New France was serene and beautiful again. During the next six days, members of the family, sons, dispersed from San Francisco to New York, sped homeward for the funeral. When the funeral mass was intoned in the little chapel the family was complete. This was the last service performed in the sanctuary of Our Lady of the Forest.

Alas, the storm and the cold weather was followed by the torrential rain and a thaw, turning the old road into a mire from end to end. The always ingenious Acadian workmen devised a way to transport the coffin out to be buried at Weymouth. My grandmother's own ox drawn sleigh, which she had named her Chariot, and which she had used on her first trip to New France in 1895, and enjoyed so much over the next fourteen years, was made ready. The coffin was suspended high over the mud and the wet, resting on slings, tied between uprights fastened to the floor of the sleigh. Tied securely, it could swing gently over the bumps, the corduroy road and the swamps.

It was a sad, silent cortege that moved off on that wet and dreary March morning, as the last embers of the last fire in the fireplace of the chapel died away into white ash. Johnie-à-Marc, the faithful teamster of the Chariot ever since that first beautiful July day of 1895 when the lovely lady of forty-five arrived from France and trusted herself to his skill, now ever so carefully coaxed his oxen to a slow start on her last journey.

Immediately behind, the old broken hearted Alsatian had lost his erect military bearing, as he slumped into his saddle. The sons followed on their horses and in carriages. The daughters had to stay behind.

After a long three hours journey, they arrived at the Corner, where they were met by a horse drawn open hearse, and several wagons to take them the rest of the way to the cemetery just outside Weymouth, on the road to New France. The remains were sealed in a cement box so that they could be returned to France some day when her husband would return home.

In its issue of March 4th, 1910, the *Digby Corrier* wrote:

> "Report of death of Madame Stehelin at age sixty-one. Madame Stehelin's death is the first break in a large family, and her demise will be heard with sincere regret by a large circle of friends in St. John, Halifax and all over the Maritime provinces. Many notable people of three provinces have occasion to remember pleasant visits under the roof of their hospitable home. Besides

her husband, eight sons and three daughters survive. One daughter is the wife of Captain Kay. She was the heroine of a thrilling rescue at sea, several years ago, when Captain Kay, his wife and crew abandoned the Digby barque — *Florence B. Edgett*."

The Old Gentleman with his remaining five children tried to carry on, but it soon became only too clear that this big house could no longer be the happy home it had been. At times, it seemed cold and dreary. Life was without joy and laughter. It was becoming routine and dull. The home had lost its soul. The grandchildren had come from Church Point and stayed for the rest of the winter. They brought back some gaiety to the house which nevertheless seemed to be getting too big and too quiet.

During the month of April my grandfather decided to move out to Weymouth. He could not stand to live at New France alone any longer. When he came to Canada, he maintained his property of St. Charles, ready to be occupied again whenever he wished to return. When he left new France, the house remained furnished. He still hoped that at least one of his sons would settle in it and revive the old way of life.

In Weymouth, he rented the house just north of St. Thomas' Anglican Church. The furniture that had been brought from France, such as the family oak desk, and the Pleyel, were hauled to Weymouth. The office furniture and records were taken and an office was set up in one of the buildings owned by the family in Weymouth.

It was not more than three months after the funeral that the Old Gentleman, his remaining sons and daughters, each to his or her own meditation, looked for the last time at their home of the last fourteen years, years of happiness ending in cruel grief. One of the last painful acts had been to dispose of the flock of white pigeons in the loft at the top of the barn. Faithful General, getting older too, carried his master for the last time. The girls rode in the wagon, drawn by Kit, a young mare that was to serve the family for many years ahead. Two dogs, one of them the famous Major and an Irish Terrier frolicked and barked joyfully on the way.

It was a day full of sunshine, but after they turned the first corner in the old road, the silence of abandon descended upon New France, The Electric City. That night, there was only darkness and haunting stillness. No more electric lights, no more dogs barking, no more ox bells, no human being moving about the square. The mill was stilled forever and no more ringing song from the anvil in the forge. Deterioration began almost at once, along with vandalism that was soon to follow. It was not long before rumors spread of strange spirits wandering and rummaging about the empty place.

The flowers kept blooming every year around the houses. They were the last reminders of the years of work and joy there. The apple trees, nurtured with such care, continued to bear fruit until they too went wild. Ever so slowly, inch by inch, the forest moved towards the square, cutting off the view of Langford Lake, Casino Beach and Little Tusket Lake.

In Weymouth, a new way of life was beginning. There was a fairly large field between the verandah on the south side and the church below. There were a few cherry trees along the back line and a barn large enough for the two horses. Young Kit, harnessed to the old wagon, was the only conveyance back and forth to the woods. Dear General, getting old, was retired, spending his days in the sunny field and his nights well sheltered in the barn. His master, getting old too, never climbed into the saddle again. He seemed to spend most of his days sitting in the sun outside on the porch, reading, dozing, but always smoking the twenty cigarettes he had made for himself after breakfast. The girls spent time visiting old friends, making new ones and collecting new wardrobes from Eaton's catalogue. There were whist and bridge parties, garden parties and dances. Maybe they even thought of looking for husbands. Alas, Therese was already thirty-eight, but Simone was only a young twenty-five, healthy and fresh as a temple vestal, never having used make up. She was a much sought after bridge player.

Life was not the same. There were no more visitors passing through, or staying for a while. There were no more walks through the woods, along the rivers and lakes. The finer customs of living brought from the homeland and fostered with such care by a perfect hostess were not maintained with the same dedication. The busy life, yet full of peace and rest, was gone. The whole of New France had been like a healthy, vibrant, living place, almost human and everyone of the family and others who had known it, could not but feel that it should not be dying, abandoned.

If one believes in the evolution of matter towards life, as man knows it, then perhaps the founder had reached this perception. The mind influences matter, but his mind, that wrought New France out of the forest, that loved and nurtured it, as he would a creature, was not powerful enough to keep it growing and ensure its permanency. Man does not know when the matter he fashions has to die. And so as the years went by, New France was remembered in the way one remembers a friend gone into the beyond.

The hunters and the fishermen passed through with a certain respect for the past. But others were not so high minded and it was not long before the houses were broken into, furniture stolen, the electrical fixtures torn out and taken as souvenirs. The dynamo in the mill was taken apart for the miles of copper wire it was made of. The equipment in the barn and the forge gradually disappeared. Even the furnishings, bear rugs and religious objects were carted away from the little chapel.

Nothing could be done to curb this vandalism. Strangely enough, however, old New France found a protection of sorts, in the appearance of ghosts. Both white and black people, were very superstitious and terrified of spirits. At least the ghosts stopped some vandalism and squatting. As the stories spread, eventually no one would spend a night at or even near New France.

According to the stories circulated widely, there was a ghost in the old mill. When someone went into it to get some firewood, the ghost banged and rattled the saws and machinery still left about. The intruders ran away never to come near the settlement again. When trespassers would settle themselves in the house for the night, another ghost, or the same one, would scare them out of their sleep by banging the doors or slamming the lids of the big kitchen stove. One ghost was credited with rolling a big wheel from the railroad down the stairs in the middle of the night. They said these wheels weighed about four hundred pounds and sometimes they would be heard rolling on the roof or in the attic, making a terrific noise just like a train roaring by overhead. The strange thing about these disturbances was that sometimes perhaps only one or two men of a party of several would hear them. This ghost was a clever one too. He would let a party settle down for the night and when they were sound asleep, he would perform his deeds and scare people out of a sound sleep. Most decamped in the middle of the night and ran home, miles away, as fast as their legs could carry them, never daring even to look back in case the ghost was chasing them.

Of all the stories of weird happenings, undoubtedly the one that terrified people most, was the one about the Fiery Rider. Those who claimed to have seen him, and there were many, vowed never to return to the abandoned settlement.

The Fiery Rider always made his appearance at dusk and always went through the same routine. But let one man who saw him tell his story.

"The year in question, my friend and I went up to Fourth Lake on the Sissiboo River (hunting in the fall). On our way back, we arrived at New France as it was getting dark. We were quite tired and we sat down by the side of the road for a smoke and a chat. It was very quiet. One could never imagine that we were on what had been a few years ago one of the liveliest spots in Nova Scotia. I had seen sidewalks all lighted by electricity, the locomotive puffing into the village and light and music all over the place. For there, as you know, the old Stehelin gentleman and his large family lived. They were a lively bunch I can tell you. Now all was dark and silent. Just a few stars lighted the abandoned settlement.

All of a sudden, my companion tapped me on the shoulder. "Hear", he said, "Hear the bell", and sure enough, I could hear what sounded like a small church bell ringing as if calling people to prayer. I am certain there was no bell within hearing distance but I am sure I heard it plainly as it kept ringing. Then we heard a noise in the distance. It sounded like the galloping of a horse. Soon after, we could hear its hoofs pounding on the rocks in the road. The sound came nearer and nearer and suddenly at the turn of the road, out of the woods, we saw a horse coming at full speed mounted by a man. Arriving at the place where once had stood the little chapel, the horse stopped short, the man dismounted and the bell stopped ringing. Needless to say how scared we were. We did not move but we looked on. The horse was very large, jet black and it seemed that smoke and fire poured from his nostrils as he stood there motionless. The rider was a tall man, well over six feet, with long white hair and fiery eyes. He was dressed all in black and a light seemed to shine through his very body. In his belt, he carried a large glittering sword. As if gliding along rather then walking, he did not seem to touch the ground as he went towards the spot where the chapel had stood in days gone by. There he knelt and seemed to pray. My friend remarked, "He is not a devil because he prays". Motionless as we kept on looking, we noticed that the horse had no tail. After a few moments, the man stood up again and made a low bow. I thought he would break in two.

    Again, as if gliding on air, he went towards the old mansion. For a moment he looked at it, but to our surprise, he did not enter. Instead he went around to the old wine cellar at the back of the building. As he stood by the broken down door, he drew his sword that shone in the night, and then walked in. At that moment, we heard the most terrible noise human ears can hear. It was the noise of fighting in the cellar. We heard yells, the clashing of swords. This did not last long but it was terrifying to hear, then a long cry that ended this battle and everything became silent again. We waited a while but everything was quiet and after we quieted our nerves a bit, we went towards the cellar. We had flashlights and we went in. It smelled smoky and warm. There was a strong smell of rum which did not surprise me too much because I know many casks had been kept there in the old days. We looked around everywhere but saw no one. We got out rather quickly and went away as fast as we could. When we went by the site of the old chapel, the black horse had gone.

    When I think of what we saw on that cold fallish night I

still shiver. I have never been back there because for nothing in the world did I want to see that black horse and its fiery rider again." (*Digby Courier* Jan. 28 — 1954)

Of course, the business had to continue but now it would be managed from Weymouth. An office was set up in one of the family buildings. There was a general office and a smaller private office. Office furniture, books of accounts and records were brought out from New France and a safe was purchased locally.

This was a good time to reorganize the business, something my grandfather had decided to do some time before when the dispersal of so many sons had taken its toll and because he had to face his diminishing ability to control the operation. The four sons remaining with him (Charles, Louis, Paul, and Bernard) would have to assume greater responsibility. Thus the firm E. Stehelin and Company came into being. Perhaps he was even thinking of returning to live at St. Charles, once satisfied the enterprise was solidly set up.

Louis would be responsible for running the financial aspects of the enterprise; contracts, banking, and all such usual management tasks. He would also assist in operating the mill and arranging for the hauling of the lumber to the wharf.

Charles would be responsible for looking after the proper storage of the lumber on the wharf, for the loading of vessels, which included hiring stevedores and keeping a final tally upon loading.

Paul was given the two most important jobs; running the logging operation and the mill. Besides he was to make the hay and firewood, the fuel for two homes (the family home and Charles') and the office. This meant that he spent most working days in the woods, returning home for weekends, which in those days was Sunday only. Zozime was his trusted helper.

Bernard was to help at the office, purchase bulk stores and other supplies, and store them in the family building at Weymouth. He also did most of the shopping for the house.

The portable mill was moved as and when necessary in order to be always near a good supply of logs. They always built a comfortable little camp for themselves near the mill, eating at the men's cookhouse.

The mode of travel, summer and winter, was by wagon and sleigh. General having been retired, Kit was the only horse left for this task. Horseback riding to and fro was discontinued, chiefly because some supplies always had to be taken in.

The Old Gentleman never went back to New France nor visited the mill. Simone, with some friends, occupied the big house for holidays each summer. Therese never went back. To keep in touch with the business, however, he had the telephone installed in the house, the office and the little camp cum office by the mill.

The office was some distance from the new home, but my grandfather often, if not everyday, walked down the hill, across the bridge and looked over things. On those days, perhaps due to inclement weather, when he did not go out, the routine was well established; Bernard brought the mail to the house in the morning and in the afternoon. If Bernard was away, Josie made the trips to the office.

The economic boom and the resulting great demand for lumber of the early years of the new century had been due, in great part, to the international situation of the time; the Boer War, the troubles in China and Japan, the development in South America and the U.S.A., and the long established trade with the West Indies, Spain, Portgual and Britain. Small villages like Weymouth were able to participate in all these active markets because sailing ships, many of foreign flags, could dock there to take on cargoes for any destination in the world.

There was a significant slackening of the demand for lumber beginning in 1907. However, markets in the U.S.A., the West Indies and South America remained bouyant. But the export business became difficult due to the gradual disappearance of the sailing ships. Foreign vessels were the first ones to disappear and as the Canadian ones became scarcer, it was increasingly difficult to find some to charter.

Steamships were coming in fast, but they were too deep to come up rivers like the Sissiboo, making shipping very much more costly. Shipping by freight train from Weymouth for transhipment in Halifax was too expensive. The Government built a wharf at Weymouth (Weymouth North today) with sufficient depth of water to take fairly large ships, which helped materially. The demise of the pulp mill was due in great part to the too high freight costs.

Many smaller lumber exporters went out of business. The Stehelins, however, weathered these negative changes. They seemed to find sailing ships to charter and managed to still make a profit. The Advent of the First World War brought back, if only for its duration, the boom of former years. Schooners were being built again in every hamlet by the sea and they were back at Weymouth Bridge taking on lumber.

For the family, settling in Weymouth after having lived somewhat by themselves, away from daily social contacts with the various elements of a mixed community, was a new experience. From the beginning, however, they adapted very well. All of them embraced the new experience with much enthusiasm, and soon they were full partners in the life of the community. They all spoke English, especially Simone and Bernard, who were really more proficient in it than in French.

The first year of operation of the new Stehelin company went very well, and the four sons were much happier. They all became active in community activities; Bernard, because he had a good education, was asked to accept a Commission appointing him a Justice of the Peace. He accepted and with the aid of a few impressive statute books, supplied by the Government, performed useful legal services within the authority granted him. Charles became very active in the affairs of the I.O.O.F. Paul, however, never seemed to have enough spare time to participate extensively in anything. He was all work and business. In fact, in 1912, he and Emile Jean, at Church Point, purchased a portable saw mill and moving it about, took sawing contracts.

Louis quickly made friends with the elite of Weymouth and Digby, who were about his age. There was the dentist, the doctor, the lawyer, the druggist, sportsmen all, fishermen, hunters, and cricket players. In time, he involved himself in politics, and became a hard working Liberal supporter.

Very shortly after the move to Weymouth, Maurice was on his way to New York to visit Jean Jacques. He liked life in New York and decided he would stay. After a short apprenticeship in his brother's business, he set up his own factory making silk tassels, cords and passamentaries. He formed a partnership with a newly acquired friend and was in business under the firm name of Stehelin and Frankenbach. The business prospered and besides Maurice was having a grand time socially, being appointed President of the New York Yacht Club. When war broke out, he left his partner in charge and went to war. By the time war ended, he had new ideas and didn't return to the business. However, when he did return to Canada in 1953, he went looking for his old haunts everywhere, and in New York, he found his old partner, a millionaire now.

Paul and Bernard also visited New York, but after visiting Weymouth friends working in Boston and looking around, they were delighted to return home and stay there.

As much as the Stehelins assimilated into their new environment and enjoyed it, they did not however adopt the lifestyle of Canada in their home. The ways of life at New France was exactly what it had been at St. Charles and they liked it that way. Albeit, moving to Weymouth, there had to be some changes, but none would have wanted to give up their French cuisine, the wine with meals, their long evening dinners followed by the quiet time in the "salon" over black coffee, liqueurs, cigars and good reading. This explains perhaps why only two sons married in Canada, and why those others who did marry eventually, chose French wives in France.

ANOTHER WAR, ANOTHER BLOW

Life at Weymouth was very different than it had been at New France, St. Charles or Alsace, so mused my grandfather, as he sat on the verandah, in the shade of the hot afternoon sun. Gone were the receptions, the guests, the long family evenings filled with music, laughter and much discussion. The soul of the home, the mother, the companion, the organizer of home life was sorely missed. Therese was a good cook, when she had time, from her new social life in the village, to concentrate on it. Simone also was very busy outside the home. There was always a servant in the house, a faithful, cheerful Black woman, and a new acquisition; Josie Goldspring. Josie, about twenty-five years old at the time, was half-French, half-English, effeminate and a little simple minded.

In the sitting room, the old Pleyel was closed, never heard anymore. The many familiar chairs brought from France were around. On the table were fine kerosene lamps, with wide shades, but the bear rugs and moose skins had disappeared. There was only one moose head in the hall, used as a hat rack. The guns, used infrequently by Paul and Bernard, rested on their rack on the wall. The fishing rods, in their cases, stood nearly forgotten with the canes and the umbrellas in a stand in one corner of the hall. The stereoscope and its glass views, the magic lantern, the games, that had provided so much enjoyment on winter nights at New France were gathering dust in the attic. The once clean and polished saddles hung in the barn, abandoned and covered with dust. The presence of General, enjoying his retirement, seemed to be the only remaining link with the past. Every day, his old master visited him in the pasture to give him, one at a time, his four sugar cubes and a pat and a scratch here and there.

The Old Gentleman was lonely.

(Translation) 3 Dec. 1911

My Dear Mathilde:

Another year has passed, the same as the others, sad nearly discouraging which adds itself to other years without lightening their load.

At the first frosts, I slipped on the ice, fell and broke my left arm which inconveniences me a lot. The fracture is perfectly back in place but complete healing will be slow and I am limited in my activities as a result of this ridiculous accident.

I wish you a Good New Year, one that will bring some relief to your sorrows of all sorts and at least one during which God will give you courage and strength to support them. I kiss you with all my heart and I think of you often.

Emile

Business was not as buoyant as it had been in the days of the sailing ships and the markets of far away countries, which had taken great quantities of heavy timber, were nearly gone. Now the United States market for building lumber was the best outlet but it was a hard market because the Americans were hard dealers. They would not contract for delivery on ship or rail car. The only firm agreement was as to price per thousand board feet on their own tally once the shipment arrived at destination. The seller was at the complete mercy of the buyer.

Life in Weymouth Bridge was busy. The Green Lantern, the community hall, was pleasant, situated on the road to Sissiboo Falls, just behind Goodwin Hotel. All patriotic celebrations such as Victoria Day, Commemoration of the relief of Mafeking and, of course, Dominion Day, took place there. Suppers were served by the ladies and there were dances, concerts and plays. There were few holidays in the year, but all were celebrated as a community affair. There was always a parade in the morning with floats and a brass band and lots of flags and bunting hanging from houses, stores and telephone lines.

The coming of the year 1914 marked another turn in the history of the family. The year began on a worrisome note. Prosperous Germany under Kaiser William was rattling the sword. But in little Weymouth, so far away from Europe, certainly the only man who worried about it was the old Alsatian. He knew the Germans, and only too well did he remember and understand the greed and insane ambition of the "sale Boche". He recognized the drive of the old Teutonic dream of world domination. France, still struggling from her ruinous defeat in 1870 was no obstacle by herself, to German domination of occidental Europe. Russia would be pushed back into the east and Britain would be held at bay from the continent while its supremacy at sea would be taken from her. With the Balkans, Turkey and the colonies of England and France swept away, Germany would rule from the North Sea to the Persian Gulf. This was the dream of the whole German nation, solidly behind its Kaiser. War would be the industry of the whole nation. All classes, from the intellectuals to the workers were united and ready.

The French papers and magazines that arrived home could hardly disguise the anxiety of the French nation and its government. There was some bravado and cries in the streets of "La Revanche," but those who reflected knew very well that France was no match for Germany. Her fate would depend on the actions of the English, the Russians and perhaps the Americans.

All that was needed now was a pretext for the Germans to start the conflict. And it came on June 28th with the assassination of Francis Ferdinand, heir to the Àustrian throne, at Serajevo in the pocket kingdom of Serbia. That fatal shot reverberated even as far as the little home in Weymouth, where the significance of the event brought fearful certainty of impending disaster. The old veteran knew that the goosestepping hun would soon be on the move again over the frontiers of innocent victims.

The usual diplomatic routine took its course. Fearing that the crisis might be cooling with the passage of time, the Germans declared war on Russia on August 1st and on France on August 3rd. The Kaiser's plan was very simple. Crush

France quickly, then the Balkans and Turkey and finally take on Russia. But the unexpected happened to slow down the invader. Belgium defended herself heroically, England entered the war and France did better than had been expected and held her line of defence at a dreadful cost in human lives.

At Weymouth, to the Alsatian, this spelt the dashing of his hopes to return to St. Charles soon, and to his sons it spelt military service, from which he had tried so hard to shield them.

Within a few days of the declaration of war, mobilization orders from the French Consul in Halifax arrived. Roger left his ship and came home. Maurice couldn't wait to get going. With Charlie, Paul and Bernard, it meant five sons called out. My father was exempt from the French draft because he had seven children. Louis and Jean were exempt for health reasons.

It was with a heavy heart that the old father gathered his sons together, simply to tell them to do their duty towards France and England. As they were all naturalized Canadians, they had hoped to join the Canadian Army. Alas they soon were told by the Consul that they remained French citizens. France did not recognize their British status and should they fail to answer the call, they would be considered deserters, subject to serve punishment, even execution, should they ever set foot on French soil again, even as Canadian soldiers.

They were all concerned, as they thought over their situation. In the end, they mustered their courage and prepared to meet the order to be in New York by August 10th, to board the French troopship *Santa Anna*. There was little time even to say farewell to their friends. Bernard was very popular at the tailor shop, where some eight or ten nice girls worked. He brought them the sad news. There were humid eyes but pride too. He was a well bussed young man by the time he left.

On the day of departure, nine members of the family were gathered for a last dinner together. The proud but very sad old father presided over the conversation and he was listened to. In those days a father was not only respected but he was also loved and gladly obeyed, because a family had to have a head, and he had the wisdom of years of experience. The toasts were drunk with more thought and perhaps meditation than at other more merry times.

When it came time to go to the train, the old father took his cane and led the whole family down the road, the short distance to the station. When they arrived on the platform, they were surrounded by a large number of friends who had come to say "Au revoir — safe journey — and come home safely". Flags were flying and the children carried their ubiquitous Union Jacks. This was the first of many such demonstrations as subsequent groups of Weymouth boys gathered at the station, going away to war. The old village and its surrounding area gave over four hundred brave soldiers to the cause, many never to return, today lying in the beautiful Canadian cemeteries in France.

The whistle of the approaching three o'clock train to Yarmouth was heard and the time was here to say the last farewell. The old gentleman gathered his sons closer to him and giving them his fatherly blessing, a cross on each forehead, and a kiss on each cheek, with his last words, "God be with you. You know where your duty lies, be sure you fulfill it well". The train was there and Charles, Paul, Roger, Maurice and Bernard climbed aboard and from the open windows of the coach waved and waved as the train moved off. They would take the Boston boat and be on time at the rendez vous with the ship carrying repatriates to war service, to the hard life of the French Poilu, to receive in pay, one franc per day.

The Old Gentleman wended his way back home, on the arm of Louis, the only son remaining with him. On the porch, in the setting August sun, father and son sat in silence, each to his own thoughts. Now began the long vigil. It would be filled with anxiety and constant apprehension over the fate of loved ones in battle. It would not be easy to stay there and just wait, pray and hope. Within the next three weeks, the same scene at the station was repeated. Six Campbell boys left for service to "Flag and Country." There were two proud fathers in Weymouth, even if worried and sad.

The long day closed with a quiet meal, with only three children left around the table. In the dim light, there was little talk, everyone sensing that a new page was coming up in the destiny of the old family.

Life in the village soon began to change and its tempo accelerated very quickly. Suddenly there was a brisk demand for lumber of all types, as training camps were being built and the export market increased its demands. The ship building industry suddenly sprang into being again, all over the Maritimes. Within a radius of ten miles of Weymouth, nearly ten yards were abuilding as fast as they could. In Weymouth itself at least two vessels were on the stocks year round. The launching was an occasion for celebration. The ship was decked with flags and bunting. Large crowds gathered and at high tide, workmen knocked at the last wedge whilst at the bow, a lady, usually the owner's wife or daughter, cracked the traditional bottle of Champagne, decorated with colourful flowing red, white and blue ribbons. At the same time, the Godmother named the ship. Shouts went up from the crowd as the vessel started on her way along the slipway, then crashed into the water, righted herself and was towed away to a nearby wharf.

Wages and prices were going up. Carpenters working at the shipyards earned up to three dollars per day and a boss or foreman, five dollars. A barrel of flour cost five dollars now. Master Workman pipe tobacco cost fifteen cents a plug and Napoleon chewing tobacco ten cents a plug. Fruitatives went up to twenty-five cents for a little bottle. These little red pills were advertised as the "deadly enemy of constipation".

The family lumber business took on new impetus. The newly built schooners were back at the wharves, taking on lumber. Louis became the sole manager and operator of the business. Only one sawmill was operated but working longer hours, it could produce all that was needed.

For my grandfather, it was a life of thinking and waiting for hopefully better news. His homeland, far away, once again was cruelly afflicted, its cities devastated and the flower of its youth mown down by superior enemy machine guns. Within his heart, the spirit of revenge for his lost Alsace was very much alive and he hoped that soon he would not have to pay yearly land taxes to the Germans. He prayed that this was the dawn of La Revanche. He lived by himself and every day he looked for the papers and then regularly the magazines, *L'Illustration* and other papers from France. Letters from his sons were few. Sometimes the only news came on a field post card. There was no radio but the Western Union Telegraph office was just down the road from the house. It was in the old Hogan house, just above the railway track. Twice a day, and more often if some important news came over the ticker, bulletins were posted in the window for people to come and read. A long bench was provided outside under the window for people to sit and wait, or just pass a bit of time talking with a friend, also there for the news. My grandfather, with his dog and his cane, went down at least once every day. At home, he kept a situation map up to date. He had some worrisome days when the German Army was advancing into France at an alarming pace. At one time it looked possible for the enemy to take even his St. Charles.

In the midst of all this sudden prosperity, people were beginning to enjoy life but the manpower requirement of Canada's war effort was felt among the young. Men were needed for the services and recruiting drives were constant reminders of one's duty. Many young men volunteered but as the casualty lists started coming home, and with life so good, fewer men were joining up and the new word "slacker" began to be heard.

In Weymouth, like in all towns and villages in Canada, a great wave of patriotism permeated the very life of the community. There was the Khaki Fund, which raised money for comforts for the "boys at the Front." It was the same old routine of working hard for a few dollars, pie socials, dinners, suppers, selling flags and red, white and blue home made lapel rosettes. The ladies knitted socks and other articles. There was the Red Cross of course and the Purple Feather fund for the wounded. The Khaki Wedding was very touching too, a boy in uniform getting married before leaving for overseas. There was the patriotic society of the King's Sons and Daughters which busied itself in some area of the war effort.

When a draft of recruits was to leave the village, there was always a big supper and party at the hall called "The Farewell to Our Boys," followed by the send off at the train the next day. But it was the same people who belonged to all these groups. The same women who cooked, sewed, knitted and danced, the same mothers and children who waved the flags. Sometimes casulty lists were part of these events. They were public news and the names were read out in the churches and written up in the *Digby Courrier* too.

But there was time for many other social activities. Auction bridge was becoming the craze. The railway put on an excursion train between Halifax and Yarmouth, now that people had money to spend on travel. As a result, the honeymoon took on new dimensions. Newlyweds could now go to Yarmouth or Digby for a day's honeymoon. Sometimes they could afford Halifax and a night there too.

Paul, Roger, Maurice and Bernard were raw recruits, having come to Canada before reaching the age of compulsory service. They did their training with the infantry regiment of Normandy and stayed with it until the First Canadian Division arrived in France. Because they spoke English, had lived in Canada, and were British subjects, they were posted to the Canadian Divisional Artillery as interpreters in the rank of non-commissioned officers. They worked mostly at brigade and regimental headquarters. They were very happy to meet fellow Canadians again, some from near Weymouth, Bear River and Yarmouth.

In 1915, news arrived that Roger had been wounded. A few weeks later, news arrived that he had won the Military Medal. In June of that year, a letter Charlie wrote to his friend in Digby, Sheriff Smith, made the *Digby Courier*.

May 4, 1915 — East of Ypres, in a dugout; weather favourable after night's rain. Address: Charles Stehelin, I Brigade C.F.A. I Can. Div., France.

My Dear Harry,

Some time since I gave you any news from the Front. The accomodation is really so poor that it is almost impossible to put two ideas together. I will try anyway. Since the 22nd Ult. when we were called in a hurry to take positions here, I am in the thickest of the battle, what the papers will probably call the second battle of the Yser. Not being a pen artist, I do not know how to go at it to give you an idea of our situation. Anyway my residence is two feet wide and four feet deep, dug in the bank of the Yser Canal facing west. I am in an observation post with my colonel and staff of I Brigade, C.F.A. The German trenches are 1500 yards in front of us. We can see them plainly with the glasses. Our guns are one mile behind us and we simply direct the shots from here by phone. It makes me think of Salmon River banks full of rabbit holes with soldiers in them, French, Belgian, Algerians, kilts and Indians, quite a mixture as you can see. From my hole on one side, the devastated country toward France, with horses dead in the fields, cattle roaming around pigs hung to trees by soldiers, wagons smashed, corpses rotting, farms burning, prisoners going by, wounded men straggling along, all the worst pictures at the worst corner of the worst battle still going on. If I turn east and peep above the canal towards the German trenches, I see the backs of the French troops lying down in their holes waiting to attack. If I look up, I am sure to see a few aeroplanes flying around. If they show the black cross on the wings, I take my Lee-Enfield and pop at them. We downed one yesterday. Here I am sitting on some straw with my rifle on one side and my water bottle on the other, thinking of dear Nova Scotia, home, friends, etc. Down hearted? No not a bit of it. But it is simply terrible, Harry. That is for the scenery. What are we doing you will ask. There are about 700 guns, French and English in the vicinity. Last Sunday I counted over 500 shots in five minutes and that goes on all day and sometimes all night. It is hard on the nerves the first day, after that you don't mind them. These are the shots going east. Well east too — for those that came from there, you need a little caution because they are made to hit you. But you hear them coming and down you go until they pass. The rifle shots are worse, they seem to come swifter. So far I have dodged them all, but we have casualties every day. A nice young officer yesterday morning. I shook hands with him. He went up to the trench, two minutes after, shrapnell got him. He is buried nearby; can see his cross from here.

You will ask me; what about the war? Harry, we don't know anything at all, except that we are fighting to hold our ground and go ahead as soon as we can, no papers, no letters, nothing — we are lost to the world, with the only consolation that our friends might think of us once in a while. It is no use to think of the splendid work of the Canadians. The papers have said all about it, but not enough yet, because it has been splendid. I saw them going up the trenches singing and laughing, mowed down by hundreds, still going on. It is something one can never forget and that makes me proud to be a Canadian. Anyone will say "I was at Ypres", that is enough for me. Since we have been here we have to repulse attack and attack ourselves every day. Today is the 4th day of May, yesterday we were quiet. It commences now again. The French 75 is snapping and our 15 pounders making the base. Rifle fire commences from the other side of the canal but happily we don't see any gas. The 22nd when the Germans surprised us with their gas they raised simply hell. It was the first time they had used it, but now we know better. Last Sunday they tried the same game but got badly left. About 4 p.m. we saw a big green cloud over the trenches. They had thrown the gas onto us. Our chaps simply fell back to the next trench and waited for them with Maxime guns and the whole outfit and when they came down, it was simply slaughter. The German bodies were piled four feet high. The French did not make any prisoners, except the ones they had not time to kill. It is getting pretty hot, Harry.

I had to stop to go with some French officers to reconoitre positions. I came back safe anyway, but have lost the thread of my letter. I think it is better for you, Harry, so I will close for this time by just saying this: It is an awful war. It will take a long time to finish it. The Germans are strong, have lots of ammunition and if their spirit is down, they go just the same like machines. We found some tied to their guns so they could not go back. It will take, unfortunately, the best of the English, Canadian, French and Belgian blood to get hold of that D. Kaiser. Let's hope that we will fix him in a proper manner so he will not be able to do any more harm. We are not to the end of our sacrifice. The boys at home must be ready to do even a little more. Those out here are alright. They prove themselves to be thoroughbred, every one of them. I feel proud and full of confidence until the happy day of return. Give my regards to those who inquire of me. Write occasionally, Harry. I have not had any letters from home for the last two months. Tell me the news and where the boys from Digby are.

Sincerely,

Charles Stehelin"

Charles was forty-three years old when he wrote this letter, a bit old to be in the trenches, but that was French law. If a man had no children, he was liable for service up to sixty years of age. The number of children he had determined when he was called to serve.

Charlie enjoyed moments of the war too, when he could get away on leave or be assigned to some special task, which took him back into the world. One duty he enjoyed particularly was to be asked by his Brigadier General to go out and forage for food and wine, for special occasions. He also liked the theatrical and one day he returned from a foraging expedition at a gallop, on a beautiful horse, leading a magnificent landau, drawn by a span of horses — driven by his batman. It was loaded with wines, champagne and the best variety of fine foods the farms behind the lines could produce. During his absence, however, the front line had moved back and suddenly he found himself in no-man's land. The Germans, probably bewildered by the sight, did not fire at him and he wheeled around and returned safely to his lines. Needless to say, Charlie was a hero that day.

Maurice led a charmed life, until one day in 1916 when he was wounded and sent to hospital. He took this just as another adventure and settled down to enjoy it. At thirty-two years of age when he was called to the colours, he had already learnt to get around in this world and get as much out of it as possible.

In 1915, Emile Jean, the sixth son to don the uniform, received his order of march from the French Consulate in Halifax, his exemption having expired. He reported to the transport officer in Yarmouth. He was then forty-five years old. While in Yarmouth, a telephone call came from Headquarters Military District 6 in Halifax, passing a message from the French Consul, advising that it was all a mistake, that as father of seven children, he was not a conscript. To that was added the suggestion that he could join the Canadians, and land in France without incurring problems with the French Government. Because he had done his military service in France and had been discharged to the reserve as an officer, he was offered a commission at once. He underwent training in Halifax, served with an infantry unit, but was soon posted to the Acadian Battalion, the 165th. The Regiment was recruited to strength and in due time, he commanded a company at St. John, New Brunswick. It was not until 1917 that he sailed with the Regiment for England, thence to France where the unit was broken up, most of the companies going as separate units to the Forestry Corps. He spent the rest of the war in the south of France running a logging and sawmill operation in the magnificent pine forest of Les Landes.

My grandfather had few friends left and visitors were rare. Contact with the College at Church Point, still run by the good Breton Eudists were few. It was not the same since his friend Father Blanche had left. Besides, the war had brought a little coolness, because some of the younger French Fathers, of military age, had not answered the call to the colours. They were in the same position as his sons and any other born Frenchman, whether naturalized or not. They were, in law, deserters, and he called them just that.

Going along the road, a passerby knew when a man from a house was at the Front. A special flag flew from the mast below the Union Jack or from a short pole extending out from an upstairs window. This pennant was about 28 inches wide by about fifty inches long. A white field about twenty-six inches by thirty inches was surrounded by a red border about eight inches wide. In the white field were blue maple leaves, each one representing a member of that family serving in the war. The Old Gentleman's had six maple leaves and he displayed them very proudly.

From the age of five years, I gradually began to form

impressions about my grandfather and his home. We loved him because he was kind, gentle and loved us. When my father joined the Army, he sold his horse which left us dependent on the train to go to Weymouth. We went up on the morning train and returned home on the afternoon one, which gave us a few hours with him. We rarely stayed overnight. If Grandfather asked us to stay over when we were alone with him, we were to refuse, lest we be accused of having asked him to stay on. If he invited us when the aunts were present, then we could accept.

The dinners, I remember, were sumptuous — roast beef, or chicken or ham every day, while at home we only had these viands on Sundays. There was always wine on the table, one bottle to be shared between two people. The desserts were always delicious. The Black servant woman did most of the cooking, and all the waiting on the table, besides the usual housekeeping work. Josie was busy cleaning up in the kitchen. This Black woman was very wonderful to us. She was always cheerful, warm and spoiling us when she had a chance. I remember how much I liked having her put me to bed at night. She must have been a wonderful mother. My grandfather never set foot in the kitchen, but he knew by the noises emanating from it when something was going wrong. I remember one day, from the living room, one could hear the slamming of pots and pans and my grandfather, saying to himself, but I heard it, "tempers again, the bills must be high this month."

After dinner, the Black servant brought the coffee and the little rum carafe to the living room. My grandfather would put a sugar cube on his spoon, dip it in the black coffee, then into the rum, and give it to me. To us, very young children, all this added up to dream living.

For the aunts and uncle Louis, this was living at ease and in comfort, with a social life that seemed to take them out of the house, afternoons and evenings. Louis had a fine Chevrolet coupe which cost the then large sum of nearly seven hundred dollars. The aunts got fifty dollars a month each, and Louis one hundred, all found, all their bills paid.

As for my grandfather, he adhered to his old way of life. I doubt if he ever got into the car. Alone through many long hours, in his solitude, I can now sense that his mind must have wandered far away, into the past. No doubt he must have wondered if he would ever see St. Charles and his beloved Alsace again.

At the beginning of the war, he had thought it looked much like 1870 all over again. Paris was threatened and saved only by the brave service of the Paris taxi drivers who rushed the soldiers to the breaking line. Gisors was even in danger of being shelled. Contacts with his friends in France were sad. They were loosing their sons. His own sons wrote that they had visited the old home and described how it remained as the day he had left it. All this made him think of the family life, the social life of those past civil, if worrisome, days. The old cathedral, also in danger now, had been not only a place of worship, but also the place where the deeds of valour in the wars of the motherland were enshrined. Stained glass windows and private little altars had been erected to the memory of officers fallen in battle. Families were very proud and consoled when they read such epithaphs as: "Bon sang ne peut mentir" (Good blood cannot lie). The bishop was an aristocrat, the Comte de Meaux, and he presided with all the dignity of the old days at the Court of Versailles. And there was the canoness, the Comtesse de Brye, a lady with the dress and manners of the Old Court too. One of her functions was to take up the offering at high mass on an open silver plate. She moved with great dignity on the arm of the Suisse and made a perfect curtsy to some gentlemen. If she didn't curtsy, every one knew the offering had been very unworthy of her favour.

And this made him think of faithful Ringback. He had been with him in the war of 1870 and had come to Gisors with him. The Old Gentleman thought how proud of his Ringback he had been when he performed as the Suisse (Master of Ceremonies). He even felt it had been an honour to himself and the family. Ringback, in his splendid uniform, feathered cocked hat, blue azure jacket, red trousers and silver buckled shoes, carrying his sword and halberd, preceded the Bishop and served the Canoness in the carrying out of her many functions. He had a particularly important role to play on St. Hubert's day, November 3rd, the day the hunt opened. The hunters came to church wearing their colourful hunting gear and the ladies their hunting habits. The ladies did not ride in the hunt but participated by meeting the hunters at specified places in the field with baskets of food and champagne. Thus in church, in an atmosphere of pomp, social niceties, the barking of the dogs and the sounding of the hunting horns, the chasse à courre was blessed and set on its way, to run all day and in the late afternoon end up at some chateau to feast and make merry all night. O tempore O mores.

All these memories came to him, as he sat looking at the recently received photograph of his five sons in uniform and on horseback, taken in the garden at St. Charles, where they had spent a leave. They didn't tell him they had found the wine cellar bricked over and how they had discussed at length whether they would force it and how they had finally agreed they would not break into it. They knew their father in Weymouth had the key to the inner door.

As he dozed away in his chair, I can still see his peaceful and serene countenance. His hopes must have been nourished by his pride and strong faith in victory and the safe return of his sons.

When Charles, Paul and Bernard left for war service, hopefully to return at war's end to rejoin the family and the business, Louis took over the entire responsibility for its continued operations. The prosperity of the older days returned very quickly and he somehow had to cope alone.

Louis worked hard, more than fully occupied looking after production, selling and running the home. The Old Gentleman was increasingly inactive in the business. A trip to the mill or the logging operation and back took a long day, from day-break to late evening. Sometimes Louis slept overnight in the cabin by the mill or at New France if he had to go there for some reason. When he got his car, travel in the winter over the well packed snow, was a pleasure indeed, taking less than an hour each way.

But it was not all hard work for Louis. He still found time to visit newly made friends in St. John and partake of the social life in Weymouth. He was very popular indeed, always the impeccably turned out gallant and fun loving very eligible bachelor.

During the war, he built himself a very comfortable and quite spacious camp at the foot of Langford Lake, well situated for fishing in the well stocked dead waters of the Silver River, and for hunting in the low country across the lake. Every spring the same party, he and his special friends went fishing, and every fall, they went moose hunting. They were a happy, jolly group and they did things well, served by a guide and a cook, and supplied with the best wines and spirits available in those days of supposed prohibition.

Gradually, Louis ran the home, perhaps involving himself in too much detail. Neither sister was about to let the other become the boss. There was the hiring of the servants, keeping Josie happy, untangling little family problems, doing the daily shopping, a job not done by ladies in those days, and being at the beck and call of his father.

We at Church Point saw very little of Uncle Louis during the war when we visited Grandfather. He always seemed to be away and when he came home for late dinner, it was near our bedtime.

SOLDIERS REUNION

During the month of October, 1916, the home at Weymouth was thrown into great excitement and joy. News arrived that the five sons would be granted a furlough to come home early in 1917. They would have three weeks with their father, after which they would return to the Front.

The Old Gentleman seemed to spring into that great directing activity of former years, as he took charge of preparations and gave instructions to his daughters and to Louis. The Present house was much too small. When they had moved into it in 1910, the family had shrunk and the visits of those away were always spaced. Now they would all be there at one time, like in the olden days at New France. He rented the big house on the south side of St. Thomas Church which belonged to Dr. Elderkin and was known as Black's Hotel. It needed a lot of repairs, which were undertaken at once. The family moved in on December 1, 1916, on a three years lease. Germaine came home for Christmas and stayed on to help get the house ready. Jean came in January and it was arranged that both would return when the brothers were home.

February 7, 1917 was indeed a day of great celebration in Weymouth. At the station, there was a large gathering to welcome the five brothers as they stepped down from the Digby train at three o'clock. The proud old father was there and the band played the family and a large following home. It would be impossible to describe the emotion and the joy of the old Alsatian, who knew what it was to be a soldier. He kissed each one on both cheeks and walked home with them, at a smarter step than usual, head high and proud blue eyes that lightened his face. He had suffered, he had prayed, he had waited, while his sons had done their duty, as he had done in seventy.

That night, there was celebration and talking way into the night. Even though the country was dry under the prohibition law, good wines and champagne were available, and of course, a barrel of rum was ready as it always had been at New France.

The five brothers had come via New York and St. John. Their brother, Emile, was then at St. John doing garrison duty with his regiment, the 165th. There they met him and spent one night together, waiting for the next day's boat to Digby. The officers' mess gave a dinner in their honour and that evening, they were invited to a performance of H.M.S. Pinafore, by the ladies of the Red Cross. Seeing Charlie in his fine uniform, someone suggested that he be made the subject of a living tableau, "The French Poilu" at the end of the performance. As the curtain slowly rose, there was Charlie standing in a huge gilt frame, resplendant in the dress uniform of the 14th Hussars, immobile, facing slightly to one side. His uniform was the blue horizon of the French Army. He wore a red képie with silver braid and on the back of his shoulder hung loosely the dark blue cape, lined in red. The French tricolour and the Union Jack hung motionless, one on each side of the frame. There was complete silence for a few seconds until the orchestra struck up La Marseillaise, when the audience rose and sang the anthem and then God Save the King. Charlie was so taken with emotion that, as the curtain started to come down, with tears in his eyes, he grabbed the two flags in his arms, as the ladies rushed to hug and kiss him. The old Palace Theatre probably never again witnessed such a patriotic display.

Paul, Roger and Bernard spent a quiet time at home with their father. They appeared at a few recruiting rallies, visited friends and visited with some nostalgia, the old home at New France. Bernard was a hero with his ladies at the tailor shop. Roger took a quick trip to New York on business and Germaine and Jean were home. The soldier sons had to talk about their experiences, the battles they had been in, such as the Retreat from Mons, the Marne, the Somme, and of course, the near fall of Paris. People in Canada had not felt the war and it seemed news to them that in France food was scarce, utilities were restricted and families in battle area had lost everything and become refugees.

Charlie travelled about more and his war stories created great interest. He had brought back a German officer's dress helmet, taken from a dead Boche. Made of black hard leather surmounted by a gilt spike, it had a gilt chain chin band, and mounted on the front a bronze eagle with wings outstretched, it carried the motto: "Mit Gott Fur Koenig unt Vater Land". It was on display as a recruiting aid in stores and halls along the shore from Yarmouth to Digby. Charlie was driven up and down, being well received everywhere along the way, always offered a glass of "something".

Maurice was not to be outdone, and he soon set himself up as the super spy catcher. His imagination invented an idea and his intelligence worked out the plan to carry it out very thoroughly. There were no policemen in those days, so he had the field all to himself. He found a few willing helpers among his friends, and he went to work having a good time in his own way. First thing was to set up a trap for spies who travelled only at night. The narrow Weymouth bridge was the ideal place for such a trap. After dark barbed wire was stretched across the bridge and cars were stopped and the occupants questioned at the point of a revolver in the hands of the French officer, charged by the Canadian Army to catch spies, known to be operating in the area. During the mornings, well placed secret information would leak the tale that the night before Lieut. Stehelin had caught one, two or three spies, who had landed from a submarine and had sneaked into these parts from St. John. What had happened to them at the hands of Maurice was a deadly secret. One can imagine the rumours. Maybe Maurice had shot them, because he always carried his revolver.

The job he had invented for himself gave him certain privileges too. He could commandeer cars, anybody's car, to chase spies, set up barricades, search cars. But the population got their thrills too. They would be treated to a real spy chase when a car would roar past in a cloud of dust, going at full speed, with Maurice leaning out the side with his revolver at the ready, to shoot a spy who was supposedly in a car, just a few miles ahead. Some simple people were awed at such bravery and the old women prayed and crossed themselves for the safety of that brave Maurice.

One might wonder what his father thought of all this. Probably he was not too concerned, as he had seen many such fanciful activities on Momo's part ever since he was a child. All his sons had a streak of the "fantaisiste" (whimsical) in their make up, which was not surprising, considering that they had been brought up in an age of chivalry. Their minds had been fashioned to some extent by stories, like the one that was often told, of the count of some noble leniage who, in the middle of a duel over the honour of a lady, had stopped the engagement to drink a toast in champagne to her with his adversary. Then there was the wonderful story of the bravery of Kaiser, a worker at the family felt factory. As a very young man, he had been a trumpeter in the Guard at Crimea. He had been wounded at the battle of "Mamelon Vert" (Green Hill), in the following circumstances. One day it seemed that the troops were hesitating to go over the top and charge the enemy lines. Brave Kaiser mounted the parapet, took his pants down and with his backside to the enemy, blew the "attack". The troops jumped over the top and charged the Russians with such spirit that they carried the day and turned the whole course of the battle. As for poor Kaiser, the Russians, having been highly insulted by his action, let him have some steel in the posterior. But all ended gloriously when Kaiser was decorated with the Grande Croix for exceptional bravery.

My grandfathe was indeed a happy man. Not only did he have his sons around him, but news from the war fronts had been particularly good lately. The French Army, led by Marshal Petain, had at last taken the offensive and was moving into stolen Alsace. For forty years, he had paid taxes to the hated Boche and now at last he sent his cheque to the French city of Than with a very moving letter which was placed in the public archives of that city. He was so happy that he began to make plans to return to St. Charles and Alsace after final victory, which could not be too long delayed, especially since it looked as though the Americans were on the verge of joining the Allies on the battlefields of Europe. Indeed, he said he was the happiest man in the world.

During my uncles' furlough, I visited at the new home with my brother and sisters. Uncles Lolo and Momo wore resplendent uniforms compared to the drab field dress of Uncles Paul, Roger and Bernard. What I remember most clearly were the interminable discussions at the table. Once again my grandfather had a participating audience. The names of the politicians and the generals were bandied about in the discussions about the war and the state of the governments of the Allies. Clemenceau, the Tiger, was the greatest hero of them all. There was news of the sufferings and misfortunes of old family friends. News of St. Charles and of the few old servants looking after the property. The talk concerning the return to peace after victory seemed to develop on the assumption that the family business would return to its pre-war status.

The home leave ended and the soldier sons returned to their respective units in France. There was not the gnawing worry and fear that they had all experienced at the parting in 1914. Victory was assured now, and with God's help, they would return again. There was a fine crowd at the station to wave the five brothers off once again. Their father, as in 1914, accompanied them to the station but he had returned to the house much happier and very hopeful, proud to be a British subject, whilst still a Frenchman.

Life returned to its quieter pace. The new house was much too large now, but it was comfortable. There was a wide verandah and sun porch with a view down as far as the Goodwin Hotel and the activities around the railway track at the top of the hill. It was a shorter walk to the Western Union now, and at night the fireplace was a real comfort, a reminder of happy evenings at New France.

In 1917, the famous Military Service Act was passed. The coalition government eventually lost power over it, and those liberals who had joined it were thrown into oblivion by their own party. The Act required every male citizen between the ages of 20 and 34 to report for examination and service, if medically fit. Exemption Boards were set up in every town to grant certificates of exemption in certain cases defined by law.

In the Weymouth area, generally the young men had responded well to the call for voluntary enlistment. However, many had no intention of going to war, and set about to circumvent this law. The first step was to try to be boarded out by the medical examiner. If this failed, other ways were tried and the final act was to run away, sometimes in the woods, and hide. Unfortunately, for some, this method was not too successful because at about that time the flu epidemic, that killed thousands, was raging in the area like everywhere else, and it was very risky to be attacked by the disease while hiding in the woods. A few died in lonely cabins which scared others.

The most encouraging event of the time was the entry of the United States in the war. It had been hoped for, and seen coming for some time, but the declaration of war gave the conclusive boost to the hard pressed Allies. It was not long afterwards that news came that Roger had been requested by the Americans. An American citizen, now a Captain in the American Navy, he was put in command of the port of Bassens. He remained in that position for the rest of the war with a terrific jump in pay.

Another piece of unexpected news reached Weymouth in that summer of 1917. It was a telegram from Maurice informing that he was coming home on convalescence leave.

At first he was very happy to be home, and what was rather unusual, quiet and satisfied to sit with his father and talk. He must have felt off colour indeed, but he stayed on a diet and sucked his two eggs per day diligently.

After a while, time began to hang heavy, but as always his fortunes were about to turn once again, very favourably indeed. A telegram from military headquarters in Halifax cheered him up, bringing as it did a possible release from the already dull life at home. It ordered him to report for a medical examination, and if found fit, undertake secondary military duties. He would be posted to a recruiting mission in the United States. Momo was overjoyed when the doctor declared him fit for the job. He knew he had landed on a good thing, and within a week, in his best military attire, he reported to the British-Canadian Recruiting Mission in Boston.

The Mission had an organization of about thirty British and Canadian officers and non-commissioned officers, who had been invalided from the fighting zone. Its function was to recruit British and Canadian citizens, or former citizens living in New England. There were many Acadians and French Canadians in that area, which explains, perhaps, the reason it was felt Maurice would be a good man for the job.

The Mission soon became well known, very popular and esteemed. Maurice, in his little jurisdiction, was doing well and having a good time as well. He was often invited to speak and he became a drawing card to swell attendance at all sorts of meetings. He talked exclusively of the war in France, the heroic deeds, the hardships and the good times here and there, in the life of a soldier. At that particular time there was much concern about German atrocities inflicted upon civilians, especially women and children. Stories about the terrible poison gas warfare always moved people very deeply and made them hate the Hun or the Boche. Stories about spying worried people because even in the United States, no one was safe from this unseen menace. For all these reasons, young men were invited to enlist and go over to support their brothers who had borne the brunt for three years.

Besides the stories of their own experiences, the men of the Mission used all the props they could get. They had lots of captured enemy equipment, helmets, rifles, bayonets and uniforms. Maurice drew loud applause when, at the end of a speech, well warmed up to his subject and with great anger, he would spit on a German helmet. They also showed allied equipment and they had a pipe band in full regalia. Later on they got a Britania, the first British tank that surprised the Germans.

The Mission was a success. Thousands of Americans had enlisted in the Canadian Army before the United States entered the war. Many citizens of Britain and Canada returned and enlisted in their respective armies. They even got together and sent to France, a contingent of women. They were the Telephone Girls, consisting of Acadians, French Canadians and French girls.

Early in 1918, Maurice was posted back to France, at Divisional Headquarters of the Canadian Artillery where he finished the war.

At Weymouth, the family lived well and seemed to enjoy the social life of the village to the full. However, as the spring of 1918 approached, the health of my grandfather seemed to decline perceptibly, but he kept on doing the same things he had always done, including his daily trips to the Western Union. As summer came, it was apparent that he was not well. His condition deteriorated, and in his diary, he complained of the bitter medicine prescribed by the doctor. The family away from home were not informed, neither were the grandchildren living only seven miles away. It was, therefore, a terrible shock to all, and especially the grandchildren, to be informed on the 8th of August, that Grandfather had passed away that day. He had not been spared to rejoice over the end of the war and victory. Before he died, however, he could foresee the defeat of the Boche and the return of Alsace to France. Finally the Revanche for which Frenchmen had hoped and prayed for since the defeat of 1870 was at hand. He had visions of airplanes overhead, flying, he said, to the last battle of liberation.

At near eight years of age, the shock was a deep traumatic experience to me. My mother hired a car and we were in Weymouth within hours. There was our beloved grandfather, on his bed in his room, fully dressed, a peaceful expression on his stilled features, his old rosary entwined in his very white fingers. On the wall above his head hung his flag with six maple leaves and along the side wall hung the large picture of his sons at war. Flowers were laid around his head, and a lonely lit candle, on a table at his side, seemed to keep the last vigil.

The funeral was early in the morning. My brother Mitt and I walked with Uncle Louis immediately behind the hearse to the church and after mass, to the cemetery nearly a mile on the New France road. Behind us came Uncle Jean and the Aunts in the family horse and wagon. Behind them came our mother and my two sisters and finally a long procession of men, women, and children, many of them Blacks.

The Digby Courier, in its issue of August 23rd, concluded the obituary in these terms, "The late Mr. Stehelin was the soul of business honour. The high esteem in which he was held by the residents of Weymouth was evinced at his burial, by all classes of the community."

There remained New France and St. Charles. What would become to these lands that had been so carefully looked after and cherished by the father of eleven children?

NEW FRANCE FADES INTO LEGEND

The war did end very shortly after the death of my grandfather. In Weymouth, like in every city, town and hamlet of Canada, there was great rejoicing and celebration. The reaction was spontaneous. There were bonfires, parades, and Thanksgiving services, in the churches and outdoors. Church bells rang out long and loudly and the whistles blew, from the sawmills, the ships and the locomotives. Everyone who owned a gun, or a rifle, was outside blasting off in the sky. One sport was to set up an effigy of the Kaiser and invite one and all to fire their guns at it, after which, doused with kerosene, it was set alight to the shouting and claping of the populace. Some of the more ardently patriotic went out at night with their guns and blasted at the chimneys at the homes of "slackers".

It seemed that every day there was a welcoming party at the station to meet heroes coming home. At intervals, there were suppers at the Green Lantern to "Honour our Heroes". The villagers turned out, and lined the road, for their soldiers who, in uniform, marched to the hall behind the band in military style and in perfect step.

Paul was the first of the Stehelins to return, early in 1919. He was very anxious to get the family business going again. However, nothing could be done until the estate was settled. He lived at the family home, with Louis, Therese and Simone. He busied himself at New France, doing the hay, and making repairs to the buildings.

Settlement of the estate had to await the return of Emile, who being the eldest, would be required to take out Administration. At the end of the war, he had been loaned to the French Government, to cruise timberlands on the Atlas Mountains and help the Regie Morocaine prepare a plan for their exploitation. He returned to Canada in late summer of 1919 and took on the administration of the estate.

Roger returned to his ship in the Pacific bypassing Weymouth completely. Bernard married in France in May of 1919 and never returned to Canada. This was an unexpected development, as he and Simone were the most Canadianized of all the family. Furthermore, he had always been deeply attached to the family business and New France. On furlough in 1917, he and Paul had visited the old home several times and had planned to resume working together.

Maurice was very busy in France, full of business and plans to marry in September, 1919. On November 8th, he and his bride arrived in Weymouth on their honeymoon. He did things in a grand way, returning to France via New York to visit Jean and old friends.

Charles returned home in June of 1919. His wife Marie was in hospital in Halifax and lived only one month after his return. After settling her estate, by early autumn he was on his way back to France, never to return to Canada.

Discussion between the heirs as to whether they would sell, or keep the business going, seemed to go on without reaching any agreement. There were too many heirs involved, with such diverse interests and plans for the future. Meantime, the lease on the house in Weymouth was approaching its end, December 1st, 1920. Therese had decided to return to France. Louis and Simone were staying in Weymouth and in preparation, Simone bought a house in June of 1919. A nice bungalow with all conveniences, two bedrooms, well off the road, with trees on the lot. She continued to live at the family home until the lease expired when she furnished her house from the home, and moved in, taking Louis with her. Simone was a thorough Canadian, with no thought of ever returning to France. She had her friends in Weymouth and Halifax, was popular, an avid bridge player, and an artist of some talent. She was still young and not yet despairing of landing a husband.

General Nox, the faithful horse we met so often during the lifetime of New France, was getting old now, but was still cared for with affection, if not gratitude. He had been the only mount of the Founder, and he had played his part in the vicissitudes of the family over the years. In the hours of great need, General was galloping in the darkness around and over the boulders of that atrocious road bringing Doctors Elderkin or Hallet safely to the bedside of a mother in labour and a declining grandmother. At other times he brought visitors, relations from France, not to forget Father Blanche.

One morning, late in November of 1919, when Paul went to the barn to feed the horses and put them out to pasture for the day, General was missing. He was not in the field and not anywhere in the village. No one had seen him. A few days later, Paul went to New France hunting, and as he turned into the deserted square, he saw General, lying in front of the stable door, dead. Paul was certain that good old General had come home to die. Like his departed master, he had not been to New France since he had left on that sad spring day of 1910.

Settlement of the estate proceeded very slowly. My father, as administrator, had to make an inventory of the assets. This proved to be a very simple matter. There was no money in the bank, no investments, no insurance. In the last few years of my grandfather's life, Louis, with a power of attorney, had run the business and the house. When it became clear that the heirs would not release their shares to him, Louis had to stop operations on the land. He took the mill out and went in business for himself, but the household continued to live on funds of the estate and allowances continued to be paid to Louis, Therese and Simone. Over the years, the two sisters had accumulated a considerable nestegg which stood them in good stead, making it possible for Simone to buy a house and Therese to settle herself in France.

In order to establish the worth of the property, an independent survey of New France was carried out by Howard Steele, who had advised Jean on the purchase of the land initially and a surveyor. They reported as follows:

1. "Nine thousand five hundred acres of forest lands, extending from Long Tusket Lake — Bear Lake to Cariboo River including down water privileges and control.

2. The settlement of New France, consisting of dwellings, barn, office, water sawmill, electric plant and other buildings.
3. Several pieces of property forming the course of the railway to the public road at Weymouth.
4. A marshland at Weymouth with front on the Sissiboo River and the Stehelin wharf.
5. The above mentioned wharf at Weymouth containing eighty thousand square feet with two buildings on it facing Weymouth Public Road.

All these lands are free of any encumbrance.

The timber estimate is as follows:

— Eight million superficial feet of merchantable spruce, and seventy thousand cords of pulpwood.
— Two hundred million superficial feet of hemlock.
— Three million feet of merchantable hardwood and a very large quantity of cordwood.
— The farmlands, the cut lands, and the burnt lands, about one thousand acres.

There were about twenty-one pieces of land, thirty feet wide forming the right of way for the railroad.

The value of the peoperty was estimated at four hundred thousand dollars. Now the decision whether to sell or continue the business had to be made. Paul argued that it would be very difficult to sell even for the valuation amount established. Besides Emile, Louis and himself could operate a good business and provide a good yearly income to each heir. Jean and Roger supported the plan, putting up a further point that the property could always be sold later, if necessary, certainly at a better price than it would fetch now.

Correspondence with those in France dragged on without arriving at a consensus. December 1920 arrived, the lease on the house was up. Louis moved with Simone to her new house. Therese and Paul moved to the Goodwin Hotel. On January 21, 1920, Therese sailed from St. John for LeHavre, never to return to Canada.

Paul kept hoping that the property would remain in the family, but during that winter, he realized that it could not be.

Those against his plan, made it plain that they wanted money now. There was no point arguing further and the property was put up for sale. With a heavy heart, Paul made a last trip to New France and on April 21, 1920, boarded the *S.S. Tunisian* bound for France, never to return to Canada. He started farming on the lands at St. Charles, living in the house with Therese. About a year after his return to France, he married and began buying land around St. Charles. He would be a farmer and he started negotiations to buy St. Charles from the estate.

In Canada, for a long time, there were no serious offers for New France. A number of inquiries came, mostly from the United States. The Nova Scotia Timberland Co. Ltd., an American company, made a ridiculously low offer, sensing that the property would be hard to sell.

Three years went by before New France was sold on July 10th, 1923. The New France Lumber Co. Ltd., a new company with head office in St. John, New Brunswick, formed expressly to exploit New France acquired title for a quarter of a million dollars, an amount considerably below the appraised value, but some heirs were virtually clamouring for their share. Those who had wanted to keep the land and exploit it were proven right, but alas too late.

The new owners repaired the buildings, and built a magnificent lodge, at the foot of Long Tusket Lake, which they named Hemlock Lodge, in honor of the two huge hemlock trees that formed an entrance way onto the verandah from the long stairway to the beach below.

At the end of a year or so, the company had no plans of operation. The big shareholders were American paper and newspaper companies, who seemed unwilling to put up the required funds. New France was sold to Nova Scotia Timberlands, who had wanted it from the start.

Nova Scotia Timberlands built a road from Kemptville, Yarmouth County to New France, about eighteen miles, skirting Bario Lakes and the Silver River. At the outbreak of the Second World War, New France was acquired by La Croix Co. of Quebec. Another road was built with government grants from above Seven Pence-Ha-Penny to Lake Doyle,

Calibri Lake, Long Tusket Lake, ending at New France. This company did some cutting of pulpwood to feed its paper mill at St. John, New Brunswick. Woodsmen were brought in from Quebec. They lived in the big house and New France seemed to come alive once more. The road was very good and visitors again came for an evening of dancing and singing to the music of the fiddlers from Quebec.

With the end of the Second World War, New France was again abandoned, until around 1948 when it was sold to the Mersey Paper Co., its present owner. From 1918 until recently very little exploitation of this resource was carried out. A great loss to the economy of the area.

By the fall of 1926, Simone decided she would take up Paul's invitation to spend a few months at St. Charles. She enjoyed the change and stayed on well into the spring. In the early fall of 1927, she was on her way to France again, but returned very early the next spring very excited, announcing her forthcoming marriage to a widower in France. She sold her house and I helped her prepare for an auction sale of her furniture. At eighteen, I was excited too, because this gentleman had a daughter whom Simone said I would marry some day. I was to go to Simone's wedding, at her expense, where I would meet my fiancée. Simone left late in June, but alas there was no marriage, and I never dared mention it to her, ever.

It must have been in 1927 that Paul invited Louis to spend the winter with him at St. Charles. When he returned to Weymouth in the spring, he looked a new man. He had put on some weight, had good colour and seemed much happier. Whilst he carried on his business, it soon became apparent that it could not maintain him in the lifestyle he had become accustomed to. In the summer of 1928, he sold his mill and by the fall, he was on his way to St. Charles where he made his home with Paul for the rest of his life, teaching English in colleges nearby.

Paul had from the start offered full valuation price for St. Charles for which there was no other prospective buyer. Finally in November, 1929, it was agreed that he would buy the house for three hundred and fifty thousand and eighty

(350,080) francs.

The furniture and effects in St. Charles were not part of the sale. These were divided into eleven lots by a notary. The heirs living in France, no doubt, got their respective lots. The heirs in America left their shares in the house, as it seemed impractical and too expensive to ship them.

The last actors of the adventure that was new France have left the scene. Unforgetable characters all, in the latter years of their lives, they felt and said that the days of their youth spent in the freedom, comfort and peace of the paternal domain at New France, deep in the forest by the clear lakes and limpid streams, had been the happiest time of their lives. The grand design of their father and mother had been to find peace and security and to shield their children from the suffering and devastation of always recurring wars in old, tired, broken but belligerent Europe.

Unfortunately, the course of fate was stronger than the father's will and his children and their children did not escape the hardships of two world wars. Most of them, living in France again in the Second World War suffered the agony of France in her ignominious defeat and occupation by the same "Boche" of 1870 and 1914. Refugees, they suffered hunger, lived in fear, St. Charles, damaged by bombs, occupied by the enemy. In this suffering, no doubt they thought of life in Canada. If only they had stayed there.

Two letters from Simone to a friend in Canada tell the story of danger, fear, hunger and suffering which was the lot of all Frenchmen.

May, 1945

"There isn't much left of Gisors. The main part of it, Therese's house included, was destroyed by the Germans in 1940, and the rest of it, or nearly all, was destroyed last year. Therese was quite lucky, the house was blown almost to bits but her floor was miraculously preserved. The stairs below and above were burned, in fact the ceiling of her apartment became the roof (she lived on the first of a four-story house); even her door was scorched, but it all stopped there. The house was in such a state that looters didn't even think to go in. But one day

Maurice went up with a ladder, and there wasn't a thing touched! He and Paul took out all her belongings through the windows. Her big mirrors weren't even cracked and her radio worked on turning the button! I don't believe she lost a pin.

I can't tell you how good she was to me these last years, sending me things to eat; meat once in awhile or a bit of fat or a bottle of milk, and all that not of her abundance but of her miserable rations."

August 25, 1945

"To think that it's already a year since we saw the last of the Germans in Paris, and that I am still here! When I think of this day last year I can thank God I am still alive to tell the tale. I don't believe I told you that I found myself in two regular battles that day. Since a few days, fighting was hot here, and whenever you were out, you didn't know how far you would go or if you would ever come back. Still, I heard on the radio the night before that French troops had actually come into Paris and you can imagine I was anxious to have a word with them. So I called up my friends who live at the other end of Paris from me, two hours walk exactly — that was what I took to walk to Church Point from Weymouth — and said I was coming over to see what I could see!

Well, it was worth while, I tell you. I hadn't walked twenty minutes when I was stopped by truckloads of our boys pouring in, and crowds cheering all along the Avenue, throwing bouquets at them, etc. I joined in with the crowd for awhile and then proceeded on my journey. I had left home at about 11 a.m. When I got to the City Hall, the place was alive with tanks, jeeps and everything, so I stopped there awhile to chat with some of them. When I got to the Louvre Palace and Tuilerie Gardens, another stop, but this time I had no choice, firing was heavy; the gardens were filled with Germans hiding everywhere, in the bushes, up in the trees, and they had tanks, their big Tigers firing on everything and anything in sight. Our boys were crawling along the hedges and along the buildings under constant fire. One of them came and said we must have the tanks. So a few minutes later along came some of those I had seen at the City Hall. They got in position and opened fire

— first the machine guns and then the big guns. Three shots were enough for one Tiger, then another was put out of action. The noise was terrific. I wasn't exactly scared, but I must say I said a prayer. Prisoners were taken, and I remember an old woman who was captured firing a gun! Whether she was French or German I don't know.

But I was still only half-way to my destination, and it was nearly 4 o'clock so I tried to move on, but they wouldn't let me. "Unless", one soldier said, "You try to go along the riverbank". Perhaps you remember there are trees along the banks of the Seine there, so I went down and started dodging behind the trees, and the guns were firing on both sides of the river. Such hellish noise you can't imagine! It was awful. But I had to come back, it really wasn't safe, so I came up on the Avenue again and managed to get along a little further. At the Place de la Concorde, another battle, more prisoners; and then the road was clear, and finally I reached my friend's house. There I fell into the most magnificent parade you can imagine. The Leclerc Division was pouring in; since noon, one tank after another, one almost touching the other, were going by right under my friend's windows. She and the children were all in the street cheering, the children kissing the soldiers — the wildest enthusiasm, as you can imagine. Oh, it was grand! And every now and then a sniper would fire from some roof or window, machine guns would enter into action, the crowds would scatter, and five minutes later the street was packed again. Oh, what wonderful hours we lived! The last tank must have passed around 8 a.m. Of course I didn't go home that night; as you may suppose I was a little tired."

If one returns to New France today, he would find but a lovely, very still clearing in the middle of the forest. The buildings were razed by Mersey Paper Co. and already firs, pines and spruce have all but obliterated the outline of their foundations. The old apple trees, tangled with the branches of encroaching trees are still struggling to live a little longer. A few hardy little blue flowers still defiantly poke their heads through the debris of rotten wood and fallen chimneys. The roofless wine cellars by the lake will soon disappear, when new trees fill their space.

Sitting on some ruin by the cellar stones of the big house, I imagine the busy life that once throbbed all over, as far as I can see. I see the work, I hear the talk and the laughter, the sounds of harmonious chords from the piano in that corner, dancing feet and singing to the accompaniment of the strident notes of the fiddle, the harmony of the mouth organ and the Jew's harp, coming from the cookhouse over there. Perhaps it is Saturday night and the men line up to pass by the little glass wicket in the office to get their week's pay. Myriads of sights and sound envelop the whole area before my mind's eye.

Finally, day is done, and I see my grandfather wrapped in deep meditation. As the last rays of a friendly sun, sinking behind the trees of the darkening forest, cast a warm glow through the wine coloured panes of that big window of the chapel, perhaps enshrining the consoling countenance of Our Lady of the Forest, inviting him far from home to accept the condition of the remaining days ahead. Man proposes, God disposes and Man complies.

Slowly but relentlessly, nature levels the works of man as if to bury all trace of his efforts here, but the story of new France will live as it passes down through the generations of all those who worked in building the dream. In its perpetual silence, the forest will slowly but completely swallow up all traces of man's work here and lock up some secrets remaining of that great adventure of the gallant Alsatian, his beautiful wife and his large family.

EPILOGUE

Our story ends with the sale of New France after the First World War. This epilogue will take the reader through the remaining years of the lives of the sons and daughters of our great Alsatian ancestor.

EMILE JEAN

In France, the eldest son is born possessing birth-rights which give him a seniority voice in the family's affairs. Emile Jean was therefore destined to some day be the head of the clan and to manage the business. In preparation, he was given a university education followed by management training. Considered equally important was a fine training in the social arts of being an accomplished gentleman, fit to take his place in the Chateaux social life of the family environment. His father would arrange a brilliant marriage for him and he would live a meaningful life.

Unfortunately, the forced sale of the factory abruptly ended these plans and Emile II, instead, found himself in a tar paper lumbering camp in Canada, pioneering the future settlement of the family in the deep woods.

At war's end, he returned to being a lumberman. Alternately he worked for big companies and on his own account until 1929 when business ground to a halt, and he suffered heavy losses in the stock market crash. He became the Postmaster at Church Point.

His greatest adventure was the short period of military duty with the French Foreign Legion; participating in skirmishes against the rebel Berber Tribes in Morocco. He loved these men of the Legion, whose past was their own secret never pried into and whose only allegiance was to the Legion and the comrade in arms.

Living at Church Point was lonely. The large family lived within itself. Anne Baldwin was a brave woman, a wonderful wife and mother, who kept tradition, English and French, and who inspired her children to work for a good future. One English custom she kept over the years was to gather the family around the piano every Sunday morning to sing a hymn and say a prayer for all the sailors at sea.

The coming of the radio was a great boon. I remember the emotion when King George V broadcast the first Christmas message by a reigning monarch to the nations of the Empire. His message was preceded by Choirs of Great Cathedrals and the booming of Big Ben striking noon.

The Second Great War was a blow, but the fall of France overwhelmed him, cut off completely from his brothers and sisters and relatives in France, not ever learning what happened to them. However, he found relief in plunging into all war work he could find. Being a great patriot, he became a popular speaker, in his broken English, at war rallies, Cenotaph memorial ceremonies, service clubs and even religious services. He was instrumental in setting up an Officers' Training Corps at College Sainte Anne, and Cadet Corps in the schools. The war work of the Legion also received his help. He became a member of a Committee set up in the County of Digby whose task was to plan the rehabilitation of service men and women who would be returning home at the end of the war.

Alas, like his father in the War of 1914, he was deprived of the great joy of victory and seeing the same "Sale Boche" of 1870 and 1914 finally defeated, hopefully for good. He died prematurely in 1943, without ever knowing what happened to his brothers and sisters in France.

Beside Jacqueline and Paul there are the twins Agnes, Catherine (Mrs. Merritt), and Anne Marie (Mrs. d'Entremont).

JEAN JACQUES

Jean Jacques continued to prosper in New York. He

married a second time in 1906 and had a son and a daughter. He and his family visited at Weymouth until the family home closed in December of 1920. He always travelled in a luxurious Oldsmible driven by a chauffeur.

Early in the twenties, his health began to decline, finally causing his retirement and sale of his business. He chose to retire at Hampton, New Brunswick, where he died in 1925 at the young age of fifty-five.

Jean had done excellent work, organizing and setting up the family domain and business at New France. However, perhaps sensing that in time, difficulties would arise, he decided it might be wise to go on his own before it was too late. This seemed to have been a good decision on his part. He never returned to France, and to New France only once to be with the family at the death of his mother and her last religious service in the little chapel of Our Lady of the Forest. Children were: Jean William and Christine Amelie (Mrs. Britton).

CHARLES

Returning to France in late 1919, Charles lived for a time at St. Charles, with Paul and Therese. He then settled in Paris where he took a position with a firm of timber merchants, specializing in fine woods for furniture making. He tried to import burl hardwoods from Nova Scotia, but the French franc was so low in relation to the dollar that trading was impossible.

Beginning in the mid-twenties, his health gradually deteriorated until he died in 1930, at the age of fifty-eight. In his latter years, he filled the role of grand uncle, and always remained the jovial, good comrade and gentleman. His knowledge of English and his experiences in Canada and the war made him a fine recouteur sought after as an after dinner speaker in Paris.

THERESE

Therese settled at St. Charles in early 1920 with Charles and a little while later Paul, when he finally returned. When Paul married in 1922, she moved to an apartment in the nearby town of Gisors.

She busied herself in community work. One of her projects was getting the Boy Scouts movement organized. The boys were enthralled at the stories she told of her life in the deep forests of Canada amongst wild animals, and about the hunting and fishing. They imagined her as the Amazone of Jules Verne's stories.

During the Second World War, she, like all French people under the enemy occupation, suffered greatly. She was a refugee fleeing, she knew not where, begging for her food, sleeping in barns. In time, returning north, she found her home bombed out. Although she was already nearly seventy years old, she picked up her courage, fixed up a home somehow and helped others wherever she could.

When liberation came, she was the most enthusiastic demonstrator greeting the Canadians as they fought their way through Gisors, up from the beaches of Normandy. She died in 1963, at the good age of ninety.

LOUIS

When Louis returned to France in 1928, he made his permanent home with Paul at St. Charles. For many years, he taught English in several Colleges in Normandy.

He was already sixty-five years old when he found himself a refugee, fleeing to the south, with nothing but a little pack on his back and a walking stick. Like the others, he had to return to St. Charles and live the hardship of the German occupation, under constant surveillance with little food. How he must have wished he had stayed in Canada; the family home, the Goodwin Hotel, his friends, his camp, his cars. He never married and died in 1957 aged eighty-two.

ROGER

Roger resumed command of ships of the American Hawaiian Line, trading mostly from the Pacific Coast to the Orient. His record as a Captain was unblemished. The company permitted him to engage in small trading on his own account, using limited cargo space. Roger imported fine silk from the Far East and made considerable money.

In 1925, he retired comfortably at the young age of fifty, still a bachelor and returned to France, to St. Charles of course. The following year, he married a rather young widow of thirty-six, settling down to a comfortable retirement in her Chateau in Central France.

Living in the unoccupied zone of France during the war, he suffered less than those in Normandy. Unfortunately, however, he suffered a long illness, causing his early death in 1943, at the age of sixty-seven.

PAUL

Paul always had very strong feelings for family tradition and solidarity. He settled in the home of St. Charles and decided it must stay in the family. Immediately he opened talks with his brothers and sister to buy the entire property, which included good farmland. He bought more land and married in 1922.

It took until 1929 to finalize the sale to Paul. After that, he wished St. Charles always to continue to be looked upon as the family home, always open to receive brothers and sisters, be they from France or from America.

His farming enterprise was a success. Besides raising crops, including grain, he kept a herd of beef cattle and in time raised race horses of good blood.

When France fell, with his wife and young son, he went through the agony of the occupation. St. Charles was bombed, looted and occupied by German troops. The bulk of the food he produced was taken from him. He had been wise enough, however, at the start of the war, to foresee the possibility of a debacle and he had buried all his precious wines, guns, jewelry and papers somewhere on the property. The Germans never found his cache.

Life returned to some normality after the war, but Paul was already sixty-seven years old. He said that he had been so near starvation that he would devote the rest of his life to eating fine foods and drinking fine wines. During those hard days, he dreamt of the comfort and peace of his life in Canada and of the fare of the cookhouses in his logging camps. He died at his beloved St. Charles at the age of eighty-four, leaving one son, Paul Auguste, the present owner of the old family home.

GERMAINE

In Brooklyn, Germaine experienced some hard times. Her husband was much older than she was and he retired from the sea in ill health when she was still young. Then in the Stock Market Crash of 1929, much of the family savings disappeared.

But the old family spirit she had always displayed came to the fore once more, and at fifty-five, she took up nursing, qualified, and practised into her seventies. After her husband died in 1948, she visited St. Charles many times. She was still an attractive woman and she boasted that she received several persistent marriage proposals long past seventy.

Around 1956, she retired in a Convent in Ottawa, where her niece Jacqueline was a sister, which took lady boarders of every age. She was very happy there, soon becoming the grandmother of the younger women and the confessor of those with problems. She died at the advanced age of ninety-two years.

MAURICE

From the war's end, Maurice was busy the rest of his life. Married in France in 1919, he successively operated a general farm, a stud farm, and finally a factory in Paris.

When the war came, he was mayor of his village of Eragny and he jumped into the underground when the German occupation began. The speciality of his group was picking up English airmen downed in Normandy and through an elaborate network, passed them through into Spain and freedom. Because he spoke English, he was invaluable as a first contact. He saved many Canadian airmen also, for which he received commendation from the Canadian government.

In 1953, he came back to Canada on a visit which extended itself until his death in the veteran's hospital in 1958. He started a business selling hearing aids, he himself being deaf. He visited his old haunts, his old friends, especially his old girl friends, now grandmothers. He gave lectures on the hardships France suffered during the war to Legion and Army groups. He was warmly received at his Alma Mater, Saint F.X. University, where he met a special old friend, now Dr. Hugh MacPherson.

He left a son and a daughter, Maurice Auguste and Germaine.

SIMONE

As mentioned before, Simone settled in Weymouth with no thoughts of ever returning to France. She was very happy there, very popular, very busy. She kept chickens and rabbits and had a garden. She had a very good friend in Babe, also a single lady who had a Model T Ford. Simone's job was to crank the engine which she did very easily. Unfortunately, this fine friendship came to an abrupt and permanent end when Babe accused Simone's rabbits of devastating her garden.

When she returned to France, she visited family for a while, finally settled in Paris for good. For many years, she regretted having left her bungalow and serene life in Weymouth. The hardships she endured during the war are well documented in her letters of her girlhood friend, Miss Killam of Montreal.

Simone died in Paris in 1975, aged ninety years.

BERNARD

It was a surprise to everyone when Bernard remained in France at war's end. He was a thorough Canadian, along with Simone, and Maurice, all three having come to Canada very young and having been well educated at English universities. He married in 1920 and had a daughter and a son. He lived at Aurillac and died there at the age of sixty-three, leaving one daughter and one son: Claude and Bernard Guy.